The Infidels

by

David Anderson

authorHOUSE™

1663 LIBERTY DRIVE, SUITE 200
BLOOMINGTON, INDIANA 47403
(800) 839-8640
WWW.AUTHORHOUSE.COM

First published by AuthorHouse 01/27/05

ISBN: 1-4208-2058-3 (sc)

Library of Congress Control Number: 2004195262

Printed in the United States of America
Bloomington, Indiana

This book is printed on acid-free paper.

www.InquiryAbraham.com

A Prayer for the Wall

My Jewish friend and I were talking about a mutual friend who had just been taken to the hospital. He had suffered a severe seizure and was close to death. This friend of ours was a former Roman Catholic and an outspoken atheist. My Jewish friend paused for a moment and then said to me: My son lives in Jerusalem. I would like to have him put a prayer for our friend in the Temple Wall. I was taken back. After all; the Temple Wall is one of the most sacred spots in Jewish religious and national consciousness. His offer clearly was a hand extended out of true compassion across a wide bridge between his religious tradition and mine and then to an unbeliever who time and again had, in my conversations with him, repudiated a belief in any form of God.

Later, when I thought more about this heart felt expression of genuine concern, I said to myself: is one prayer for only one person enough? Shouldn't there be other prayers? What about the thousands who have suffered in the past and are suffering today as a result of the absolutist religious certainties that have grown out of our common Hebraic foundation? And, as for the history of Wall itself, don't we now see eerie parallels between 70 C.E. when the Romans destroyed the Temple and massacred the Jerusalem Jews and the threats to Israel today from the hostile Muslim nations that now surround it. In fact, the Islam these Muslim nations practice, with their suicidal adherents, has now become so absolutist and extremist that the nations not only present a threat to Israel, but to all of Human civilization. Given the present growth trajectory of this religious fanaticism, the future human loses could be in the tens of millions.

It was then that I realized why I wrote this book. It is my prayer for the victims of these three religions of Abraham, not limited to those of any one faith, but encompassing those of all faiths. It is a prayer asking you, the reader; Jew, Christian, Muslim, agnostic, atheist, even non religious secularist, and the millions like you, to join with me in my quest for an understanding of where each of the religions have gone wrong, and how each must now right these wrongs, at the same time plumbing the depths of their greatness for their far reaching intrinsic values; all to bring an end to the human suffering we now see unfolding before us.

Ominous Echoes from Our Past

The recent flare-up between Islam and the West has brought to the surface an urgent question about our three religious faiths. It is the most important of our time. It extends even beyond the current world religious conflict into the planetary crisis in which we now find ourselves. It is a question about the very survival of our species. It asks whether these three Hebraic religions we call our own are leading us down a fiery path toward an Armageddon. It asks: Are they through their own intentionality driving us toward their own self fulfilling prophecy, that which they in ages past predicted *the end of times*?

To answer it we are forced to explore others: Where did these ancient religions come from? Who is this God who so dominates them? How did He spell out the relationship between us and our planet? How did He spell out our relationship to Him? How strong a power does He have over our thoughts and actions? What does this mean for us today?

The stakes are high. What we see before us as the Islamic threat is only a small part of our problem. It is just the tip of the iceberg. There are other far reaching forces at play, all interconnected to our belief in this God.

All of these forces are converging at an alarming rate. Some of them are clearly visible to us; others are forming under the surface of our awareness: We have entered an atomic age where we can destroy each other in unimaginable numbers. Extremist factions in Islamist states are taking control over advanced atomic weaponry. There are indications that we will use it. We witness sudden weather changes. The bio chemistry of many living forms is being altered in a self destructive way. Vital world resources are being squandered

Exacerbating all of this is a population explosion that is producing a permanent under class living in abject poverty, and with no hope for the future. As the world economy expands, the line between these world citizens living at or below a subsistence level and those in society consuming resources to excess is being more clearly drawn. The later remain oblivious to the profligate nature of their appetites. They resist change, retreating into the comfort of their excessive consumption. They overwhelmingly benefit from their power over the earth's recourses, oblivious to the disenfranchised billions on the margins of society who barely survive.

That the three Abrahamic religions under the power of their God are failing to give adequate guidance is becoming increasingly clear. Moreover, in many ways this God of Abraham seems to be the major cause of the dilemma in which human civilization finds itself

Why do we think the way we do? The early Greeks gave us the answer. There is an interaction that takes place between ourselves and the God or Gods we worship. We become like them and they become like us. This interaction is dynamic and all powerful. It follows that for Jews, Christians and Muslims, and not just at the extremes but many others within the envelope of these religions forming the fabric of their cultures, it is the God first of Abraham and then of Moses who drives their thoughts and actions. All three have used this God as the foundation for their perception of GOD. They use the persona of this God they worship to determine who they are.

We are entrapped by this interaction. In an attempt to find a way around the seemingly intractable bind of our past and present conflict, some try for inter religious dialogue, but that is not working. Others take the atheistic view, but that too—as recent history so clearly proved—leads us into unknown paths where we find no resolution. Either way, we find ourselves searching for a new and different basis for an understanding of ourselves and the world around us, but none is found.

How did we reach this point? We must look to the origins of our God for the answer. In Judeo/Christian/Islamic society believers and non believers live under the spell of the powerful ancient mythological images that formed the God of their three religions. These images envelop their world, working in their subconscious, patterning their thoughts, controlling their actions. They are the Sumerian/Hebraic images that originally formed the persona of this God. They grew out of ancient myths and epic tales first passed orally from generation to generation and then recorded in the Hebraic scriptures. These images form the internal archetypal structure of Abrahamic religious belief.

The mythological Hebraic images that formed the basis for these religions are more than just tales from the past. Contained within them is a durable and lasting power that gives shape, form, and identity to a common vision of their God. These images also define a relationship to this God. It is a relationship that is a codependent one, with the God of Abraham always remaining the central and controlling figure.

Jews, Christians and Muslims are reminded of these images every time they read from their Torah, Bible and Koran. To keep them current, each tradition in its own way has established self enforcing rituals. Today in the 21st century these images from the past remain as alive as they were when they were first formed. We deceive ourselves if we think this is not so.

Without these Hebraic myths and the images that have grown out of them, the God of Judaism, Christianity and Islam would cease to exist in the form given Him. He would have to exist in some other form. These images from the past exclude any possibility of other forms. They reveal to believers in definitive terms who this God is and who He is not. They deny any other form or forms.

Under the surface of their consciousness believers become empowered by the ancient mythological images that surround this God. They determine how Jews, Christians and Muslims individually and in corporate form think and act. Whole societies, including those within them with no particular interest in religion, even atheists and agnostics, fall under their spell.

How is this God revealed in the three Abrahamic religious traditions? Since their foundations are the same, He is revealed much the same way in each of them. He is revealed as a father. We are His children. We watch His every move. Like children, we want to be like Him. He is our mentor. Like a child observing his father, we look up to Him in awe. Like a father, He always remains in control. Like a father, He always has the last word. We want to be like Him. But, as much as we try, we find He will not let us. So we can only pretend to be like Him.

It does not end there. Real fathers die. They leave us. He does not. He is always there with us. He is alive within us. Like a living father He remains a living part of our lives. We find that we can not make decisions apart from Him.

We say to ourselves: If He can destroy infidel non believers who do not believe in Him as I do; I too can destroy those who do not believe in Him. If He could bring on a great flood and the end of His creation, and if He said He will do it again, I need only watch as a bystander as I now see once again the end of his creation in sight. If He can be angry with me—which He often is, I too can be angry with others. If He can have retribution towards me, I too can have retribution towards others. If He can punish me, I too can punish others. If He can "slew" His enemies, I too can destroy mine. If He can destroy the Sodomites, I too can denigrate and destroy those who are not heterosexual.

This brings us to the question: Is this image of God, God? Is it valid? Or, is God some other form? Is what we see before us in our religious belief not ultimate reality but an aberrant form of God that is no more than an ancient and incomplete version of ultimate reality? And, if it is an aberration, then is this early Sumerian/Hebraic image leading us astray? Is it leading our planet toward Armageddon? Is it turning us against each other? Has, in our modern world of today, the ancient Yahweh lost His relevance? Is He in His archaic anthropomorphic form holding each of us individually, as well as all of humanity, back from becoming what it can become?

There is an even greater question we must face: If all of this is true, then how can we escape from this God/Image that has been with us for so long? How can we escape from the powerful forces within this "God Spell" without releasing within ourselves other equally powerful dark and destructive forces? How can we as a society break away from this ancient God image and create a new image, with new forms of belief that will allow us then to create a more equitable and humane society and an ecologically balanced and sustainable planet?

And finally, a question to every Jew, Christian and Muslim living today; do you have the courage needed to face this reality?

CONTENTS

Note: Some of the chapters are followed by numbered "Reflections", the contents of which support the conclusions of the chapter preceding them. These reflections draw on many different forms of religious and philosophical thought. They express a "progressive" view in line with current liberal religious scholarship. They run against all Abrahamic religious orthodoxy. They are shared by many progressive thinkers in all three faiths.

Author's Note

The following explanation is given to avoid any possible confusion on the reader's part with respect to capitalization of all letters in the word "God" and expressions referring to God, such as "Him" and "Word of God". The author has chosen to use the rules that existed before the advent of the modern word processor; as a great deal of religious writing remains in this form and, in the author's view, *The Chicago Manual of Style* which gives the modern rules does not allow for the subtle distinctions that are called for in this book. The rules used by the author therefore are as follows:

- GOD—The God of all Creation

- God—a general definition of GOD, i.e., the God of the Jews, the God of Islam (Allah), the God of Jesus, pagan Gods, etc.

- HE, HIM, HIS, CREATOR—used sparingly for author's emphasis to refer to the one true GOD

- He, Him, His, Creator—used generally

- WORD OF GOD—used sparingly to designate what any group of believers believe to be the inerrant word of GOD

- Word of God—used generally

Another distinction must be made. By using the masculine HE, HIM, HIS and He, Him, His, the reader should not assume that the author considers God to be masculine. Also, with respect to the use of the masculine form, i.e., "man" as in "man's spiritual nature", the reader is directed to the author's use of the word "woman" whenever possible such as when he uses the expression "man's and woman's" and "his and her" spiritual nature. In some cases the use of the word "man" is used alone, but only to ease the flow of the idea being expressed. In those cases the reader should understand that the word "man" should be taken to mean *huma(e)n beings* ,that is members of the huma(e)n species, men and women taken together by GOD as one.

There are many forms of Judaism, Christianity and Islam. Hopefully, the following chapters will adequately describe them, at least for the purposes of this presentation. Some explanation is, however, necessary as we begin with regard to Christianity.

The use of the term "evangelical Christianity" refers to any form of Christian denominational worship that demands, without metaphor or allegory, a literal belief in the words of the King James Version or an equivalent modern version of both the Old and New Testaments. This fundamentalism is not limited to the well-known fundamentalist denominations like the Southern Baptists and Pentecostals but cuts across worshiping segments in many protestant denominations such as Lutheran, Presbyterian, Episcopal, etc..

In Roman Catholicism there is an altogether different meaning to the word "inerrancy". Roman Catholics believe scripture alone is not a sufficient authority for faith. It is the authority of the church as it has interpreted scripture over the ages that provides inerrant authority.

An Open Letter to Those of the Three Religions of Abraham

This letter is being written to those of the Jewish, Christian, and Muslim faiths. It deals with a number of very important and urgent questions that each must soon face.

They are questions about how all of us from the same Hebraic tradition, with our diverse historical backgrounds, can live in peaceful coexistence and with common purpose. They are the most important questions we can ask of ourselves. They are of such importance that their answers will determine not only the quality of the lives of ourselves, our children, and the children of future generations, but possibly even the survival of the human species as we know it.

There is a far-reaching spiritual dimension to these questions that this generation is not addressing. Many think they are; however, they are living under an illusion.

The reality is that those in all three of the religions of Abraham who hold fast to an orthodox view of their beliefs are embarked on a dangerous spiritual and ideological—as well as geopolitical—miscalculation, one that already is having dire consequences for all of human kind. Recent world events have shown that the beginning of the tragic outcome of this miscalculation is coming fast upon us.

There can be only one way to remove ourselves from this dilemma. As those who will become the next generation and then those to follow grow into adulthood and form their own thoughts about themselves and the world around them, they will have to face far-reaching questions about the religious beliefs of their mothers, fathers, and mentors. The way each and every one approaches these critical questions will make a difference in some way, large or small, for the entire world.

As they have done from the beginning of their history, Jews, Christians and Muslims today are searching for the truth about who and what they are and must become in relation to their God. And, as in the past they are passing this knowledge on to the next generation. The question each must now ask is: Does this knowledge reflect the ultimate truth about human existence?

Many think the truth can be acquired through blind belief in inerrant scripture or dogma or by following the words of clerics. They are wrong. This human failing is the underlying reason for the pain and suffering growing out of current world conflict. Religious history too has proven this to be true. All scripture and dogma and the words of clerics must be critically examined. For many Jews, Christians and Muslims, this will call for a repudiation of past belief. It will mean the abandonment of past perceptions of the God worshiped by their mothers, fathers and mentors. This will be particularly painful for those who look to their scriptures as being inerrant.

Answers will require an examination of the perception of the nature of the one God of our universe and our relationship, both individually and corporately as the human species, to that one God. This is a search for truth that can only be found through painful self examination of past belief. There is no other way.

It is my belief that this God of our ancestors can not be confined narrowly to the present belief system of any particular religious institution that is today a part of Judaism, Christianity or Islam, or to the vision of any select group of clerics, or to any national or tribal identity. I believe the God of our creation is beyond that.

I believe God has only one plan for our destiny as the human species. It is not an apocalyptic plan nor is it a plan where one religion conquers another. It is a plan conditioned on whether we, not as any chosen religious group, but individually through a process of searching to the very bottom of our very being, can elevate ourselves into a knowledge of His presence.

This is the purpose of our existence. It is the awesome task given by our Creator to each and every person during the time span of their lives here on this earth.

David Anderson

I

The Role of Religion

September 11 by the enormity of its horror, as well as the American reaction to it, was a marker in world religious history. It said that fundamentalist religious extremism grounded on the inerrancy of ancient Abrahamic religious texts has been forever left behind. It has no place in an interdependent scientifically advanced 21st century world.

Since then, the world has been looking for answers beyond those being given by religious leaders, politicians, TV commentators and the mass media. Whether in the Jewish, Christian, or Islamic world, we only find a confusion of extremist religious demagoguery.

As the crisis deepens, political leaders and their advisors who hold the levers of domestic and international political power secretly hold fast to their own deeply imbedded religious beliefs. These are beliefs that often simplistically define choices as being between those who think the way they do and those who do not, between *them* and *us*. As they make choices—choices that often affect the lives of millions—they are convinced that the actions that spring from them are in some mysterious way the Will of their God.

Without them realizing it, their actions are being driven by an underlying archaic religious image of the God firmly rooted in their minds from their childhood; an image that has continued into their adulthood; an image that patterns their every thought and every action; an image that overwhelms their adult sense of reason.

In the political discussions that take place, this image of their God is subsumed. There is a political correctness holding back any kind of open critical discussion of religious ideas. Diplomatic discussion and debate therefore has the appearance of superficiality. Strategies take place on the surface of a chessboard. As the pieces are moved, the underlying religious motives driving decisions are never brought to the surface and examined openly as a part of the dialogue. Deep seated religious differences remain hidden. The assumption is that we are all basically the same.

1

Words to describe events and the reasons for them are carefully chosen so as to be religiously correct, with the result that they only have limited meaning. An example is the usage of the word to describe Islamic terrorism. Muslim terrorists are singled out and defined by the single word *terrorists*. At the same time, the complexities of Islamic thought leading to terrorism are kept silent.

The result is that the interactive causes of world terrorism are kept from the conversation. To find them one would have to examine multiple breeding grounds. There is a reluctance to do this. If there were an examination, we would first find that many of the underlying beliefs of the Muslim terrorists are shared by hundreds of millions of Muslims world-wide. This includes Muslims in America. These Muslims silently support the terrorists and in a sense therefore are terrorists themselves. As it did in Nazi Germany, culpability must extend to the general population. Next, and more shocking, we would find that many of the Islamic beliefs leading to terrorism come from the same roots as those found in Judeo-Christianity. Therefore, there are in effect not one, but three breeding grounds. Terrorism now becomes not a single force but a complex interactive one.

An example of this interactive complexity is the Israeli Palestinian problem. As fanatical Orthodox Jews tenaciously hold on to land with a centuries old Palestinian claim, in their silence, American politicians and the American media are viewed by Muslims as defending the Jewish right to occupy the West Bank and parts of Jerusalem. Many Jews look upon this land as their Holy Ground, land given to them in their Bible by their Yahweh. Discussion of Palestinian Muslim rights and claims is muted.

We see this same muting of Muslim claims by American evangelical Christianity today as it supports unbridled Zionist expansion into the Holy Land, if only for the reason that the Nation of Israel for these evangelicals will fulfill apocalyptic scripture. All other views relating to the geopolitical complexity of the Israeli presence are left out of the conversation. We saw this myopic vision of the world during the Bush administration, when an unspoken religious correctness allowed powerful evangelical extremists to take center stage and drown out moderate voices. These evangelicals judgmentally lashed out and attacked those who opposed them. Only they were right. Everyone else was wrong. Only they had found the Word of God. Only they would be saved. These self proclaimed Christian spokesmen pronounced 9/11 as God's punishment of a decadent, corrupted American society. In their exuberance they felt empowered by God Himself to invade Iraq.

2

History has shown that those following the religions that grew out of the Hebrew Bible, along with their positive acts of "goodness", have repeatedly violated the sanctity of human life, inflicting pain and suffering on those not of their own kind who did not think as they do. As this was true in the past, it is true today.

This book exposes the underlying flaws that are built into each of these three religious belief systems; and although it leaves it to the reader to decide, argues that culpability for world terrorism lies not only with the extremism of Islam, but also with the extremism of Judaism and Christianity. It shows these flaws as having been present from their very beginning. It presents the argument that certain of these flaws are today so serious that they may over time lead to the self-fulfillment of Biblical Apocalyptic prediction.

The book begins with an examination of the ancient anthropomorphic Hebraic image of GOD. It traces the development of this image through Jewish biblical history into the radically different image presented by Jesus Christ. It discusses the disconnection between the Jesus image and the Hebraic one. It draws a connection between the image presented by Jesus and Hellenistic, as well as Buddhist, thought. It explains why Christianity never completely abandoned the Hebraic image.

It discusses the formation of the Christian Canon from an historical perspective and introduces new insights in light of the Gnostic Gospels and other writings found in 1945 at Nag Hammadi in Egypt. It suggests that without this new view of the nature of GOD shown in this discovery, Christianity—as well as Judaism and Islam— will remain incomplete in their understanding of who and what Jesus was. It suggests that many of these newly discovered Gnostic images of Jesus could be seen as erasing the last vestiges of the early Roman Catholic Hebraic and later Protestant ones.

It explains why, suddenly after years of stand off with the Soviet Union, the western world is suddenly being challenged by Muslim countries such as Afghanistan, Saudi Arabia, Lebanon, Syria, Pakistan, Iran, Iraq and Indonesia. It explains why this list continues to grow. It answers the question of how long this will continue and more importantly what must take place in the religious beliefs of Muslims before it ends.

The reader will find that criticisms of institutionalized orthodox Christianity, Judaism and Islam are equally harsh. The central idea that the archaic religious beliefs in each tradition to one degree or another must bear much of the blame for present world conflict is the overriding theme. It is the rigidity of each belief system that goes to the core of the problem.

The book departs from a belief in the inerrancy of religious scripture and offers a view of the nature of GOD and our relationship to Him from a different perspective. It views religious scripture from all forms of belief, Jewish, Christian, Muslim as well as all others, as man's attempt through his eyes and ears and inner being to define the nature of GOD. It concludes that as man is fallible, so too can scripture be. It disputes the value of many parts of Jewish, Christian as well as Islamic scripture and the dogma that has followed it. It contends that man, ever since the beginning of his consciousness as a spiritual being, has been defining GOD from his own perspective, making GOD according to his own imagined man-made image, and that this may not necessarily be GOD'S.

It does look to certain mortal humans who have lived on this earth as being closer to a reflection of the image of GOD than others. This includes those from many different faiths, some of them well known and some not known at all. It looks to the life of Jesus as one of these, not as it was defined by the Roman Church centuries after his death, but as we are now seeing it defined based on recent discoveries.

It views every life on the face of the earth as precious in GOD'S sight. No one is excluded. It sees GOD'S covenant not with any select group; Jews, Christians or Muslims, or any other religious belief group, but with each of us individually during our lives. It is a covenant that covers every human being. No one is predestined or pre-selected. It lasts only for the brief moment of each life. The relationship is direct. It is between each of us and GOD. Each must make the critical decision as to how to form his or her life in response to GOD'S purpose for that life.

We enter the world of our existence alone and we leave it alone. There are no religious institutional intermediaries. In the short amount of time HE gives us, we are charged by HIM with the awesome responsibility to search our lives for glimpses of His perfection and to live our lives for HIS purposes. We put at risk our eternal destiny if we do not find HIM. HE gives each of us the gift of life here on earth as a prelude to our eternal destiny. How we live our lives determines our eternal destiny.

This is a book that forces every Jew, Christian, and Muslim to ask: Why do we have world conflict? Is my own religious belief system at fault? Am I at fault? Am I part of the problem? How can I be part of the solution?

II

The Beginning and the End of Religious Diversity

Sometime in the distant past, between 3500 and 4000 years ago, a small Semitic tribe of wandering *herdsmen* surrounded by highly sophisticated and literate ancient civilizations began to look inward to form its own theology. It would be a theology that would change the course of world history.

In forming this theology, the tribe redefined many of the myths and legends coming from the civilizations that had existed before it. It also added many of its own. Out of this grew a new and radically different view of the nature of GOD and man's relationship to GOD.

This new view saw a monotheistic God, not only as an all-powerful creator of our Universe, but also as a God demanding a new kind of moral order from His people. This moral order extended far beyond the moral order demanded by the Gods of the other religions.

In setting out this new theology, the myths and legends from the past as they were redefined were no longer thought of as being from some other realm or mythical dimension.

The Garden of Eden and the Great Flood were not events to be viewed in mythical terms as they had been in Sumerian literature, which dated back another 1000 years or more. They were events that happened on earth and they were real. The first man, Adam, was real. Abraham, their first patriarch, was real. The tablets brought down from Mount Sinai by Moses containing the Ten Commandments were real. Later in their history, King David was real. These stories as well as the laws that grew out of them that were subsequently spelled out in their Hebraic language were from their own tribal God, Yahweh, and they were real.

The historicity of their belief, an idea that would set the foundation for their religion over the coming millennia, was formed in their tribal consciousness. Twenty first century Jewish, Christian and Islamic fundamentalism and orthodoxy was born.

As they looked inward in their search for the meaning of their existence, this small and unknown Semitic tribe also began to see themselves as unique among all other tribes. They saw themselves as being *Chosen*. The idea of being separate from others in GOD'S eyes was born.

At first they passed all of this on from generation to generation by word of mouth and then later in writing in their Torah. According to one story, their Nation of Israel represented a favored brother, named Jacob, whom GOD loved. The other brother, named Esau, representing all other nations, GOD hated.

With this Covenant came the call for obedience to their God. He told them what He expected from them and what they could expect from Him. He had chosen their nation to carry out His Word. He had chosen them to fulfill a special role in His great plan. To do this, they must obey only Him.

The idea of Monotheism was their idea alone to hold on to and to believe. He was their God alone. The Gods worshiped by the other nations were powerless and irrelevant. He told them:

Thou shall have no other Gods before me.

Over the course of many generations, with this belief in a direct line of authority from GOD, came the seeds of argument, debate, and ultimately conflict. The message was from GOD, but the interpretation of the message often had different meanings. The interpreter of the Word was always human. Was the interpreter getting the message right? Was he to be trusted? What did the message of their God really mean? Why were there ambiguities in interpretation?

These ambiguities became even greater when, 1500 years later, men began to write about the life and death of Jesus, the long awaited Messiah, whose coming had been prophesied in the Hebrew Scriptures. Now, for many, both the Hebrew Bible and the canon of new scriptures depicting the life and death of Jesus Christ were the WORD of GOD. For the followers of Jesus the cycle was now complete. The nature of GOD was fully revealed.

Most of the Jews did not accept Jesus and his teachings. The view of the nature of their God had suddenly become very different. And their relationship to Him had changed. He was not the same God. He was not a harsh judgmental God to be feared as He was shown to be in the Hebrew Bible. He was now a God of love and compassion. He was incapable of inflicting punishment on His people. In fact He was a God who showed sorrow over the pain and suffering of His people. He had offered His own son as a sacrifice to show the depth of His love. And His covenant was now with all of mankind—and with womankind—not just with the Nation of Israel.

In many other ways, this new concept of GOD clashed with the one that the Jews had accepted from the very beginning of their history. As a result, the argument over the interpretation of the WORD of GOD and HIS relationship to those interpreting HIS message became more complex and increased in intensity.

Then came another change. Six hundred and ten years after the appearance of Jesus, in the ancient Arabian city of Mecca, angels began to speak to a merchant named Muhammad and a third interpretation of the nature of the God of both the Hebrew and Christian Bibles was declared. A new religion was born. The Prophet Muhammad proclaimed that the Hebrew and the Christian view of GOD had been corrupted, and the only true view of GOD was the one given to him by the Angel Gabriel.

If the view of the nature of GOD had changed, then how could all that had been written and said about Him be true? These questions did not find solutions in scholarly disputes. They gave rise to deeper issues. For Islam there followed a series of great battles, resulting in an empire that expanded westward and eastward from Mecca, destroying all other religions in its path, and covering a land mass from the shores of Morocco to Afghanistan as well as into parts of what is now Spain.

But Islam was not the end of the search for GOD. Fifteen hundred years after the death of Jesus Christ came another cataclysmic event that reshaped the view of the nature of GOD and how humans are meant to respond to HIM. The Protestant Reformation had begun. The Christian Church itself was split in two, leading to generations of bloody warfare. Who is right and who is wrong? Who is *Chosen* and who is not? Who is saved and who is not? Who is predestined and who is not? These became the bloody contentious issues.

To this day, these issues, Jewish, Christian, and Muslim have not been resolved. They still simmer and fester. As they have in the past, they continue to be a major underlying cause of world conflict. Pointing to the inerrancy of their scriptures and their own interpretations of these scriptures, fanatical factions within nations and in some cases the nations themselves brazenly justify their actions as the will of GOD. They claim to be *Chosen* to carry out His will. This fanaticism has spilled over into social and political conflict of such proportion and potential danger that it may now threaten civilization itself.

For the religions of Abraham, after over four thousand years of religious history, this is the dangerous and unstable path on which they find themselves as they enter the 21st century. It is a path strewn with the corpses of those who have perished as a result of the visceral disdain of Muslim fanatics toward Jewish and Christian infidels. It is a path of wanton secularism where large numbers of people look at all religious belief with cynicism. It is a path of defiance of respect for the idea that there are natural laws set in place by a greater power, laws that control our environment and will determine the survival of the human species on Planet Earth.

How did we get to this path? Where is it leading us? How much time do we have to change course?

The author says in this book that the time has come for thinking men and women concerned about the human condition in the 21st century and in the centuries beyond to examine the foundations of the three religions of Abraham, taking from their strengths and rejecting their weaknesses—and not with the mentality of those who have placed us on the path: Catholic Bishops, Rabbinical scholars, Islamic Ayatollahs, American television Evangelists, and Apocalyptic *Pop* Christian evangelical authors.

The time has come to look at these religions with minds liberated from the bondage of past belief tied to the inerrancy of the Hebrew Bible, the Christian Old and New Testament, the Koran, and the theologies that have grown out of them.

This book was written to open religious minds, to open new paths for all Jews, Christians and Muslims in new and unexplored directions, directions that may determine the future of not only their religions but also human civilization over the coming millennia

III

The Legacy of Hebraic Religious Belief

"What is Life?

It is the flash of a firefly in the night,

It is the breath of a buffalo in the wintertime,

It is the little shadow that runs across the grass

And loses itself in the sunset."

(A Blackfoot Indian Chief as he was dying)

Circ 1890

The words above were spoken to an American missionary by a Blackfoot Indian Chief as the Blackfoot Indian Chief lay dying. They express a sense of wonder at the magnificence of GOD'S creation. They speak to no moral rightness or wrongness. They are simply the reflection of a dying human being in his last hours, acknowledging the existence of his creator.

These two men coming together on the American prairie were bound together by a common inescapable human link; however, each viewed the world around him from an entirely different perspective.

The American Missionary came from a society with a belief system built upon ancient Hebrew Scriptures and prophecies. An essential part of his value system was the belief, made explicitly clear in the very first book of the Hebrew Bible, that it was man's God given right to subdue nature for his own purposes.

The Blackfoot Indian Chief came from an earlier form of social organization dating back to the very beginnings of mankind, perhaps extending as far back as 250,000 years. He came from a value system that looked at nature not in terms of domination or subjugation but in terms of harmonious accommodation. It was a value system that held to the belief that mankind was placed on earth to live in harmony with nature.

David Anderson

His was a pre-agriculture civilization of hunters and gatherers. It looked at the world, the stars, the mountains, the plants, the animals, from an entirely different point of view. It was a view that saw all of nature at one and in harmony with the mystery of the Creator of the Universe. It was a nature not to be subdued or dominated by man, but to be revered and looked upon with respect and awe, even as in the poem of the Blackfoot Indian Chief, to the very smallest part—the flash of a firefly in the night.

The Blackfoot Indian Chief has now been gone for over 100 years, yet his eyes are still with us in his last words as we too picture this scene in our own minds. We see more than just a picture of a dying human being painted in words. We see our own never-ending search for GOD.

The world today has little of the sense of awe that the Blackfoot Indian Chief expressed. Not only are we caught up in our religious history, but also we are caught up in the frenetic pace of our lives. We have lost sight of the wonder of GOD'S creation all around us. We look for our answers not to the firefly in the night and the breath of the buffalo in the wintertime, but to our reliance on reason and modern science.

We look to Quantum Mechanics to extend our knowledge farther and farther into the smallest parts of matter. We use our advanced instruments and our analytical knowledge to break down matter into its smallest composition. But as we do this, we are left with mathematical constructs that behave in less and less predictable ways and only open up new and profound mysteries. We also extend our knowledge the other way, out into the vast depths of space in our Universe, and as we do this we are left with the same uncertainties. As scientists delve into these mysteries, they long for a *Unified Theory* that will bring this all together, knowing all along that there will always be another side to the reaches of their knowledge.

Our world has undergone far-reaching changes since the Blackfoot Indian Chief lay dying. We not only know more about the physical universe around us but we also know more about what makes human beings act the way they do. Both the social sciences as well as the physical sciences have moved forward at exponential rates of speed.

This has not been the case with religion. We have not seen the same far-reaching changes. In fact, we have often seen a stubborn resistance to change. Advances in religious thought are held back by the rigidity of past belief, which is grounded on the inerrancy of ancient religious texts.

Those belief systems most intent on resisting change carry many different labels, the most prominent being that of Orthodox, Ultra-Orthodox, Conservative, Fundamentalist, and Evangelical. In all cases; however, there is a common denominator. Presuming the superiority of their belief system over all others, believers proclaim that only they are right and everyone else is wrong. The beliefs of all others outside of their own belief system are devalued.

These *believers'* generally hold to certain common convictions and follow certain practices in order to establish in their own minds the superiority of their own particular belief system. On the surface these can seem benign, and even necessary for individual religious fulfillment; however, they can also lead to unintended consequences. These consequences can lead to pain and suffering among those both within and outside of a particular belief system.

Some generally followed are:

- Only we have an understanding of the true nature of GOD

- Only we will be at one with GOD after death

- Only we have a true covenant with GOD

- Only we have been endowed with a mission as the moral catalyst for all humanity

- Only our rituals and observances have value and are the path to GOD'S grace

- Only our scriptures come from GOD and are without error

- We are surrounded by an alien, hostile, threatening, and immoral world

- All society outside of our own religious belief system exists in ignorance

- All society outside of our own religious belief system has been overtaken by evil

- Those who hold ideas other than our own have been overtaken by evil

- There will be a messianic age concurrent with an End of Time when only we will be saved by GOD

All of these beliefs and practices to one degree or another can be found in Judaism, Christianity, and Islam. None of the three Hebraic religions can escape the criticism that, in one way or another, they enable their own believers to say: "I have value in the eyes of GOD and you don't because you don't believe what I believe."

With this separateness come both intended as well as unintended consequences. We can see this in our recent history. Some examples are:

- The silence of Lutheran and Roman Catholic Germans—as well as many others in the west—who, during the Hitler era, looked at Jews and their religious beliefs and practices as being inferior. For them, Jews **held ideas other than our own** and therefore were **overtaken by evil**. As the Holocaust unfolded, many German Christians who believed that **only we have a true covenant with GOD**, silently stood by, seeing Jewish lives as irrelevant and having little value.

- Jewish intellectuals at that time who, rejecting the divinity of Jesus, preached the rabbinical idea of their own *particularity*, a word the rabbis used to describe all Jews, which defined them as unique among all of civilization—because of their Torah and its definition of covenant. Believing in this, these Jews openly considered their religion not only to be superior to Christianity but also a religion **endowed with a mission as the moral catalyst for all humanity.**

- In more recent times, evangelical Christians who believe that both The Old Testament and The New Testament **scriptures come from GOD and are without error**, and therefore interpreting the Gospel of John 3:16 in its most narrow sense, openly condemn those in society who do not express a rhetorical belief in Jesus as the Christ, saying that they will not be saved at death but will pass on into the fires of hell.

- Muslims throughout the world who believe that every word of the Koran **comes from GOD and is without error** and all Jewish and Christian scripture is corrupted. They believe that their thoughts and actions are encouraged by Allah, to include the murder of all enemies of Islam, even by means of suicide if necessary. They harbor a demeaning view toward non Muslims to include Christians and Jews as well as secular atheists and agnostics. They are told by their clerics to believe that all infidels are *najis* (unclean) and will remain so until they convert to Islam. (See www.sistani.org Grand Ayatollah Ali al-Sistani's Ruling 107 where he defines an infidel or Kafir as person who does not believe in Allah and His Oneness, as being *najis*.) He then defines *najis* as follows: "the entire body of a Kafir, including his hair and nails, and all liquid substances of his body are *najis*" (Islam generally defines *najis* substances as urine, dead bodies, pigs, dogs, sweat of an animal that eats unclean things and menstrual blood).

In each of the above we see one group of believers assuming superiority over the other, and we see an unwillingness and inability to change. Each religious group proclaims that ***only we have an understanding of the true nature of GOD***. This feeling of superiority acts as a negative force freezing old religious patterns of thought and works against the acceptance of new religious ideas originating from outside the bounds of the narrowness of a particular group's religious orthodoxy.

These responses can affect geopolitical events in both positive and negative ways with broad and far reaching results. Politicians, religious leaders, and intellectuals may be at the forefront; however, it is the general population with its underlying beliefs that become the supportive driving engine. It is the power of this "silent majority" that allows what happens to happen.

For Jews the idea that ***only we have been endowed with a mission as the moral catalyst for all humanity*** began at the end of the 18th century with the Emancipation movement in Europe, a movement that allowed Jews to assimilate into European society by giving them fuller political and economic rights and educational opportunity. This in turn at the end of the 19th century led to the Socialist movement. This Jewish utopian idea of social consciousness as it spread throughout Europe ultimately led to social democratic reform in many of the European countries. It also was largely responsible for the world's experiment with International Communism, a system that tragically released the darkest side of human nature. This social consciousness, as European Jews immigrated to the United States, gave political impetus there to the International Trade Union Movement as well as other forms of social activism. The idea of Judaism acting as a force toward social goodness as well as the idea of the *particularity* of Jews and the special place of Jewish thought continues to exist in the United States as a liberal political dimension of Reformed Judaism.

For evangelical Christians the identical idea of one's religion being ***the moral catalyst for all humanity*** in recent years has expressed itself politically in exactly the opposite way in contradiction to the aforementioned Jewish thought. Resting their case on the breakdown of morality in American society, in the 2000 and 2004 Presidential elections the evangelical Christian *Moral Majority* exerted considerable political influence and turned the election both times in favor of a Republican Presidential candidate holding to a conservative ideology in line with their evangelical Christian conservative political agenda. Their interpretation of *social consciousness* was in stark contrast to the recent historical one of Judaism that had traditionally expressed itself through the Democratic Party. One can debate the question: Is the Reformed Jewish concept of *social consciousness* more like the message of Jesus than the Christian conservative concept of *social consciousness*?

What is most important to observe here is the power in the United States—as well as throughout world—that religion has to establish and sustain political power. Examples of this on the domestic front in the United States range from the abortion issue to gay marriage to stem cell research. Two examples on the international front are the influence of American Jews on the policies of the United States toward the Nation of Israel and the decision to preemptively wage war on Iraq, where the president made reference to his being guided by a "higher power."

This conviction that only *our* particular religion as interpreted by *our particular group* can be seen as ***the moral catalyst for all humanity*** is often based on the belief that certain supporting scriptural texts, as well as certain interpretations of them, are from GOD and therefore are without error. This can manifest itself in many different ways.

Many Jews today believe that the Hebrew Bible and the rabbinic law and exegesis that grew out of it are from GOD. They believe that ***only we have an understanding of the true nature of GOD***. In fact, when a Rabbi is interpreting the Torah, in Judaism it is GOD who is speaking. This authority has led some Rabbis to pronounce that the land of Israel was given to the Jews by GOD, and the restoration of the Temple there is directed by GOD.

Muslims, as has been noted, believe that the words of the Koran were given to Muhammad by Allah himself. The Sharia law that grew out of the Koran is sacrosanct. Sharia law is Allah's law for all humankind. A Muslim must live his life under Sharia law. Islam is to be ***the moral catalyst for all humanity***. Therefore, the conquests of Islam cannot rest until the world has become a clerical state under Sharia law.

Christianity has followed much the same pattern. The idea of being ***the moral catalyst for all humanity*** is central to all Christian belief. Also, there is an emphasis on the *chosen ness* of the individual believer—covered by the complex and often debated concepts of predestination and election.

The idea that ***Only our scriptures come from GOD and are without error***, taken to an extreme, can be seen in the approaches to two concepts common to evangelical Christianity, namely the concepts covering the end of the world and evolution.

Evangelical Christians believe ***There will be a messianic age concurrent***

with an End of Time when only we will be saved by GOD and they eagerly await for this time, which they call the Apocalypse.

As for evolution, in their arguments against Darwinian, as well as the more recent scientific theories of evolution, they refute all but the biblical creation account. Archeological and anthropological discoveries are to be ignored. Carbon dating is from the devil. Darwinian evolution was a hoax. Man began as Adam. Eve came from the rib of Adam. The Universe was created in six days. GOD flooded the world because He was angry with mankind. Only Noah and his family were saved.

These Christians look outside of themselves with myopic eyes seeing scientific progress as something to be feared and rejected. They look with suspicion at all other religions open to a modern scientific view of evolution and those in them who believe in any other way.

From the very beginnings of man's search for a knowledge that would free him from the cycle of birth and death, he had woven into his history a written record of his beliefs. Whether is was the lessons of the Vedas, the Greek classical writings of Plato, the Koran of Muhammad, the Hebrew Bible, or the Canon of the Christian New Testament scriptures; the expression of religious thought at some point in its development always took on a written form. Fundamentalist religion says that this written form was the word of GOD and it cannot be changed. It refuses to acknowledge that any of it could be from the mind and hand of man.

If this were merely an academic exercise, it would have little relevance for the world of today, but this is not the case. In fact, it has become the cause of much of the present world conflict, and it promises to be the cause of future conflict. It has in a sense taken over the conflict of the past century between the two political ideologies, Communism and Capitalism, and grown to express itself in the form of international terrorism with potential dangers even greater than those previously faced.

Pointing to the inerrancy of their scriptures, fanatical factions within nations and in some cases the nations themselves brazenly justify their actions as the will of GOD. They claim to be exclusive or *Chosen*.

The texts supporting the arguments over which these conflicts have arisen represented the efforts of past civilizations to explain the nature of GOD based on their ancient level of understanding of themselves and the world around them. Much of what was written has limited relevance in the world of today if taken in literal form.

A case in point is a famous passage in the Hebrew Bible:

> *It shall be done to him as he has done; fracture for fracture, eye for eye, tooth for tooth; the injury and disfigurement he has inflicted upon another shall be in turn inflicted upon him.*
>
> (Leviticus 24:20)

and in the Koran:

> *It is life for life, eye for eye, and nose for nose, and ear for ear, and tooth for tooth, and reprisal in wounds....*
>
> (Sura 5.45)

This may have been a legitimate way for Hebrews to control a tribal society in the desert 3500 years ago, and Muslims their society in the Arabian desert 600 after Jesus Christ, but clearly it is not the way human beings should respond to each other in our modern age where in an escalation of violence planes can be flown into buildings, suicide bombers can blow themselves up in night clubs and atomic bombs can be detonated in major cities.

Modern day Jews will argue that this Leviticus passage is now for them in the 21st century interpreted only in a legalistic sense; however, recent events in Israel prove that this is not the case. The same can be said for Muslims who will point out that their Koran goes on to say: *... but he who forgoes it, it shall be an expiation for him....* The dangerous outcomes of these archaic thought patterns cannot be passed off in such an intellectual fashion. Once these ideas are fixed in the minds of the believer, they remain in the subconscious.

An example of scriptural thought patterns acting as a driving force in decision making is the Palestinian/Israeli conflict over the settlements in the West Bank near the city of Jerusalem. This land for Orthodox Jews was mandated to them by Yahweh in their scriptures. As they aggressively expanded these settlements in defiance of world opinion, Palestinians respond in turn with suicide bombings. Then, Israelis in turn respond with the killing of Palestinian terrorist leaders as well as innocent Palestinian civilians caught in the crossfire.

We need to acknowledge the power that scripture has over our thoughts and actions. We are rapidly becoming one world of one human race. No longer can we hide behind our past tribal, national, and religious identities as a justification for our actions. The time has come for religious scriptural self-examination. Not only Christians, Jews, and Muslims, but all peoples of the world of all religious beliefs must examine the validity of their beliefs and ask the following two questions:

- Are we being held back in our social development as a world community by our belief in the inerrancy of ancient religious texts that no longer relate to our new knowledge?

- Is it possible that many of these texts have more to say to us, but by holding fast to the inerrancy of their language, we are missing new and deeper meanings?

Here is where debate among religions of all peoples of all nations should be taking place, not over the inerrancy of any scripture of any kind. The past has given us glimpses of GOD'S revelation, not a lock on the truth. As human beings we entered the world with the commission to search for the truth.

To find the truth there are two questions that every religion must address:

- Does the GOD we worship ask us to honor each other?

- How do we honor each other?

This today is the challenge to all people of all religions. Each of us must take this road in search for GOD. Whatever the traditional religious background, all of mankind from its very beginning has been moving towards this same goal. We should not be held back now by ancient religious texts. They should enhance our knowledge, not restrain it.

Challenges to Christian New Testament writings and to the Hebrew Bible (Christian Old Testament) have come from many different directions. Some have come from archaeological discoveries and some from the physical and social sciences. Some have come from simple observation of the human condition and recognition of the inadequacy of religion to correct its failures. At the same time the expansion of knowledge relating to our world and our universe has been exponential, and as this has occurred, there has been a clashing with orthodox biblical belief. What began with Copernicus and Galileo continues with even greater violence.

As this debate over the inerrancy of scripture continues, there is arising an entirely new issue that is largely being ignored. In recent years we have heard scientists question whether our human species, given its present pace of resource use and the accompanying environmental degradation, can survive for as long a period as it has already existed. The fragility of our earth is illustrated in the photographs that have come back to us from our satellites. Our scientists are warning that the earth may not be able to sustain us if we continue to pollute and destroy. Clearly, issues such as this call for a reassessment of our relationship to our natural environment, as well as to each other. They also call for a reassessment of the adequacy of the role of religion in addressing the future.

The religions grounded on the Hebrew Bible should be examining these issues. They are not. Rather, they are wasting their time and energy in a constant battle as to who is theologically right and who is theologically wrong, who is saved and who is not. As far as the future of the world is concerned, arguments over apocalyptic prophecy take center stage. There is an assumption that the day will come when the world will no longer be. GOD is viewed as the destroyer. He will end it all as He did with the world in Noah's time, but this time totally.

The question must be asked of those Jews, Christians and Muslims who believe in an Apocalypse: Is yours a self-fulfilling prophecy, which over the centuries has rested on a false foundation, that of man's god given right to *dominate nature*? What if the Blackfoot Indian Chief quoted at the beginning of these remarks was right and all of nature should be looked at as being at one in harmony with the mystery of our Creator? What if GOD intentioned a continuation of HIS creation here on this earth towards the beauty of HIS perfection and we humans are a part of that perfection? Is apocalyptic thinking a death wish for all of humanity? By their own belief in the End of Times are they, the sons and daughters of Abraham, subliminally setting the stage for the end of the human species? Are they selfishly saying to future generations: We want it all now. We don't have to care about the future of the world. GOD will be destroying it anyway.

Those of the tradition of Abraham believe that man was told by GOD that He has dominion over nature, He can dominate it and to use it for His own purposes. The Book of Genesis tells man that he is to:

> *rule over the fish of the sea and the birds of the sky and over the cattle and over every creeping thing that creeps on the earth.*

(Genesis 1:28)

From the beginning of his history this is what man did, and it allowed him to prosper. It is only in the last century as scientists have observed the irreparable damage being done to Planet Earth that man has looked back and realized that the power to dominate nature also gave him the power to destroy it. To his horror he is seeing that by degrading and destroying the environment that surrounds him he is setting out the pathway to his own extinction. Humankind is seeing the first glimpses of the end of the human species, not coming from a punishing God in some apocalyptic act of final judgment taken from Hebrew scripture, but from his own actions.

Could this assumption that originated in the ancient Hebrew Bible and became such an important part of the theology of Judaism, Christianity, and Islam be wrong? Have we been misguided by the words of these ancient texts? Were the words of the Hebrew Bible that laid the foundation for Judaism, Christianity, and Islam directly from GOD or were they merely from an exceptionally gifted and introspective people living in a desert wilderness looking for the answers to their existence? Are other assumptions made in the Hebrew Bible, The Christian New and Old Testaments and the Koran wrong? Should we be searching for greater knowledge elsewhere?

There may be a great deal that modern man can learn from the Blackfoot Indian Chief quoted at the beginning of this chapter and those who lived before him. The Blackfoot Indian Chief looked at all of nature as being at one and in harmony with the mystery of our Creator, a Creator who intended a continuation of everything in His creation here on earth, a creation forever moving towards perfection. The Blackfoot Indian Chief would have had no quarrel with parts of the Book of Genesis, but he would not have agreed with all of it. He too believed that what GOD had created in the world was all *Good*. For him, GOD was a creator of beauty. HE was a creator of the mystery of life. HE was also a God who looked upon every man, every woman, every bird, every animal, every living thing, even to the very smallest—*every creeping thing that creeps upon the earth*—as an interdependent and sacrosanct part of the mystery of that creation. The Blackfoot Indian Chief saw each and every living thing, as well as non-living thing, to be honored and respected, not to be ruled over or dominated.

For the Blackfoot Indian Chief the breath of the buffalo in the wintertime was the spirit of GOD saying to him:

I am here with you. See me in the beauty of my creation.
Die in peace.

(This author)

The words in this book are addressed to everyone, from those with the same faith as that of the Blackfoot Indian Chief to those holding complex faiths grounded on ancient writings and philosophical discourse. They are also addressed to those with no faith at all. They give due credit, but largely leave aside for other writers the positive role that religion has played over the course of history towards the advancement of human civilization, and rather concentrate on the shortcomings of religious belief in the world of the 21st century. They come to the conclusion that the underlying cause of world conflict today is religious belief.

The three Hebraic rooted religions, Judaism, Christianity, and Islam, exist suspended in a time warp going back thousands of years. They are unable to change. It is for this reason that they are unable to act in concert as a positive force toward the advancement of human civilization. In very many ways each has become an impediment to advancement.

As for Christianity, many of the ideas in this book are in opposition to accepted Christian doctrine as it was grounded by the early church bishops in the authorized New Testament texts. The message sides more with the revelations taken from the Nag Hammadi findings, and in particular The Gospel of Thomas discovered at Nag Hammadi. Knowledge gained from this Gospel is used in the argument against the inerrancy of the New Testament as well as the Hebrew Bible and the Koran. It is also used as an argument against all institutionalized religion.

The Jesus portrayed by Thomas said that GOD does not limit His presence to those of any single earthly religion. He said that the relationship between human beings and GOD is direct and without the need for any religious institutional intermediary.

He told Thomas that GOD exists in the here an now and not in some far off dimension looking down on human beings and judging them as to whether or not they are following the laws and observances called for in their religious texts. Nor will there be a final judgment day. He said GOD exists at every moment within and around each and every one of us. We are a part of Him and He is a part of us.

There is a caveat though. Jesus told Thomas that the road might not be an easy one. For some it will be very painful. He said we cannot find GOD within until we have cast aside from our lives everything of this world that by defining our wants and desires is distracting us. We must first know in the depths of ourselves on what side we have placed our lives, what God or Gods we have allowed to define us. He said it is only after we have done this that we can then begin the search to the depths of our very being to find answers to the most penetrating questions about ourselves, questions that we may never have dared before to ask, questions about who we really are. Only then can we discover the one GOD who is within. Only then can we reach HIM. As Jesus told Thomas, only then can HE reach us.

According to the Thomas Gospel, the God we find within will not be the anthropomorphic God of the Torah. Nor will He be the God of the Christian Old Testament or much of the Christian New Testament or the God of the Koran. He will not be a judgmental God. He will not be a God capable of anger. He will not be a God to be feared. He will not be a God who requires us to obey 613 commandments or to pray five times each day. He will be a God of awesome power and pure love, but a God who demands that we show this same love to each other.

This is not the definition of the God revealed in Hebrew, Muslim, and Christian religious texts. Christians have come close to the Thomas definition in the New Testament, but they nevertheless continue to hold on to the Hebraic definition of the angry, judgmental, and fearful father God of the Old Testament. They define Him that way as the inscrutable father God of their Trinity.

The time has come for humans to face a number of questions: Have these three religions wrongly defined the nature of our Creator? If the thoughts and actions of those following these religions are being conditioned by their belief in this ancient God, is this patterning their behavior towards each other and the world around them? Is this a primary cause for present world conflict? Does it threaten future human existence? Was Thomas right? This book is an exploration of these and other questions.

Our thoughts can not escape those of the Blackfoot Indian Chief. Like his, they come from all of nature that surrounds us. There is little difference between us. We all have the same sense of awe as we see in the depths of our minds the

"... flash of the firefly in the night

... breath of the buffalo in the winter time

... little shadow that runs across the grass

And loses itself in the sunset".

IV

The First of the Infidels
The Story of Jacob and Esau

Which ones can make the claim to be loved by God like Jacob; the Jews, the Catholics, the Presbyterians, the Baptists, or is it the Muslims? Which were from the very beginnings of the foundation of time destined to be the *Chosen* ones? Which were not?

The God of the Hebrew Bible made a distinction between the two brothers. Jacob He loved, Esau He hated. The Nation of Israel that sprang from Jacob He loved. All other Nations and all other people He hated.

It was a distinction not made on merit or lack of merit, on being good or being evil. It was not related to what either brother did or did not do to please the Hebrew God. It was a distinction made seemingly without reason. It was a distinction made before their birth, before either one even had a chance to make his own choices. Jacob was included in GOD'S grace. Esau was excluded, cut off. The Nation of Israel was included in GOD'S grace. All others were like the brother, Esau, cut off.

Is the story of Jacob and Esau as it was recorded in Genesis simply a primitive tale of little relevance today, or does it remain a part of our 21st century world? Should we dismiss this story about the beginning of a special covenantal relationship between GOD and the Nation of Israel as just an elitist notion?

For the Jews this is a story that established their belief that they were elected by GOD to be His *Chosen* people. Later, for Christians the belief in election and predestination looked to this story for its meaning. When the Prophet Muhammad was receiving his messages from the Angel Gabriel six hundred years after the death of Jesus, the distinctions between Jacob (Yaqoub) and Esau (Ishaq) were not made, but the idea of superiority was there and this story formed the basis for his belief that only those who accepted the Islamic faith were to be among the *Chosen*. He (Allah) was able to say in the Koran:

Fight those who do not believe in Allah...they are in a state of subjection.

(Sura 9.29)

*O you who believe! Do not take the Jews and Christians for friends; ...
Allah does not guide unjust people.*

(Sura 5.51)

*And the Jews say... And the Christians say... Allah will destroy them;
how they are turned away!*

(Sura 9.30)

*The Children of Israel. All this—the evil of It—is hateful in the sight
of your Lord.*

(Sura 17.38)

This was a story that had a lasting impact, first on Judaism, then on Christianity, and then on Islam. Was it really from GOD Himself; or, did it merely grow out of the mind of an early Jewish patriarchal tribal nation looking for a personal God for its own protection? When Jacob and Esau were born, was GOD present at all? Did Jacob get the upper hand not because he was loved by GOD but simply because he was devious and deceitful? Were the early Jewish writers merely transferring their own emotions of love and disappointment toward their male offspring into an anthropomorphic paternal God of their own definition and by so doing giving him their own human frailties, having him be like any father, favoring one son over another?

The answers to the above are unimportant. What is important is the lasting impact this story has had on western thought and how this is leading to conflict in the interdependent geopolitical world of today.

It is a story that begins in Genesis and extends through the Old Testament and then into the New. Then it takes hold of Islam. It builds in intensity, as the idea of GOD'S covenant with the Nation of Israel becomes more and more a part of Jewish religious thought. It is the story of two brothers. The role of GOD behind the scene at first does not appear. The full written explanation of the why of GOD'S choice between Jacob and Esau only appears fifteen hundred years after their births, in the Book of Malachi when we find a confusing yet definitive explanation. The Prophet writes in the person of GOD Himself:

*Was not Esau Jacob's brother? ... yet I (God) loved Jacob, and I (God)
hated Esau.*

(authors' brackets)

(Malachi 1:2-3)

Malachi makes it clear that GOD not only favors the Nation of Israel—a metaphor for Jacob—, even with all its faults, but He dismisses all other nations and their people as marginalized. As with Esau, He turns His back on them.

Malachi's revelation that GOD chooses as He wishes to choose, favoring whom He wishes to favor did not stop with the end of the Jewish Bible. The words of Malachi were brought into the Christian New Testament. The Christian idea, of the *chosen ones* being only those who believed in Jesus Christ as the Messiah, was born.

The Apostle Paul and later the Roman Catholic Church placed this idea of exclusivity and superiority in the forefront of Christian theology where it has remained ever since. It was called Election and Predestination and it was to be available only to believers in Jesus Christ. With the presence of the Messiah, no longer would any kind of special relationship be available for the Jews. GOD had turned His back on those in the Nation of Israel who did not accept Jesus as their Messiah. The covenant that had only been available to Jews and the *particularity* of individual Jews in the eyes of GOD had ended. They were to be like Esau, separated from the love of GOD.

The Apostle Paul looked to the messianic prophecies of the Hebrew Bible for his claim that only those who believed in Jesus Christ were favored by GOD. He began his argument with the story of Jacob and Esau. We see a reference to Malachi in Paul's Letter to the Romans where he says:

As it is written, Jacob have I loved, but Esau have I hated

(Romans 9:13)

He ties this in with the concept of election when he says in Romans:

For the children being not yet born, neither having done any good or evil, that the purpose of election might stand, not of works but of him that calleth.

(Romans 9:11)

Then, to make sure that this special place, as it had been over the years for the Jews, would apply regardless of Christian human frailty, he again quotes again from the Hebrew Bible:

I will have mercy, and I will have compassion on whom I will have compassion.

(Romans 9:15)

In his Letter to the Ephesians he then makes the final claim:

According as he has chosen us in him before the foundation of the world, that we should be holy and without blame before him in love, having predestined us into the adoption of children by Jesus Christ, to himself, according to the good pleasure of his will...

(Ephesians 1:4-5)

Sixty years after the death of Jesus, Paul had drawn a line in the sand. Only Christians can stand in the place of Jacob.

This challenge to the Jews did not end there. There was yet to come another challenge. The Prophet Muhammad said both Judaism and Christianity were misguided religions. Their writings were corrupted. He drew another line in the sand. Muhammad was to be the new Jacob, chosen by Allah Himself and the Nation of Islam under Sharia Law the new nation. All others were the Esau. They were irrelevant. It was the will of Allah.

With each of the three religions making the same claim, the idea that only *we* were chosen by GOD took on a new and potentially dangerous dimension.

For Judaism the idea of being the *Chosen* people had become the foundation for the belief that there existed a covenant between GOD and the Nation of Israel. Individual Jews were to share in this and be singled out as being separate from others. This is the belief of Jews to this day. For Christianity with the writings of the Apostle Paul, election and predestination became the foundation for the idea that Christians are separate from all others and some, if not all, are predestined to exist in GOD'S grace. For Muhammad writing six hundred years after the death of Jesus the idea of being superior and separate became the rational for the belief that all of those outside of Islam are infidels and are doomed to either a lower status—People of the Book—or, for all others, eternal damnation.

The biblical Jewish, Christian, and Muslim scriptures quoted above came from ages past and therefore may today seem archaic and benign, but they are not. As they were in the past, they are very much alive today in our world. They have become an important part of the thinking process of 21st century Jews, Christians, and Muslims. If GOD could favor Jacob and turn his back on Esau, why shouldn't we be able to act in the same manner? Why shouldn't *Chosen* Jews or *Sharia* Muslims or *elected* Presbyterians, Baptists, and Roman Catholics consider themselves separate and superior to all others?

In recent years the Jewish concept of being *Chosen* has become the justification for the idea of the land of Israel being *their* God given land. Jews remain GOD'S *Chosen* people with a right to that land. Jews define themselves by the word *particularity*, which is as being different and superior as to their religious beliefs.

For Christianity the concept of election and predestination became the justification for the Inquisition and the Crusades. It fueled hatred over the centuries among competing Christian theological positions, as it does to this day, each Christian group believing that only its members are among the elect. Over the centuries it provided the rational for Christian anti-Semitism. As for Islam, from the time of Muhammad to the present day it has fueled the hatred of Muslims toward Jewish and Christian *infidels*.

It allowed many German Catholics and Lutherans to look silently with disdain on German Jews as the Holocaust unfolded. After all, had not Paul quoting Isaiah (29:10), referred to the Jews as "those of whom God has given a sluggish spirit, eyes that would not see, and ears that would not hear" (Romans 11:8)?

If GOD could devalue Esau and view him as a non-person, why shouldn't they, as elected and predestined Christians, be justified in viewing the Jews as non-people? Why shouldn't they look at the Jews as being separate and inferior? In the mind of GOD, as with Esau, Jewish lives had little value. Their Christian theology told them the Jews, like Esau, were irrelevant. Jewish lives had no place in eternity except among the damned. The Apostle Paul had said so. Without remorse, the Jews could be exterminated. It is not surprising that the world witnessed the Holocaust.

German Christians must not be the only ones singled out. The Holocaust was only a boil coming to the surface and erupting telling us of an underlying disease permeating all three religions. It is the disease of superiority, judgment, and arrogance. It existed then and continues to exist just as powerfully today. Jews, Christians, and Muslims must each recognize their own culpability. The idea that certain human beings "other than our own" have little or no value and we like Jacob are superior and favored by GOD is woven into all three. It is a disease that goes back to the very beginning of Judeo-Christian/Islamic scripture, to the story of Jacob and Esau.

The story of Jacob and Esau is just as pernicious a force today as it was over three thousand years ago. That only those of our own particular religious belief system have higher value in the mind of GOD is firmly imbedded in the subconscious of each. This, to a great extent in the world of the 21st century, is influencing the thoughts of Jews, Christians, and Muslims towards each other. It is also influencing their actions. These feelings today are the primary underlying cause of today's world conflict.

V

Three Different Approaches to Salvation

"The greater question those at the extremes must ask is whether
GOD is making the same exclusionary choices that they are."

(The Author)

The world has chosen to look at the three religions of Abraham as if they
were three brothers or sisters. The fact is, like siblings from the same family who
are raised by the same parents, each is very different from the other. This is most
noticeable in their separate understandings of the nature of the monotheistic
God they worship and the personal relationship of believers to that God.

The understanding of the nature of the God each worships is not the same.
How to achieve eternal life with GOD is not the same.

- **For Christians** it is by striving to live and think like Jesus Christ whom
  they believe was GOD incarnate. Their goal is to become perfect like
  he was. However, they believe that no matter how much they strive
  to become perfect like him, they remain fallible sinful human beings
  who can never attain total perfection. They believe it is only through
  the love and forgiveness of GOD that they can be at one with Him for
  eternity. The depth of that love was expressed by the crucifixion of His
  son—symbolically the ultimate sacrifice. Works alone therefore can
  never be enough to justify redemption.

- **For Jews** it is by both studying and following the law of the Torah and
  its commentaries. Torah study encompasses the whole Hebrew Bible,
  including the prophets and the other writings. It also includes the
  bulk of post biblical literature, called *Mishnah* and its later elaboration
  known as the *Gemarah*. Together they are called the *Talmud*. In
  addition to the *Talmud*, there are biblical and homiletic works called
  the *Midrashim*, a large corpus of rabbinic works. To the extent Jews
  live their lives studying these texts and living by them, they believe
  they will be rewarded after death by a God of judgment although there
  are no specifics as to "Heaven" in the Christian or "Paradise" in the
  Muslim sense.

- **For Muslims** it is by following the teachings of the prophet Muhammad and believing that he was the appointed by God to give the world His word. This word is expressed not in the Christian Old or New Testament or the Hebrew Bible or commentaries but in a code of conduct found in the Koran and the Sunna, known together as the Shari'a. Muslims are required to believe that living and thinking by these writings is the way to eternal life. All other teachings outside of Islam are considered to have been corrupted. At death, as in Judaism, it is a God of judgment who will decide the eternal existence of the Muslim.

It can be seen that the three religions that sprang from Abraham have far reaching differences. The most significant of these deals with the two most important questions any religion can ask of itself: What is the nature of GOD and what is our relationship to HIM?

For most of the believers of these three religions, there is the conviction that only they are right and all others are wrong. In the matter of salvation none of the three, a least for orthodox believers, believe that there can be any kind of compromise or even accommodation. Each believes that all in the other traditions risk exclusion from a perfect eternal union with GOD. There is a general belief, however, at least among those with moderate views in each of the three —generally not among the orthodox—that GOD will favor those from the other Hebraic rooted traditions who think and live their lives in accordance with some approximation of their own tradition.

As for the Orthodox positions, and assuming s judgmental God and an afterlife, the greater question those at the extremes must ask is whether GOD is making the same exclusionary choices that they are. If GOD is not, but is looking at some other aspect of human thought and behavior, those who live and think at the extremes of their traditions may have to face the eternal consequences of a series of questions at death:

- Could some of their scriptures, Hebrew, Christian, Muslim not be of the Mind of GOD, but of the mind of man? Could they be *corrupted*?

- Is it GOD'S divine truth that eternal union with Him is reserved just for themselves?

- What does it mean if they are wrong?

- By judging others as being excluded, are they making Gods of themselves?

These are questions with an eternal dimension. By excluding all others, their answers may place at risk for eternity nothing less than our own souls.

REFLECTION # 1

Three Monotheistic Beliefs

I. Christianity

"We are saved solely through him, out of grace and mercy, without any works or merit on our part".

(The sermons of MARTIN LUTHER

section I on Faith, and coming to Christ)

If righteousness is through the law, then Christ died for naught.

(Galatians 2:21)

II. Judaism

"God created two different time periods: The first period is called the 'period of Effort and Striving.' This is the period we are living in. In this period we live a Torah life and perform Torah commandments.... This is where we earn the goodness. This period is temporary, as it ends in death. The second period, called 'the Period of Reward,' starts after death. During that time the soul will receive the goodness that it earned. This period is eternal."

(Rabbi Moshe Chaim Luzatto,

18th Century Italian)

III. Islam

"Thus it is evident how closely connected with the Maker is the leader (Muhammad) ...who serves the purposes of the Maker's artistry... Surely the religion of God is Islam... Muhammad is the messenger of God.... If you want endless accomplishments with regard to your afterlife, walk on the Prophet's way.... By acting in accordance to the elevated Sunna of the Prophet Muhammad, one can make one's transient life produce eternal fruits to be the means of eternal life.

(WWW. islamanswers.net/sunna/loved.htm)

VI

The Challenge to Rabbinical Judaism The Continuing Revelation of the Hebrew God

Judaism Despite Christianity

The Letters between Eugen Rosenstock-Huessy and Franz Rosenzweig

"And the question (was) forced upon him (Rosenzweig) as to whether there was any purpose in the synagogue, seeing that in the reality of history the struggle between the pagan world and the message of revelation was being fought out not by Judaism, but by Christianity".

About The Correspondence

By Dr. Alexander Altman, Professor of Jewish Philosophy, Brandeis University

Judaism Despite Christianity is a book of letters written in the early part of the 20th century between two great religious thinkers of our age, one a Christian, the other a Jew. In one of the letters Rosenstock-Huessy, a Christian, directs a question to Rosenzweig, a Jew, about the relevance of Judaism in world history. It was of such poignancy that when reading it, Rosenzweig decided to abandon Judaism and convert to Christianity. But then he changed his mind.

An introduction to these letters reads: *...there did not seem to be any place (for him) for Judaism.*

This statement opens up a question that haunts the Jewish-Christian dialogue to this day. Why would Rosenzweig, a Jew, look at Judaism as being a religion that had lost its relevance, a religion that had died? Why would he then want to become a Christian? Why then couldn't he?

Rosenzweig, who had not in fact been a devout Jew before his decision, decided that before converting, he would return briefly to his Jewish roots. He wanted first to experience the fullness of living and thinking spiritually as a Jew. When he did turn to Judaism, as he later wrote, what occurred was a "religious experience that happened with the force of a conversion" but it was not like the conversion experienced by Christians. It was a conversion experience that brought him into a direct relationship with the God of Judaism without the intermediary of Jesus Christ. Rosenzweig was drawn back into his Jewishness. He remained there for the rest of his life.

Can both Christians and Jews learn something from this story? What was it about the question that made Rosenzweig, a Jew, decide to become a Christian? Why did Rosenstock-Huessy's question disturb him so deeply? What held Rosenzweig back from conversion to Christianity? Was Rosenstock-Huessy's question about the relevance of the synagogue in history valid? Does his assertion of its irrelevance have application in our world today 75 years later?

The answers center on the influence of Judaism as a contributing factor in the advancement of Western Civilization. Rosenstock-Huessy was saying that over the past two millennia the battle in the West against the forces of paganism had been fought not by Jewish Rabbinical introspection in the Synagogue, but by the openness of Christianity as it extended itself outward to all of man and women kind. He was saying that the dictum of Jesus Christ: *As you have loved the least of my brethren, you have shown your love to me* had been a driving force unprecedented in world history bringing people of all tribal, national and spiritual backgrounds into a relationship with the God of all Creation, helping them to separate and destroy within themselves the opposing de humanizing and destructive forces of evil.

Rosenstock-Huessy was saying that this revelation unveiled 2000 years ago by a Jew from Nazareth was the force that had powered the Western World into the society it is today. For the first 300 years it overcame the Roman and other hostile pagan forces that were bent upon crushing it. For the next 1000 years, after the fall of the Roman Empire and through the Dark Ages, it battled the forces of Barbarian conquest. Then, with the Renaissance it opened up the human mind releasing all of its potential and allowing civilization to spring forth into a new age of enlightenment.

From the time of Rosenstock-Huessy's letters to the present day, the revelation of Jesus relating to our relationship to each other and to GOD has continued to be absorbed in human consciousness throughout the world and to gain strength. In recent history, from the two great wars, to the standoff against atheistic socialism, to the war in Bosnia, to the battle against Islamic Jihad; the ideas expressed in the life and teaching of Jesus have been at the forefront of the struggle.

In recent history two American Presidents have framed the threats to western society in the context of the message of Jesus. It is not by accident that President Bush, a born again Christian, characterized the struggle against global terrorism as a struggle not simply against a challenge to the American democratic way of life or the preservation of two hundred and fifty years of American history, but as a struggle against an "axis of evil". On the surface this may have seemed simplistic; until viewed, as his fundamentalist Christian perspective would necessarily imply, as a struggle against the antithesis of the revelation of Jesus Christ. This antithesis has been the struggle from the very beginning of human history. It was defined by the Jews in the very first book of their Torah when in Genesis man's capacity for evil was revealed. And, it occupied the overriding theme of the rest of their Bible.

With the coming of Jesus Christ, the Jews did not reach outside of the Temple and then the Synagogue and join in this life and death struggle. In their past they had always fought for their own tribal and religious preservation, but had not made an effort to spread the ideas from their Torah to the rest of the world. At times, they had accepted some non-Jews from the outside, but just as often their armies had destroyed and left abandoned those who had challenged them and their beliefs. There was no attempt to change the world.

With Jesus as the self proclaimed last Jewish Prophet and Messiah, the new religion that he formed, Christianity, took on the great battle against evil in the world. But, the Jews rejected him. They turned inward, and as they dispersed from their homeland after 70 A.D., they hid behind their Torah in the confines of their synagogues.

Shortly after the crucifixion of Jesus, the religion of Abraham had become two Jewish religions, one, ancient Judaism and the other Christianity/Judaism. Then, Christianity itself began to change and to take on a form of its own, more separated from Judaism and in part removed from the Jesus whom the Jews had seen and heard. Four centuries later Roman Catholicism was born.

Could it be that Rosenzweig was only seeing a side of Christianity in part removed from the original purity of the thought of Jesus? If he was, then what specifically about Christianity was holding him back? Was it the dark side of the history of the Christian Church? Was it the dogma and the liturgy, the Triune God, the Nicene Creed, or the proclaimed inerrancy of the New Testament Canon of writings authorized by the fifth century catholic bishops? Could he have converted to Christianity simply by accepting Jesus in his earliest form as the Jewish Messiah and the incarnation of GOD, without accepting the dogma and liturgical formality of institutionalized Christianity? Was total assimilation into present day Christianity necessary?

A more important question concerns all Jews at the time of Jesus. Why did so few, in the years immediately after the death of Jesus, do what the Pharisee Paul did? Why did more not become Jewish Christians? Was it that Jesus had extended GOD'S hand to the entire world and throughout Jewish history they had seen only themselves as His "Chosen People". Jesus had said they would have to give up everything, including the idea of being "Chosen" and be "born again" into a new life, a life lived with GOD "indwelling". For the Jews, only they were "Chosen" and God was not "within," He was outside in the heavens.

Throughout their history being Jewish had been more than just a religious belief. Jewish atheists and agnostics still considered themselves to be Jews and were considered by other Jews to be Jews. Only under extreme circumstances would a Jew be thrown out of a Synagogue.

For Rosenzweig was this tribal attachment the stumbling block? Were the interlocking Jewish/Tribal religious practices? Were the cadence, the rhythm, the emotional ties to Jewish ritual preventing him from escaping his Jewish identity? When he did experience a "conversion experience," was it real or was it just a superficial emotional catharsis taking him back to the tribal and religious ties that bound him to the Judaism of his ancestry?

The Judaism of Rosenzweig's ancestry, during the time of Jesus, was held captive by the Temple Priests. In Rosenzweig's time it was held captive by the Rabbis; as it is today. How much authority should the Priests have had 2000 years ago and the Rabbis today to tell Jews how to approach GOD and to define who GOD is and who God is not? How much of the religious practices as defined today by the Rabbis are necessary for a Jew or anyone else to know GOD?

Putting all of this aside, could there possibly have been for Rosenzweig a synthesis? Is it possible that he could have had it both ways, to be at the same time both a Christian and a Jew? For 2000 years each side has only thought in terms of total assimilation or no assimilation at all. Jews continue to reject Jesus as a continuum of their vision of their God. Christians see Jews as ignorant because they have not accepted Jesus as the Messiah. Jews look at the early Christians as just another of many Jewish sects that existed at the time of Jesus. Christians look at Jews as being unyielding and stubborn and failing to recognize the revelation that occurred. Jews look upon Christians as being anti-Semitic. Christians look upon Jews as being exclusive, self-centered and unyielding. There has been no willingness to compromise.

It is not a question of whether there can or should ever be compromise between the two or whether one can or should assimilate into the other. These words detract attention from the real issue. The real issue must be addressed in another way. It is whether the revelation of the nature of the Creator of our Universe and the GOD of all humanity stopped at some past point in time or is a continuing process that began with the beginning of Jewish history, extended through the life and death of Jesus and even is continuing to this day.

At issue is whether along the way both Judaism and Christianity have taken on trappings which have held them back from seeing their commonality, trappings that have turned both of them inward and are not relevant to the central issue of the revelation of the true nature of GOD. Within the religions themselves these internal requirements of belief and practice have served to solidify opposing positions, and this has deflected attention from the central issue of whether there ever can be a common understanding of the revelation of GOD'S nature.

In the early part of the 20th century when these two intellectuals were exchanging their letters, Jews had been resisting assimilation for almost 4000 years. No military, political or religious power had ever succeeded in separating them from their Jewish tribal identity and their Torah. The Egyptians, the Babylonians, the Romans, the Muslims, they all tried and failed. Rosenzweig could not be assimilated any more that could his ancestors. He could not assimilate because for him it was either the one or the other. Once a Jew, always a Jew. This historical tribal and religious tie to identity conditions the Jewish frame of mind to this day. For a Jew, it is the blood of Abraham running through his and her veins. It is an identity too strong to be cast aside.

Rosenzweig did not, however, totally dismiss Jesus. He saw Christianity in the role of a messenger of the Jews extending the Torah to the rest of the world. According to him, Judaism was the coals and Christianity was the flame. So he did acknowledge that Jesus was an agent of GOD. But the question still remains, then why couldn't he totally accept Jesus as the Christ? If Jesus was just another sect leader, then how did he become such a force? Why didn't Judaism without him become the flame, a flame that burned brightly for 2000 years and still burns even more brightly today?

From the very beginning of their history the God of the Jews had identified Himself as a God of both love and anger, and of awesome power, inscrutability and mystery. He was exclusively their God and their protector. The God of Jesus was not the same as the God the Jews had identified. Much of this new definition was in contradiction to the definition of the God of the Torah. The God of Jesus did not stand behind armies as they established earthly kingdoms but changed the hearts of the enemy. He did not keep people from pain, but He gave them comfort to endure it. There was no mystery to this God of Jesus. Through his sayings, parables and his life Jesus presented a perfectly clear view of the nature of this God. He was a God of pure love. Jesus built his ministry on one simple powerful statement dealing with compassion and love, even towards enemies. He defined our relationship to GOD saying:

As you have loved the least of my brethren you have shown your love to me.

Jesus was a disappointment to the Temple Priests. They had expected a powerful mighty Messiah sent by the God that Moses had witnessed and all they saw was a poor Jew, the son of a carpenter. They expected a Messiah who would make their Nation powerful in the face of Roman power and all they saw was powerless preacher. They expected a royal burial and all they saw was a crucifixion. There was no promise of eternal holy ground, no permanence to the Temple in Jerusalem, no army to keep the enemy away.

But his words were disturbing. And the words of those who followed him were disturbing, so disturbing that the temple priests decided to persecute those Jews who became Christians. The self proclaimed Messiah had challenged the order of things. He had challenged the very definition of the nature of the Hebrew God.

Throughout their history the Jews have always wanted to know more about their God. They have wanted to see His face. From the moment of His revelation to Moses this has been their quest, to know more about their God. To find Him they first developed an Oral Torah, which was passed on from generation to generation. Around 500 B.C.E. it finally became the written Hebrew Bible.

But the Hebrew Bible did not tell them enough. They wanted to know more. They wanted to find a way to worship their God and to find His deeper meaning for their lives. They proceeded to develop another Torah apart from the scriptures of the Hebrew Bible, first as the Mishna and then as the Midrash. Along with these came elaborate rules of conduct all designed to help them worship their God. As these rules developed, they became more and more demanding. How to dress, how to eat, how to pray, what clothing to wear were all considered a way to worship and sanctify themselves before their God and find His approval in them. Levitical Rabbinical Judaism was born.

The Torah and the rules that followed were to help Jews to worship and to know their God. But did they? Did Torah enable the Jews to know any more about their God than they knew of Him when Moses came down from the mountain?

Judaism had become an inward religion dictating a required pattern of behavior to be applied only to the individual Jew. There was little or no requirement as to the behavior for non-Jews outside of Judaism. Those outside of Judaism were as if they never existed. The purpose of Rabbinical Judaism and the Synagogue was to preserve Judaism, not to conquer a pagan evil world. Judaism had no desire to extend itself outside of itself. There was no purpose to the Synagogue outside of the Synagogue.

This is what led to the question that Rosenstock-Huessy, the Christian, asked of Rosenzweig, the Jew:

"Whether there was any purpose in the synagogue, seeing that in the reality of history the struggle between the pagan world and the message of revelation was being fought out not by Judaism, but by Christianity."

The question of Rosenstock-Huessy, the Christian, to Rosenzweig, the Jew, remains. It is a question that must be addressed today by all Jews, and not within the confinement of the Synagogue. It must be taken outside of the Synagogue and addressed in the openness of world society without reference to the Rabbinate.

We cannot see the face of GOD. We learned that from Moses when he returned from the mountain and told His people what GOD had said to him:

My face you cannot see.

But we can see the presence of GOD after He has passed through our lives. We can also see Him after He has passed through our world. We can see His presence in our history. We can only see the shadow of His form from behind after He has passed. He told Moses:

and you shall see my back....

Has there been any historical evidence of this in our world over the past 2000 years? Is there any evidence that He was here and still is today? Yes, if we will open our eyes we will see that He has been in our presence. We will see that over the centuries there has in fact been a very great struggle, one that the Apostle Paul described as being a struggle of *cosmic proportions*. It is a struggle that Rosenstock-Huessy described as *the struggle between the pagan world and the message of revelation*.

It was the message of Jesus that was at the forefront of this struggle. Those Jews who continue to reject Jesus saying he was an imperfect interpreter of their Torah should ask themselves the questions: If the self proclaimed Messiah who was rejected 2000 years ago was so insignificant and unnecessary, how is it that history has proved his presence on this Earth to be so powerful? How did this new and different view of GOD when absorbed into the lives of men and women have such power against the dehumanizing forces of evil over such a long period of time? What would our world be like today if there had not been a Jesus? Without him, how would we now be facing these forces? How would we be living and thinking?

Rosenzweig's reference to Judaism being the burning coals and Christianity the flame was a correct metaphorically; nevertheless, at the same time it comes across as a feeble excuse to avoid having to acknowledge the reality of what actually happened. It refuses to acknowledge the persona of Jesus Christ as the indwelling presence of GOD working in the lives of very many men and women over a period of 2000 years. Clearly, it took more than just the *religious influence* of Judaism, hidden for all that time behind the walls of the Synagogue, to make happen what happened. This stubbornness of thought is the reason for the difficulty over history of any Jewish/Christian dialogue.

History has made the strongest case for Jesus being the continuing revelation of the GOD the Jews had been waiting for so long to see. Looking back on the last 2000 years, the answer to the question of "What would it have been like without Jesus" gives proof of his authenticity. Jesus was the metaphorical incarnation of GOD, not the Hebraic God, the inscrutable God confined to the Synagogue, but a God outside of it among and between and within all people in the world. Two thousand years of History has proved Judaism wrong to assume that the revelation of the nature of GOD exists only for them confined to its ancient form; that it ended with the Hebrew Bible and their exclusive interpretations of it.

What will be GOD'S purpose for the synagogue over the next 2000 years? Should it remain inward, encapsulated within its orthodoxy by its Talmudic law, preserving for all time its anthropomorphic God in His ancient and exclusive form? Or, should it turn outward, at the same time embracing Jesus, if not as the Messiah, as GOD'S continuing revelation to the Nation of Israel, as well as to the entire world?

VII

Was Jesus of Nazareth the Messiah?
Will He Come Again?

And the Lord God commanded the man saying, of every tree of the Garden of Eden thou mayest freely eat, but of the tree of the knowledge of good and evil, thou shall not eat of it: for in the day that thou eatest thereof thou shalt surely die.

(Genesis 2:16-17)

"Humpty Dumpty sat on a wall:

Humpty Dumpty had a great fall,

All the King's horses and all the King's men

Couldn't put Humpty Dumpty together again."

English nursery rhyme from

Alice in Wonderland

by

Lewis Carroll

❧

Author's Note:

    This chapter speaks as the voice of a progressive Christian. It is the voice of a progressive form of Christianity that is fast taking hold throughout the world. At present, it is being overshadowed in the clamor of the media and the publishing industry from evangelical Christian fundamentalism and traditional Roman Catholicism by the noise they create; nevertheless, it represents a powerful force among both Christian intellectuals as well as the general public. The academic works of these Christians show that much of evangelical belief is theologically incorrect and even spurious. As a result of this serious inquiry, we now see the emergence of a progressive form of Christian belief based on disciplined scholarship. This new form of Christianity may become the Christianity of the future. Given the realities of our 21st century world, it may be the only hope for the preservation of the Christian religion.

The following chapter presents a progressive Christian argument along the lines of this emerging progressive formulation. By use of the word "Christian" in this chapter, unless further defined, the reader is asked to take it to mean "Progressive Christian".

&

As Genesis describes us; like Humpty Dumpty, we too had fallen. And like him, we were broken for all eternity. We could no longer be the way we were.

Could we ever return to the way we were and be like we were, in *the image of GOD* before we fell into sin? Could we ever return to an eternal union with the GOD who was a part of us at the very beginning of our human existence? Could the sin that we brought upon ourselves ever be forgiven? Could the damage be undone?

Christians believe that the life and death of Jesus was GOD'S call to humanity to return to the way they were, to let Him place the brokenness of their lives back together again. Those from the same Hebraic tradition, Jews and the Muslims, do not believe this. Jews believe that the slate was clean when they were born. They themselves during their lives estrange themselves from GOD. They believe that this estrangement battle will remain until the coming of their Messiah, as literally prophesied in the Hebrew Scriptures. Muslims too live their lives in this great battle. They wait for the end of the world and a final Day of Judgment when ALLAH will examine their lives in His Book of Records. They expect that Jesus, whom they look at as the second greatest prophet next to Muhammad, will then appear along with the Prophet. For those of the other main world religions, the Christian idea of original sin and estrangement from GOD is not a part of their understanding of man's spiritual nature. They do not acknowledge the duality of human nature and the force of evil as it was described to Christians in their Old Testament. They see life as a succession of choices.

For the Jews, from the beginning of their history, and with the presence of Jesus Christ for the Christians from the beginning of theirs, the story in Genesis of the fall of man presented a vivid description of that part of the nature of man that was alien from GOD. Genesis told how sin had led to an estrangement from GOD. It declared that the result was for mankind an endless cycle of pain and suffering.

Any study of history shows this duality in the nature of man to be true. The hundreds of millions who have suffered over the ages in the hands of their fellow men is testimony to man's inhumanity to man. The horrors of history both past and present show clearly this duality of man's nature as it was described in Genesis. The Human Being, among all others in the animal kingdom, has shown without interruption through history a unique propensity to degrade and destroy.

Today, Christians view the life and death of Jesus as GOD'S call to make right what had gone wrong. For them it was a divine intervention by GOD. GOD showed men and women a way that they in their imperfection can be at one with GOD in His perfection both here on earth as well as for eternity. The coming of the Messiah had the purpose of removing man from the damnation into which he had fallen, giving him the possibility eternal union with GOD.

During the time when Jesus lived and in the immediate period after his death, his purpose was not so well defined. It took time for the universality of his message to be understood. Many at the time thought he was the Jewish Messiah; others did not. He did not, in fact, build his ministry on a proclamation that he was the Messiah. He identified his presence as being beyond the limitations of the expectations of the Hebrew prophecies. He often was circumspect as to whether he was. He avoided the Talmudic arguments as to whether or not he was. He would answer the question of whether he was with words like: Who do you say I am, or Who do they say I am?

There is a question as to whether Jesus himself believed that he was. Verses in the Gospels show him making this proclamation; however, the argument among many Christian scholars as well as non Christians is that these verses are in fact not historic in the sense that they are not a verbatim record of what Jesus actually said. It was the early Christian followers who interpreted his presence as being that of the long awaited Jewish Messiah. They needed to legitimatize the messianic Jesus among the many other Jewish prophets who had over the years suddenly come on to the scene and then had just as suddenly faded away. During the period when the Gospels of Matthew, Mark, Luke and John were being written, to make a Talmudic case for Jesus being the Messiah, they used the prophetical biblical evidence at hand.

Looking back at the life and death of Jesus, there is no question that he claimed a divinity that transcended Jewish prophecy and the Jewish historical religious experience. It was a claim of being at one with the GOD of all creation. He demonstrated a power and authority not less than that of GOD Himself. It was a power and authority that extended beyond his crucifixion. And, it revealed a God with an entirely different nature from the God defined in the Hebrew Bible.

It is clear from a study of scripture that Jesus viewed the meaning of his life beyond the confinement of the definitions of what a Jewish Messiah was or was not expected to be. He did not view himself as a King who would restore the Nation of Israel. Nor did he view himself as an apocalyptic divinity to mark the end of time. He distanced himself from the legalistic complexities of prophetic Hebrew scripture. This may have been the reason he often answered in such an ambiguous way when being asked the question of whether he was the Jewish Messiah. He viewed himself as the fulfillment of GOD'S plan for all mankind and not just the fulfillment of one prophecy or another for the Nation of Israel.

The conclusion can be made that Jesus may have understood himself to be the Jewish Messiah, but he did not build his ministry on a proclamation that he was. Both the New Testament Canon, as well as the other writings not included in the Canon, such as those that were found at Nag Hammadi in 1945, show that he viewed himself beyond the messianic fulfillment of Hebrew prophecy.

The vision of Jesus was a vision of a new and different kind of personal relationship with GOD. It was not distant, as was the Hebraic relationship. His vision even extended so far as to bring GOD into oneself, as was demonstrated in the Last Supper, a sacred act that later became the Holy Sacrament of the Eucharist.

When Jesus appeared, many of the Jews were expecting a nationalistic Messiah who would be anointed by GOD Himself and who would restore the Kingdom of Israel. In their scriptures He was described as a King of the line of David. He would lift up Jerusalem to its glory and lay the foundation for a theocracy that would rule GOD'S Kingdom on earth. This national ideal saw the Messiah establishing here on earth the Kingdom of GOD. It would take place under the miraculous intervention of the Messiah. He would reestablish Jerusalem as its center and gather the dispersed. His Kingdom would be eternal. With it would come the conquest and subjugation of the heathen who would be driven from Jewish holy land.

Another parallel line of thought existed among the Jews. In it the Messiah is described in terms of being like a Son of Man appearing on the right hand of GOD in the clouds of heaven, inaugurating a new age, not by national victory but by the exercising of the divine right to judge the whole world. This was the apocalyptic ideal, based principally on the Book of Daniel. A future age was to be ushered in by the Divine Judgment of mankind preceded by the resurrection of the dead. The Messiah, pre existent from the beginning of the world, would appear at the consummation, when there would exist a heavenly Jerusalem which would be the abode of the blessed.

This apocalyptic idea also existed among the Jews independently, without a Messiah, that is the idea that the end of the world would come and there would be a final judgment. This would be a day of reckoning when pious Jews would be recognized for their piety.

With Jesus, none of this came to pass. There was no ultimate manifestation of GOD'S Kingdom on earth. A new King did not appear to restore the Nation of Israel. Nor did the end of the world occur. All that the Jews witnessed was the son of a carpenter from Nazareth speaking about a new and different kind of God from the one they recognized in their Hebrew Bible, and even re defining many of the scriptures on which rested all of their arguments as to what the Messiah would or would not be.

The Jews therefore remained skeptical of this claim, and do to this day. Their belief that every word of their Hebrew Bible is literally the Word of GOD held them back from accepting the universality of a messianic Jesus.

They asked then and today ask the same question: If he was the Messiah sent from GOD, why was he not able to establish the Kingdom of Israel? In fact, history was quickly moving the other way. The Romans were gradually eliminating the Jewish presence in Jerusalem. There would be no hope for a unified nation, just the opposite. The Jews were being dispersed. Jesus clearly had not restored the Kingdom of Israel. And what about the *End of Time* when those who had spent their lives in the study of the Torah would be separated from those who had not, and rewarded with GOD'S eternal grace? He did not bring that either.

The early Christians attempted to counter at least the apocalyptic argument by saying there would be a Second Coming of Jesus as the Christ and then an apocalyptic period when these things would take place. The newly converted Jewish Christians, as well as the converted gentiles accepted this, and at least for the first one hundred years after the death of Jesus, eagerly awaited the Second Coming.

In view of the justifiable skepticism of Jews during Jesus' time, as well as today, based on their Talmudic arguments, the question must be addressed by Christianity: Why was it necessary for Jesus to be the Jewish Messiah? Why were the early Christians writers so quick to make this claim? In our 21st century world, is it that important? From our perspective now, looking back at the overwhelming influence of the life of Jesus on the western world over the past two thousand years; is his being a Jewish Messiah that important? Would he think it to be?

One reason for the emphasis on his being the Messiah was that for the early first and even second century Jewish converts to Christianity this claim was absolutely essential in order for them to establish their own Jewish belief in Jesus as the Christ. Without a tie into the Messianic prophesies of the Hebrew Bible, the divinity of Jesus would have been open to question. It must be remembered that for the first fifty years the church was not Gentile but Jewish. Gentile conversion was only a gradual process that came later on. Most of the early Christians had been devout Jews before becoming Christians. They all had a thorough knowledge of the Hebrew Scriptures. Even for the non-pious Jew, studying the Torah and other sacred books was an important part of life. A Jew would spend his whole life in study. In order to argue their case among their fellow Jews, it was important for the Jewish Christians to prove Jesus was the Messiah based on a Hebrew scriptural foundation. Even his lineage had to be traced to David. Everything had to be supported from the original divine source, the Hebrew Bible. The early Jewish Christians needed to see a fulfillment of the prophecies that they knew and understood and in which they believed.

Nevertheless, as the early Christian Church wrestled with this concept, there were different messianic interpretations. The concept was not one that could be clearly defined based on Hebrew scripture and commentary. As has been stated, Jesus himself had added to the confusion by his ambivalence.

Among the early Christians there were basically three interpretations of the role of Jesus as the Messiah:

1. Jesus began his messianic work when he was baptized by John.

2. Jesus began his messianic work at his resurrection and ascension to GOD'S right hand.

3. Jesus would begin his work as the Messiah with his Second Coming.

As the years passed, these interpretations lost their importance so that today it is the fundamentalist Christian view that Jesus of Nazareth from his birth was without question the long awaited Jewish Messiah. It is also their view that Jesus himself interpreted his role as being that of the Jewish Messiah.

Where did the idea of a Second Coming originate? Where did the idea of the end of the world—the Apocalypse—originate? The idea of an *end of times* had grown out of the history of the Nation of Israel. From its very beginning the history the Nation of Israel had been a painful one. Throughout all of its suffering, there was the idea that at some future time GOD would *even the score* and then evil in the world would be defeated and Jews would receive their just rewards in heaven. The end of the world would take the form of a cataclysmic event when GOD would recognize those Jews who had, over the ages, been his loyal subjects.

The early Jewish Christians were confronted with the same painful existence. The idea of an Apocalypse and Second Coming of Jesus Christ was one that gave them hope during their time of trial. They had come from a religion that stressed temporal rewards for behavior that pleased GOD and temporal penalties for transgression. As time passed they saw that their righteousness was not being rewarded. Evil had not been vindicated. GOD'S enemies were not being overthrown. They only saw persecution by the Romans, as well as by their fellow Jews. Most of their fellow Jews did not accept Jesus as the Messiah. The Jewish Christian converts therefore found themselves alone and isolated.

For these Christians the Jewish idea of an apocalyptic period when GOD would destroy the evil of this world and restore the righteous gave them hope. This idea had for Judaism itself taken a firm hold by the year 200 B.C.E., although it extended back to the writings of the Prophets. Notable is the idea of judgment referred to in Isaiah 2:12. For the Jews it was anticipated to be a period marked by a cosmic cataclysm when GOD would destroy the world. It would be the end time and usher in the Kingdom of GOD. This fit well onto the early Christian predicament.

The Disciples of Jesus looked upon him as being the fulfillment of this apocalyptic biblical prophecy. The Kingdom was at hand. But, there was no end to the suffering. And, there was no end of time. They needed a theory to solve their problem. The idea of a second coming was born.

During the early period of Christian persecution this idea of a second coming was quickly accepted and taken over by many of the followers of Christianity. It was ultimately incorporated into the orthodoxy of Christian faith as well as the Canon of accepted writings—The New Testament—so that today it is accepted by many Christians as an article of faith. The Book of Revelation became the final proclamation of Christian doctrine relating to the Second Coming, the end of the world and the final judgment.

This idea was readily accepted by many in the early Jewish Christian community as well as the gentile converts. After the crucifixion of Jesus, one of the Disciples, John, in his exile on the island of Patmos about 95 A.D., using the imagery from Ezekiel and Daniel, wrote the Book of Revelation which gave a thorough description of the event. With this book, the idea took on a dimension well beyond the traditional Jewish one.

This Hebraic and Johannine prophecy would, for the early Christians, lay the foundation for their firm belief in the Second Coming of Jesus Christ. At that time, the messianic as well as the apocalyptic predictions of the Hebrew

Bible would all be fulfilled at once, and the powerful evil forces would be defeated. Christians would be ushered into the hands of a loving GOD in heaven. Non-Christians, that is, those who did not profess a belief in Jesus as the Christ, would be left behind.

It is the view of most of Christianity today that there will be a Second Coming of Jesus Christ. They believe that in time the Apocalypse will occur according to the Hebrew biblical prophesies as further reinterpreted in the New Testament in the Book of Revelation. Then, there will be a *Day of Judgment.*

The Book of Revelation caused a great deal of controversy in the early Christian period and barely made it into the Canon we now call the New Testament. The presupposition it made as to the *End of Time* and who will be saved and who will not was from the very beginning attacked by many Christians. Recent scholarship into the discoveries at Nag Hammadi as well as historical conclusions based on other information as to the underlying power struggles that took place among the Christian bishops during the second through fourth centuries, as doctrinal matters were being settled, raise questions as to whether the idea of an Apocalypse and a second coming was a part of the teaching of Jesus at all and therefore should have been included as part of Christian orthodoxy.

Most striking is the incongruence between the idea of a future apocalyptic judgmental period and the message of Jesus itself. This, for Christians, gives rise to an irreconcilable tension. Through spiritual rebirth and the grace of a loving GOD, before they physically die, most Christians believe themselves to be *born again* into a union with GOD in the here and now. As the Apocalypse calls for a postponement of this union until there can be a *final judgment,* there arises a doctrinal inconsistency. In the 21st century, the very idea of the *dead* being resurrected from their graves is difficult to grasp. The two ideas are theologically incongruent: the one; immediate acceptance by GOD through rebirth, and the other; the raising of the body and the person from the dead and then future judgment

This theological problem, for Jews as well as Christians, is made all the worse by the fact that there were recorded actual reappearances of prophets in the Hebrew Bible. Also, for Christians there have been reappearances of the Virgin Mary. Jesus was said to have spoken to Paul long after Jesus died. Modern science has confirmed a number of cases where there has been communication with those who have physically died. Of note is the well-known Elizabeth Kubler-Ross case where a deceased patient some time after death returned. If we must wait for the Apocalypse and the Second Coming, how could all this have happened?

In the New Testament, Jesus did talk about a future judgment time, but not in Gospels such as the Gospel of Thomas that were excluded from the Canon by the Roman Catholic Church. The question must therefore be asked: Was the *End of Time* recorded in the New Testament only there because the early Christian writers wanted it there? And, did they want it that way only in order to explain away their inability to understand more deeply the message of Jesus? Were they too closely tied to the Hebrew Bible?

There never was nor is there today any ambiguity for the Jews. As has been stated, the Hebraic concept of the Apocalypse and the coming of the Jewish Messiah are based on the prophecies of the Hebrew Bible and its commentaries. At that time there will be a separation of those who, during their lives on earth have been observant, those who have lived the Torah life, and those who have not. Entrance to heaven will only take place after the occurrence of the Apocalypse, not before. This was the belief of most practicing Jews during the time that Jesus lived. It is the belief of Jews today.

Two thousand years have now passed, and there has been no Second Coming of Jesus Christ. Nor has there been an Apocalypse. Hope continues that this will take place though, especially among evangelical Christians. Because of the theological incongruity of the concept itself, however, many Christians today are asking the question: Did the early Jewish Christians simply expropriate this idea from the Hebrew Bible as a result of the *First Coming* not fulfilling all of biblical prophecy? Is the *Second Coming* then in fact an inauthentic part of the Gospels? Further confusion arises in Matthew 16:28 where Jesus says,

Verily I say unto you, there will be some standing here, which shall not taste death, till they see the Son of man coming in his Kingdom of God.

This statement, taken literally, means that his followers would see the end of the world during their generation. Of course, this did not occur. Christians over the centuries who take the Gospels as the Word of GOD have always been disturbed by Matthew 16:28. It is inconsistent with other parts of the Gospels. Could Jesus have meant that after his death, he would return, not during a future apocalyptic period, but in the hearts and minds of people, and he would then lead them into a rebirth into the Kingdom of GOD, not in some distant dimension, but here on earth?

Many Christians still await the *Second Coming* and have in fact moved its expectation to the forefront of their belief system. A recent development has been the belief, primarily among evangelical Christians, that Christians and Jews will be brought together in the last days. Then, those Jews who welcome

Jesus Christ as their long awaited Messiah will pass on to heaven along with their Christian brothers and sisters, and those Jews who do not accept Jesus as the Messiah will go to hell. The 21st century geopolitical significance of this is found in the strong and vocal American evangelical Christian support of the God given right of the Nation of Israel to occupy the territory of the Holy Land and in particular the city of Jerusalem where the Second Coming is expected to occur.

Could it be that the canonical references of Jesus to a Second Coming were wrongly interpreted and therefore wrongly recorded because of a thought process of the early Jewish Christians rooted in the prophesies of the Hebrew Bible and based on a *need to believe*? Did they only hear what they wanted to hear? Did they interpret the words of Jesus only the way they wanted to interpret them? The Gospel of Thomas, which may very well predate the Gospels placed in the New Testament canon, refutes the idea of a Second Coming and an Apocalypse.

Whether or not Jesus spoke of his Second Coming and an Apocalypse cannot be proved or disproved. What is open for debate now in the 21st century is the authenticity of the scriptures recording what he purportedly said. Orthodox Christianity stifled this debate for 2000 years claiming that all matters relating to the scriptures were settled. Evangelical Christianity makes the same claim today.

If we look at the prophesies of the Hebrew Bible and the New Testament statements relating to the end of time from the perspective of modern science, we are left with the fact that there will indeed be an end of our world; however, it will come either from a sudden catastrophe of overwhelming proportions or our own slow destruction of our environment. Either way, it is evident those of the human species who are alive, other than those able to colonize other planets—which at the present is a remote possibility—will perish. The scientific reasons for these possibilities were not understood 2000 years ago as they are today. Then, the workings of the physical Universe and the interdependence of life on our planet were all a mystery.

Until the turn of the 20th century, the Canon of writings found in The New Testament, not just for evangelicals but for almost all Christians, remained the inerrant WORD of GOD. The description of the Apocalypse and the idea of a second coming of Jesus Christ were considered sacrosanct. They were accepted on faith. The images that grew out of early Christian doctrine, defining a physical separation between heaven and earth, were required to be accepted on faith. Any thinking that did not fit into these ideas was considered heretical. Much of Christianity continues to hold to these ideas today.

Many of the ideas held as sacrosanct since the very beginning of the Christian Church are now being challenged. The challenges are not just academic or theological ones. They are challenges that are having a far reaching influence on the question of how future generations are to view themselves and the world in which they will continue, or not continue, to exist. The greatest of these challenges has come with the discovery of the lost "Gnostic" Gospels at Nag Hammadi in 1945.

These writings, and in particular The Gospel of Thomas, show Jesus talking about himself, as well as heaven and earth, in a different way. He spoke of heaven as if it were non-dimension in space and time and in fact even as if it were a part of earth. He spoke of the non-physical aspect of the human form—which he demonstrated by his reappearances after his crucifixion. These were and continue to be ideas alien to traditional church doctrine; but, interestingly, fall in line with modern scientific theory which recognizes space as multidimensional, time as purely a man made construct enabling him to understand himself and the Universe in ways that he can mathematically measure, and the human form not as physical mass but as energy particles without mass, or more specifically moving energy surrounded by vast space. The very idea of heaven as being someplace else where one physically "goes up to" therefore quickly loses its meaning as does the idea of an "end" or a "beginning" of time. Thus, the orthodox Jewish and Christian idea of one going "up to" heaven at the "end of time" rings hollow.

Three recorded statements about heaven, purportedly made by Jesus are worth noting. They show a progression in thought that could not have been understood when the Gospels were written and compiled, but can be understood now in the 21st century:

From the authorized Christian New Testament

The Kingdom of Heaven is like a mustard seed.... A mustard seed is smaller than any other; but when it has grown, it is bigger than any garden plant....

(Matthew 13:31-32)

From the Nag Hammadi Library: The Gospel of Thomas

(3) The kingdom is inside of you, and it is outside of you.

(51) What you look forward to has already come, but you do not recognize it.

(113) It will not be a matter of saying 'here it is' or 'there it is'. Rather, the Kingdom of the father is spread out upon the earth, and men do not see it.

It is interesting to observe that the Matthew description does not speak to a heaven here on earth. It simply adds descriptive definition to a Christian metaphysical reality that exists somewhere else. It is therefore no more than a further clarification of the biblical Hebraic non-descriptive and murky definition of heaven and the unknown immortality of the Jewish soul. Nor does it place us in heaven during the present. It describes heaven as someplace in our conventional understanding of *space* apart from us.

The Gospel of Thomas, however, describes an entirely different kind of heaven, and it places it on and within our plane of existence. It tells us everything about heaven we would ever want to know. It challenges us to break through our traditional Hebraic way of thinking and find it within ourselves. It forces us to find rebirth, to shed the old and become the new.

The Thomas Gospel descriptions are not found in the Hebrew Bible or the Koran or in Roman Catholic Christian Orthodoxy, and for very good reason. These are all religions of final judgment and passage to a heaven in some far distant place at the time of the Apocalypse. Passage for those with these beliefs; Jews, Christians, and Muslims can only come as a future event and then only for those who have pleased a judgmental God. As noted, Hebrew biblical definitions of what it is are murky and impossible to define. The description that Muhammad made in the Koran gives more definition. It describes a sumptuous banquet with virgins for the pleasure of men who have been devout Muslims.

These and many other definitions left open by the Hebrew Bible and the New Testament Canon were challenged with the discovery of the Gospel of Thomas in 1945 in Upper Egypt. Outside of the Egyptian city of Nag Hammadi it was discovered along with more than fifty other early Christian texts, many unknown since antiquity. They were found in an ancient six-foot jar unearthed from a hillside. After 1600 years the seal of the Christian Canon cast by the Christian Church in the fourth century was broken.

In response to a fourth century edict to destroy all but the authorized Christian canon of writings, a group of monks near that town took the so named *unauthorized* and *heretical* writings out of their library, placed them in a six foot earthen jar, and buried the jar in a hillside where it would remain for 1600 years.

The early Christian bishops who had the greatest influence on forming the theology that would become the foundation of the Roman Catholic Church had, to a large extent, rested their case on the inerrancy of the Hebrew Bible as well as certain new writings about Christianity. They alone were to decide what to include and what to exclude in the New Testament. These bishops, by and large, represented a Roman Christian consensus and not that of the provinces. As they were debating, clearly one of the Gospels that must have troubled them the most was the Gospel of Thomas. They branded it as *heretical* and ordered it destroyed.

The author Elaine Pagels in her book *Beyond Belief: The Secret Gospel of Thomas* remarks:

"I was amazed when I went back to the Gospel of John after reading Thomas, for Thomas and John clearly draw upon similar language and images, and both, apparently, begin with similar *secret teaching*. But John takes this teaching to mean something so different that I wondered whether John could have written his Gospel to refute what Thomas teaches.... I was finally convinced that this is what happened."

It should be noted that The Gospel of Thomas was written long before the Gospel of John. The gap in time may have been as much as fifty years.

To understand why early Christianity took this turn, it is necessary to look not only at this Gospel, but also at the many others and to examine the question of why they were declared *heretical* and ordered by the bishops to be destroyed. This includes all of those found at Nag Hammadi.

Strong personalities often shape history, especially when they have carefully assembled political power. This was the case with early Christianity. In sorting out what writing would be accepted for the New Testament Canon and what would not, a bishop named Athanasius, intent on bringing all Christians under the supervision of one office, in the year 367 proclaimed twenty-seven books to be The New Testament. At the same time he called upon Christians everywhere to "cleanse the church of every defilement" which are "filled with myth, empty, and polluted."

Bishop Athanasius in his selection showed a predisposition toward the inerrancy of prophetic Hebrew Scriptures as the foundational framework for Christian belief and toward the Gospel of John as the one Gospel that in effect encapsulated that prophetical belief. He would make sure that this for the early Christian Universal (Catholic) Church became the center of its belief system.

Once the writings were chosen, from that moment on the tenets of Christian theology were sealed. From then on there was only one door leading to salvation and that was the one leading into the Universal Roman (Catholic) Church.

The hierarchal structure of the Church based on apostolic succession was fixed for all time. Only those bishops who were a part of the one holy and apostolic church had the authority to interpret the word. To make sure that there would be no temptation to make changes, a council of bishops had been convened at Nicaea in 325 and an authorized creedal statement was written. This was a complex set of belief concepts about the nature of both GOD and the divinity of Jesus as the Christ. Thereafter, all who offered viewpoints apart from these creedal statements were labeled as *Heretic* and *Schismatic* and denied participation in the one Universal Church. Over the years, some so labeled were even burned at the stake.

The Emperor Constantine, the first Roman Christian Emperor who reigned during this period, was quick to accept the authorized Christian Canon and the creedal statements that grew out of them. It was a way to unify the Roman Empire through a universal anti-pagan Church during a time of imperial turmoil. The Spoken creedal phrases repeated at every worship service such as "one Holy Catholic and Apostolic church" brought unity and strength to a slowly fragmenting Roman Empire. The books of the New Testament declared by Athanasius to be the only acceptable books relating to the life of Jesus and also the creeds have not changed to this day. Around them was formed the belief system of the Christian Church over the centuries.

The authorized Gospels which became a part of The New Testament and the formulation of the Nicene Creed were the end result of a bitter battle among strong personalities and political groups, each bent on forging its own brand of Christianity. The thinking that won out came from the efforts of two individuals, beginning with a second century bishop named Irenaeus, and then finally in the fourth century the bishop just mentioned, Athanasius. Athanasius was the architect of both the authorized Canon of New Testament writings as well as the Nicene Creed formulated at the council of Nicaea in 325. He was tenacious, extremely gifted politically and from the biographical facts known about him even could be described as megalomaniac. His objective was to unite Christendom under one rule with one iron clad interpretation of the life of Jesus, based to a large extent on the literal meaning of the Gospel of John.

The Nicene Creed was accepted by the Emperor Constantine who had attended the council. It soon became the architecture of Christian belief and has remained so to the present day. Those who opposed it, estimated to be as much as one half of Christendom at the time, were expelled from the council. General opposition throughout the Christian community was eliminated by an edict from Constantine issued just before the meeting that all "heretics and schismatics" were to stop meeting and to surrender all property they had to the Catholic Church. As time passed, the New Testament writings and the Roman Catholic creedal theology that grew out of them was assumed to be sacrosanct. The conclusions at Nicaea were assumed to have come from the Holy Spirit. They could not to be questioned.

The issues at the council were very broad in nature; however, there were several that formed the core of the debate. Their resolution in favor of Athanasius had a far-reaching effect on future Christian doctrine. Their resolution served, with Constantine's active support, to assure the growth of Christianity into a well organized and popular world religion. Among scholars today, this has raised the question of whether the resolution of some of these issues may have been primarily for political purposes. This is the reason for the intense interest in the Nag Hammadi discovery. Until then, scholars had only been able to speculate in vague terms as to what these issues really were.

A very general summary of the opposition position follows:

- Every person alive has the divine within.

- We received our being from the divine, the same source as Jesus.

- Jesus is not our master, only the template for our lives.

- We can become like him as equals.

- Jesus came to show us the light each of us has within.

- Self-knowledge is knowledge of the divine within.

- All those who find the light of the divine within are saved.

- Those who don't die as if they never were.

Was Athanasius no more than a religious and political fanatic who pushed through the council a dogma that did not in fact reflect the true meaning of the life of Jesus? Was he blinded in his understanding of Jesus by his strong desire for the growth of Christianity throughout the Roman Empire? Should other views of Jesus have been included? Was an almost total reliance on the Gospel of John to define Christianity correct? Who really wrote the Gospel of John and how much of it was from the mouth of Jesus?

When we look at Athanasius from a modern psychological perspective, we see in his actions and his personality some disturbing signs. The telltale symptoms of religious fanatics are:

1. Absolute intolerance of dissent

2. Belief that if you are not with us you are against us

3. Belief that one's cause has been blessed by GOD

4. Belief that one's actions are commanded by GOD

5. Belief that the cause is not just good but the only good

6. Use of reinforcement techniques such as repetition of simple phrases

7. A doctrine riddled with contradictions

It will be left to the religious historians to answer these questions. The fact remains that Athanasius and those who supported him blocked out a different view of Jesus, and then with the backing of Constantine enforced their own brand of Christianity on the world. It was a brand of Christianity that would control the thoughts and actions of western society for the next 1700 years.

Since the discovery of the Gospel of Thomas in 1945 at Nag Hammadi, Christianity has been forced to reexamine the rational for the selection of the writings that formed the New Testament and also, as a byproduct of this examination, the creeds themselves. We now see that in the process of establishing the system of theology that would become the Roman Catholic Church, the bishops suppressed many important resources relating to what Jesus may have said. The Nag Hammadi discovery revealed that there existed a much wider range of Christian thought within the first one hundred years after his death than was previously recognized.

Many Christians today who repeat the Nicene Creed during their worship with words describing Jesus as *begotten not made, of one being with the Father* who is *seated on the right hand of the Father* and who will come *in glory to judge the living and the dead* do not give these words a second thought. Nor do those who are not Roman Catholic know that as their churches are not considered by Roman Catholicism to be the *one holy and apostolic church,* and therefore they themselves live in ignorance. Many Christians, when they repeat the words set down 1600 years ago saying that they *look forward to the resurrection of the dead,* do not in their hearts believe this. They speak of their dead Christian relative or friend who has just passed on as being at present in heaven. They do not give much thought to what Athanasius said 1700 years ago.

Nor do they have a clear idea of what position Jesus would have taken as to the constitution of the three part Trinity which grew out of the Nicene Creed, a concept that had no Old or New Testament foundation but was formulated after the Council meeting. So, they are left to ask: Do we pray to Jesus as the Christ or through Jesus as the Christ, or do we pray directly to GOD?

They are not aware of the fact that there were many other ideas about the life and death of Jesus that were never given a chance. They are not aware of the fact that many of these issues were looked upon in a different way by close to one half of Christianity during Athanasius's time.

The Gospel of Thomas found at Nag Hammadi more than any other writing brings these issues to the fore. The Catholic Church over the centuries knew about this gospel. Even though by edict they had ordered it destroyed, some fragments of the Thomas Gospel continued to exist. The official church position was that these fragments were associated with a discredited early religious movement called Gnosticism and therefore were heretical and of little value. The complete manuscript found at Nag Hammadi showed that the Gospel of Thomas was not in fact a Gnostic Gospel, but it was an authentic account of the sayings of Jesus, either predating or written at the same time as the New Testament Gospels, and possibly written by a Jewish follower of Jesus who lived in Ephesus or in Antioch, the capital of Syria, or possibly even earlier by Jesus' brother Judas (not Judas Iscariot). In any event, there is sufficient evidence to suggest to scholars that the person or people who wrote it traveled with the disciples of Jesus and may even have been one of them.

The Nag Hammadi writings show Jesus teaching about a different kind of personal relationship with GOD from that shown in the authorized Gospels. The writings speak of heaven in a different way. They speak of the Apocalypse in different way. They speak of the Second Coming of Jesus in a different way. They show that Jesus offered union with GOD; not just to those who believed in him as the Christ, as the Christianity of Athanasius based on John's Gospel insisted and orthodox Christianity insists to this day, but to each and every person born on this earth who finds the *light* of GOD within him or her self. This is identified as the same light that Jesus found within himself. It is identified as the image of GOD hidden in man, an image that has been there, as described in Genesis, ever since the creation of man. It is an image that is within every person from birth. This is a far different view from the sinful and corrupted view of man as seen by Orthodox Christianity. It is a contradiction of the description of man as seen in the Gospel of John.

To quote from Elaine Pagel's book *The Gnostic Gospels*:

"What John opposed...includes what the Gospel of Thomas teaches—that GOD'S light shines not only in Jesus but, potentially at least, in everyone. Thomas's Gospel encourages the hearer not so much to believe in Jesus, as John requires, as to seek to know God through one's own, divinely given capacity, since all are created in the image of God".

The Gospel of Thomas is too long to quote here in full. It is not in narrative form as are the canonical Gospels, but is presented as a series of 114 statements attributed to Jesus. Some of the statements parallel those in the canonical Gospels. What follows are selected words from some of the statements that run contrary to the canonical Gospels. They may surprise many readers as they already express the ideas of many modern day Christians in the 21st century, even though the orthodox beliefs of their churches may say otherwise. They also have some parallels with mystical Judaism.

(3) Jesus said .. the Kingdom in inside of you, and it is outside of you. When you come to know yourselves, then you will become known, and you will realize who you are.

(13) Jesus said, I am not your master.

(17) Jesus said, I shall give you what no eye has seen and what no ear has heard and what no hand has touched and what has never occurred to the human mind.

(18) The Disciples said to Jesus, Tell us how the end will be. Jesus said, Have you discovered then, the beginning that you look for the end? For where the beginning is, there will the end be. Blessed is he who will take his place in the beginning; he will know the end and will not experience death.

(24) He said to them, There is light within a man of light, and he lights up the whole world. If he does not shine, he is in darkness.

(28) Jesus said, ... I found none of them thirsty. And my soul became afflicted. For the sons of men, because they are blind in their hearts do not have sight; for empty they came into the world, and empty too they seek to leave the world.

(41) Jesus said, Whoever has something in his hand will receive more, and whoever has nothing will be deprived of even the little he has.

(51) His disciples said to him, When will the repose of the dead come about, and when will the New World come? He said to them, What you look forward to has already come, but you do not recognize it.

(70) Jesus said, That which you have will save you if you bring it forth from yourselves. That which you do not have within you will kill you if you do not have it within you.

(77) Jesus said, It is I who am the light, which is above them all. It is I who am the all. From me did the all come forth, and unto me did the all extend. Split a piece of wood, and I am there. Lift up the stone, and you will find me there.

(94) Jesus said, He who seeks will find, and he who knocks will be let in.

(97) Jesus said, The kingdom of the father is like a certain woman carrying a jar full of meal. While she was walking on the road, still some distance from home, the handle of the jar broke and the meal emptied out behind her on the road. She did not realize it; she had noticed no accident. When she reached her house, she set the jar down and found it empty.

(108) Jesus said, He who will drink from my mouth will become like me. I myself shall become he, and the things that are hidden shall be revealed to him.

(111) Jesus said, The heavens and the earth will be rolled up in your presence. And the one who lives from the living one will not see death.

(113) His disciples said to him, When will the kingdom come"? Jesus said, "It will not come by waiting for it. It will not be a matter of saying 'here it is' or 'there it is.' Rather, the kingdom of the father is spread out upon the earth, and men do not see it.

It can readily be seen from these statements that the differences between the teachings of Jesus found in the New Testament and in particular the Gospel of John and those found in the Gospel of Thomas reach to the very core of some of the most significant questions facing Christianity today. They are central to today's understanding and misunderstanding of Jesus by Judaism, Islam and other religions in the world. They reach to the very definition of our personal relationship to the Creator of the Universe and to all fellow human beings. They challenge us to reconsider the ancient idea of the presence of the Kingdom of GOD as if it were in a far off place. They force us to look at judgment as being not at some future time but in this time at every moment in every life. They challenge not only the exclusivity of Orthodox Christianity, but also the exclusivity of all other Orthodox religious thought. They challenge us to think more deeply and give broader definition to the words in John 3:16, *whosoever believes in him (Jesus Christ) shall not perish but have everlasting life* and ask us to use the words:

> Whosoever shall find within him or her self the divine light that Jesus found within himself will never be separated from God but will be reborn into HIS presence to be in oneness with HIM on earth and for all eternity.

(Author's Interpretation)

Because of the wide differences in interpretation of scripture brought on by the Nag Hammadi discovery, important questions relating to the teaching of Jesus as they relate to present day orthodox Christian thought call for examination. This examination is in fact being done by eminent biblical scholars, archaeologists, and historians—honestly inquisitive human beings. And this time it is being done without the accusation of heresy, as was always the case in ages past.

Few Jews today are concerned about or even aware of this conflict and debate within Christianity, nor do they choose to look at Jesus in any wider context than that of the Jewish Messiah. For them the study of the Torah remains their primary concern and therefore the question remains: According to the Hebrew Bible was Jesus the Jewish Messiah sent by GOD as a fulfillment of prophecy or was he not? They believe he was not. To them it is clear from a rabbinical examination that Jesus of Nazareth did not fulfill biblical prophecy. The rabbinical conclusions are based on a literal interpretation of prophetic scripture as well as rabbinical commentary. For them, the Hebrew Bible is the Word of GOD, and it does not show that he was the Jewish Messiah. Only its words are perfect. All else—The Christian New Testament as well as the Gospel of Thomas — is imperfect knowledge coming from Hellenistic and other outside influences.

For all Orthodox Christians Jesus was the Messiah. Their belief is based not on obscure and unfounded blind faith but on Christian interpretations of scripture developed over the ages. These interpretations are from fragmentary, but nevertheless compelling evidence in various passages of the Hebrew Bible. For them, a literal interpretation of every reference is not necessary. They believe that the ambiguity and often conflict over the many references to the coming Messiah put forth by the Rabbis should not be taken as reason to doubt. As the Apostle Paul writes:

When in former times God spoke to our forefathers, He spoke in fragmentary and varied fashion through the prophets. But in this final age he has spoken to us in the son...the stamp of GOD'S very being.

(Hebrews: 1:1-3)

Jesus time and again corrected the Hebrew Bible. As he did so, he would use the personal pronoun *I*. According to the Jewish faith only GOD can correct the Hebrew Bible and only GOD can use the personal pronoun *I* when doing so. The Christians say Jesus was GOD incarnate. He could

57

therefore use the personal pronoun *I*. In fact by using it, that proved he was GOD incarnate. The argument between Christians and Jews therefore becomes a circular one.

There is an aspect of the Christian claim that extends beyond this rabbinical argument. It is that the earthly presence of Jesus cannot be narrowly confined to the messianic vision of the Hebrew prophets and their apocalyptic predictions. This raises a question that must be faced by the Jews: Did the life and death of Jesus have a greater purpose? Did he come, not to save the Nation of Israel, but to save the world?

Surely the transformation of the western world over 2000 years from the darkness of paganism — and later Islam as it too attempted to fill the gap — into our present age of enlightenment would not have taken place without him. His spiritual power working in the lives of many individuals was without doubt the principal driving force. Without it, the decaying Roman Empire would have left us with an entirely different world. A question remains unanswered by the rabbinate: What would the world be like today if it had not been for the presence of Jesus? Would Judaism even exist today? When the possible historical scenarios are played out, there is some doubt.

Would pagan barbarism have swept through all of Europe and stayed there? What would have held it back? Certainly not insular Rabbinical Judaism. Would Roman and Greek classical thought have been placed in the far corner of some Islamic library and left to rot? Would Islam in the seventh through ninth centuries have spread like a contagion so that today Europe would be one giant Islamic clerical state under the rule of the Koran and bent on conquering by force the entire world? Could there have been a Renaissance? Even if the Muslims had not been totally successful, would barbaric Scandinavian Vikings be today the altruistic Social Democratic Norwegians, Danes, and Swedes we now see? Would there have been a U.S. Constitution?

Looking at events as they unfolded in the 20th century: After the Second World War, would there have been a reconstruction of a Japanese nation or would it have been totally humiliated and crushed with its women raped and its men murdered? Would there have been a Marshall Plan? Would the United States and Europe have stood up to the despotism of a Nazi Germany and a Soviet Union?

It is clear that the history of the entire world rested on this one individual. The burden of proof rests on the rabbinate to prove this is not so.

The course of history was changed not by the sudden adherence of mankind to a new set of rules—The Ten Commandments—or a universal church creed, but by an inner experience that transported people into a new way of thinking. It was a movement that gradually swept through all of society and influenced all of human behavior at every level. Although the Roman Church did have an influence, the change did not come, as some Roman Catholic Christians would insist, from its exclusive presence as the *Body of Christ*. The course of history was changed slowly as human consciousness shed its view—and its fear of an Hebraic fearful and judgmental God—and accepted a belief in a God of Love and forgiveness, a God who valued each person for what they were as they were and for what they could creatively become. History was changed, as Thomas described it in his Gospel, from men and women finding the *light within*.

In the very beginning of the Torah, Genesis describes the condition of man after his eyes were opened to knowledge of both good and evil as being estranged from GOD. Adam and Eve had disobeyed GOD and were sent away from Him. Where Adam was at one time a part of GOD and in His image, he was now cast away. From that moment on GOD existed far off in another dimension. There, He would look down on Adam and Eve and their offspring as a punishing as well as rewarding God, like a father looking down on His children. Men and women would spend their lives trying to please Him, but they could never rise to GOD'S call for perfection. The punishment therefore would always far exceed the reward. For the Jews, this was and continues to be the understanding of the nature of the God of the Hebrew Bible and their relationship to Him. It also explains for them the inscrutability of an unfathomable God.

To understand progressive Christian thought and the God of Jesus, we must return once again to the English nursery rhyme. If all the Kings horses and all the Kings men could not put Humpty Dumpty back together again, who could? Could GOD take something that was irreparable and restore it to the perfection of what it was before? Could He bring man back to the state in which he had existed before he was corrupted by the knowledge of evil? Could GOD bring him back from a life of alienation from Himself? Could He reverse the words in Genesis 2:17 ... *thou shalt surely die*–and replace them with the words *thou shall never die*. Jesus Christ said yes GOD could, but then Jesus Christ set a condition. He said:

I am the way

Many of the early Christians missed the full message of Jesus. They missed it because they were concentrating on the wrong picture. They were concentrating on the picture of Jesus as the Jewish Messiah. They were concentrating on the Apocalypse. They were concentrating on the second

59

coming of Jesus. They were concentrating on a fear of a judgmental and retributive Hebrew Bible God. They did not see Jesus as the incarnation of a God of pure love and themselves as having the possibility to be at one with the God that Jesus had redefined. It was easier for them to concentrate on the wrong picture. It was easier for them simply to profess a rhetorical belief in Jesus and then settle into the Hebraic religious orthodoxy. It was easier than modeling their lives after the life of Jesus and searching for the *light within*. Almost all Christians still miss this message today.

The life and death of Jesus showed us that we are no longer broken by sin. By GOD'S grace we are put back together again. We are restored in the image of HIS perfection, like Humpty Dumpty before the fall. This comes to us not by our good works but by HIS grace. Jesus showed us that a God of perfection loves us, even as we are. In spite of our inadequacy, HE sees us not as sinful human beings but as we were in our perfection and perfect union with HIM before we opened ourselves to sin.

Jesus identified himself as the way to enter the presence of GOD, not at some future moment in time during an apocalyptic period but by rebirth now, here on earth. This is what he meant when he said that you must lose your life to gain it.

He came as a final revelation to say there is no need for the Apocalypse prophesied in the Hebrew Bible. Nor is there a need for a Second Coming. He said GOD is here with us now, with each of us who will accept Him. GOD is with us through the Holy Spirit. This is how The Kingdom of GOD has come to earth. Each of us has within the same light that Jesus had in him. If we can find that light, we can walk the same path that Jesus walked. People throughout the world, who have walked in this path, people like St. Francis of Assisi and Mother Teresa were ushering in His Kingdom on earth. And there are countless others who have done and are doing the same. Many are unknown. Some do not even know Jesus Christ; they are from other religions or have none at all, but they have found His light within themselves. The include Jews and Muslims; those of the eastern religions; and those with no religion at all. These caring, loving individuals are all too few, but then Jesus said the path is narrow. This is what Thomas in his Gospel is telling us.

It is a path that leads to a knowledge of GOD'S purpose for our lives. Jesus told us about this path during the short period of time he was with us. He told Thomas it is not a path that argues whether or not Jesus of Nazareth was the Jewish Messiah. It is not a path strewn with apocalyptic and messianic argument and debate. It is not a path that pits Orthodox against Gnostic Christians. It is not a path that pits Islam against the secular West. It is not a path that says only through apostolic succession in the Roman Catholic Church can we know the truth.

Jesus took all of this away from the Roman Catholic bishops, from the Jewish Temple Priests, from the Synagogue Rabbis, from today's evangelical preachers, from the Islamic Ayatollahs. He took it away from the Muslim Clerics too who only consider Jesus of Nazareth a prophet and teach hatred to the Muslim youth, who are afraid for fear of eternal damnation to believe that they should look to Jesus and not to Muhammad for the ultimate truth.

It is an uncluttered path that leads to a God of love and love only. GOD showed us the path through the example of Jesus, which can be the model for our lives. Jesus set the example for our thoughts and our actions. He said we can become a part of a loving God right now here on earth, the GOD who created us in HIS image, or we can turn our backs on HIM. The choice is ours.

He gave us the choice to prevent an Apocalypse of our own making. He gave us the choice to enhance or degrade life and the natural environment. When GOD gave man the power to subdue nature, He also gave him the power to destroy it. He gave us a choice; we can worship false Gods or we can worship HIM, the one true GOD. How we define the God we worship is all important. The false Gods will destroy us and our world. They will lead not only to our own individual destruction but also to the destruction of the human species and the earth on which we live.

We must look at the confusing and often contradictory prophetic predictions of the end of time pronounced in ages past and question whether these were no more or less than an expression of a people searching for an explanation for the pain and suffering that they were experiencing. They lived in a world overwhelmed by evil. Their lives often appeared to be influenced by sinister forces beyond their control. More often than not, their religion gave them no protection. They saw sinners being rewarded and the good being punished. All they had for solace was their dream of a time when the world would end and those who had kept the faith would be rewarded.

Jesus by the example of his life and death offered us a way to experience a life and death free from pain and suffering. He did not eliminate pain and suffering, but he gave us a way to live with it, and to benefit by it.

Modern science has shown us that there may indeed be an end to the world for the human species, but it will not be an end caused by an angry God. It will be an end caused by a natural cataclysmic event such as an asteroid. Or, it will be an end caused by man himself as he overheats, degrades, and pollutes his environment, and poisons or manipulates living creatures, including man himself.

What the prophets of the Hebrew Bible did not understand is that we bring upon ourselves both individually and as a society our own pain and our own destruction. They saw man as powerless to change this. It was logical for them to blame God and to talk about an apocalyptic period. They did not understand that GOD does not punish, we punish ourselves when we separate ourselves from GOD; when, as the Gospel of Thomas tells us, we do not find Him.

The God that Jesus described to Thomas, unlike the God of Hebraic, Koranic, and Christian orthodoxy does not free us with dream like solutions, such as an Apocalypse, from the individual responsibility to overcome the evil in this world. He does not offer to separate good and evil miraculously at the end of time. Nor does He begin with the presupposition of man's innate sinfulness and inadequacy. He starts with the presupposition of man's goodness and ability to overcome evil. He is the one GOD who points to each of us to make this separation by ourselves and with HIM within to become co-creators of HIS Kingdom here now on earth.

Is this what GOD was trying to tell us with the discovery of the long lost Gospel of Thomas at Nag Hammadi in 1945; that we have all gone astray; Christians, Jews, Muslims, and all others, that we have opted for the easy way out? Was HE trying to tell us that to save ourselves and to save the world HE created for us, each of us on our own must separate him and her self from the comfort and paralysis of our own particular man-made religious orthodoxy and find HIM within?

VIII

The Uncertain Future of Islam

Part I
Understanding the World Wide Threat of Islam

There is No Deity Worthy of Worship except Allah

"There is no Deity worthy of worship except Allah, and Muhammad is his messenger".

Welcome to the Islam Page
Internet Site

If anyone desires a religion other than Islam (Submission to Allah), never will it be accepted of him; and in the Hereafter he will be in the ranks of those who have lost their selves in the Hell fire.
(Sura 3:85)

Before reading these three sections covering Islam, it is necessary to have some further definition of the meaning of Judaism, Christianity and Islam as they are known today.

Judaism is expressed by a wide range of thought, from that closely tied to ancient Judaism—known generally today as Orthodox and Conservative Judaism—to that known as Reformed Judaism and Kabbalah to what can be termed "secular Judaism". The orthodox forms remain very much alive both in the United States and abroad and are at present have considerable strength throughout the world, as is particularly evident in parts of Israel and Europe. Orthodox/ Conservative Judaism, like Islam and evangelical Christianity, sees its scriptures as the Word of God, and it understands this scriptural definition of God as the only true definition. Reformed and secular Judaism does not hold to this view. The European period of Enlightenment in the eighteenth and nineteenth centuries produced a Judaism with a very different face. It was an open liberal and universally socially conscious form of Judaism. It was exported at the turn of the last century to the United States under the name of Reformed Judaism. Out of the Enlightenment also came another form of Judaism, namely; "secular Judaism", that is a form of Judaism observant in the sense of maintaining "Jewish identity", but atheistic or agnostic in belief. It is important to note that Jews of all of the above beliefs, with very few exceptions, consider themselves to be "Jews" in the historical tribal sense and they openly identify themselves as being Jewish. For an excellent history of Judaism, the author suggests Professor David B. Ruderman's 24 lecture series "Between Cross and Crescent: Jewish Civilization from Mohammed to Spinoza" which is noted in the Bibliography.

In Christianity we see the same ranges of thought; the same polarities and the same recent changes. Evangelical Christianity sees its scriptures as The Word of God in a literal sense. Its God definition is based on the Old and New Testaments and is the only one that is true. Protestant liberal Christianity, which encompasses a broad range of thought about Jesus, on the other hand, does not hold to this scriptural inerrancy. Roman Catholicism presents another view altogether. Rather than holding to the inerrancy of scripture, the church as the interpreter of scripture has the final word. As with Jews, Christians—catholic and protestant—openly identify themselves as being Christian, although the feeling of identification generally does not run as deep as it does with Jews.

It is the understanding of many in the West that, as with Judaism and Christianity, Muslims can be orthodox, conservative, liberal, etc. These individuals, who include many in positions of power, say we all, after all, worship the same God. This is far from the truth. In fact, without agreement that the Koran is The Word of God and Muhammad is the greatest Prophet and that all Jewish and Christian scripture is corrupted, one can not be Muslim. All of Islam is orthodox. It is all fundamentalist. Without being so, a Muslim can not be a Muslim. This of course does not say, as with all religion, that there are no secular Muslims.

When discussing the inherent dangers Islam presents to the non Islamic world, an understanding of these distinctions is important. The reader must keep in mind that Islam is more than just one more form of Abrahamic thought within which exists varying degrees of interpretation. Islam in all forms is orthodox in every sense of the word. It is a unified system of belief and worship. Sectarian differences such as Sunni and Shi'a center on disputes over historical beginnings and concurrent levels of orthodoxy. Non Muslims must understand that all Muslims see all other Abrahamic forms of belief as corrupted and incorrect. The mission of Islam today is what it has always been; to overtake all Jews and Christians and to replace their belief system with Islam. Islamic militancy is rationalized through a singular belief system grounded on words in the Koran. This is a shared belief of all Muslims no matter the sectarian or tribal affiliation. The mission may not take the form of acts of terrorism by most Muslims on the streets of Cairo or Peoria or Madrid or London, but it must be kept in mind that the objective of universal superiority and domination has universal Muslim support. Further, all Muslims understand that it is to be accomplished, if necessary, by force. This is written in the Koran.

These three sections on Islam will explore the origins of this Islamic militancy and how it is today challenging the socio political world formed by what we now define as Western Civilization: a composite of Jewish, Christian and Greco-Roman thought.

Around 610 years after the birth of Jesus, and then over the next several years, in the ancient Arabian Cities of Mecca and Medina, the Angel Gabriel spoke the Word of God to a merchant named Muhammad. This Arabian merchant would emerge as one of the most powerful political/religious figures in human history. He was believed by his followers to be the perfect man, predestined by God himself at the Creation, a human being whose spirit was destined to pervade the entire universe until the *end of times*.

A new religion was born. Within 100 years, converted Muslim Arabs in a series of great battles swept out of the Arabian Peninsula and conquered most of the hard lands of the Eastern Mediterranean. The Muslim Empire then continued to expand further to the west and to the east from the shores of Morocco to northwestern India. The Empire had become, in a very short period of time, the most powerful military theocratic empire of its day.

Today, more than a billion people in the world claim the religion of Islam. Fewer than 25 per cent of all Muslims are now a part of the original Arab population from which it sprang. Islam continues to attract new converts in greater numbers than all other religions.

Unlike Christianity, which originated as purely religious movement, Islam originated as a military and political force as well as a religious one. Through military/political dominance, most of those conquered were in time converted. For those who would not convert, the consequences ranged from inferior status as second class surtaxed citizenry to torture and death.

When Muhammad appeared on the world scene, Judaism and Christianity, which traced their beginnings from the same Abrahamic roots, were benign religions centered on spirituality as an end in itself. Except for very brief periods in their history, Jews had only gone into battle to protect and preserve their own tribal religious identity or to gain land for themselves. Theirs' was a religion that had no interest in bringing others into a special relationship with the God of Israel. He was their own tribal God, a God not to be freely shared with other tribes. Christianity, on the other hand, was a religion that, a least at the beginning of its history, told its followers to convert all non-believers from wherever they came, but not, as with Islam, through military conquest. Christianity began as a religion of peaceful conquest of the mind. Christians were asked to demonstrate their love toward all people by the way they lived and thought. From this inner transformation came conversion—called rebirth—into a personal relationship with Jesus Christ. Christians were told to spread his word to the world making disciples of all nations, not by war, but by demonstrating to others the meaning of the life, death, and resurrection of Jesus.

The Koran, as well as the Islamic commentary about Muhammad himself, the Sunna, rested its proclamations largely on the tenets not of

Christianity but of of Judaism. As with Judaism, in the Koran there was an emphasis on obedience to the will of God, moral vigor, doctrinal conformity, and the exclusiveness of the religion as being the only true form of belief.

When Muhammad was receiving the voice of the Angel Gabriel, there were prosperous Jewish communities both in Mecca and Medina as well in the nearby desert areas where semi dry land agriculture could be found. It would appear that he and his followers had a close association with some of these communities and from this association knowledge of the Hebrew Bible and Jewish traditions. Muhammad recognized many of the Hebrew prophets, including the patriarch, Abraham. He repeated in his Koran, at least in part, many of the Jewish historical biblical events. Also, he adopted many of the Jewish food and worship requirements. For example, he called for daily prayers, increasing the number to five. But, he went farther than just a verbatim repeat of Hebrew custom, scripture and Mosaic Law. He reinterpreted all of them.

Even though Christianity had been in existence for over 600 years when Muhammad began to receive his messages from the Angel Gabriel and speak the Koran to his scribes, it was largely unknown among the tribes of the Arabian desert around Mecca and Medina. Christian ideas had reached the desert society immediately surrounding Muhammad only to a limited extent. Influential groups of Christians lived in the coastal centers along the Mediterranean facing European Christianity to the North, but this was just a sliver of influence in the vast reaches of North Africa. Furthermore, the Roman Empire itself was in the process of disintegration. The Dark Age of Christianity had begun. Therefore, the Jesus of Roman Catholicism was seen and understood in part by Muhammad, but only from some distance.

The organizational blue print of Judaism was adopted. Like Judaism with its authority resting in the synagogue and schools or learning, Islam rested its authority in the Mosque and the same kinds of intellectual centers. This was not the way of Roman Catholicism. The Roman Church had been molded around a powerful central hierarchy of priests and bishops who had spiritual and temporal authority given to them through the Holy Scriptures. At the top of the pyramid was the pope's authority, which was unquestionable. Pagans could join the church only if they paid homage to it as the one true Church, the *Body of Christ*. For these structural as well as other reasons later discussed relating to the Roman Christian concept of the divinity of Jesus and a Triune God, early Christianity and the teachings of Jesus only marginally became a part of the Koran.

The Koran was a legalistic constitutional document that presented a legalistic religion. It told Muslims how they must think and how they must act in order to please Allah. It described this God as the same anthropomorphic fearful punishing monotheistic God identified by the Jews and recorded in the Hebrew Bible more than 2000 years before, a God who laid down a very specific set of laws and codes of behavior. And like the Jewish God, he was an exclusive God, a God who had said to the Jews—now to the Muslims—you are the chosen ones in My sight and all others are misguided and live in a state of ignorance.

Like the Jewish God, the God of the Koran was a God who placed a heavy burden on his followers. He expected them to please Him by living with that burden. It was the duty of every Muslim to spend their lives pleasing Allah. Like Judaism, the emphasis remained on a God who set out the rules of human conduct down to the smallest detail. Allah had given an enlightened version of the Mosaic Law to Muhammad and He said that this is what I expect of your followers. There was room for some compassion though. Allah was a God who looked upon human beings as weak and therefore unable to come to absolute perfection in the law. Like the Christian God defined by Jesus, He required each and every person to try as best they could. Then, at the *end of times* He alone would make the final judgment. He would keep His option open to this judgment as to whether one would enter Paradise or not enter. There would be a Book of Records that He would examine to determine whether an individual had lived according to the Sharia law of Islam and was deserving of salvation.

According to Muhammad, Jewish and Christian scriptures had been corrupted by the Jewish and Christian writers who wrote them. God had spoken directly to him in the purity of classical Arabic to reveal this. Allah in His transmittal of the final Word to him had him separate out the parts of these scriptures that were corrupted. The result was the pure and final inerrant Word of God. And, more than just being Allah's Word for that particular time, it was everything anyone would ever want to know about the natural world, man's behavior towards his fellow man, and man's relationship to God. It was the final word for all time, up to the final Day of Judgment. It was never to be altered until that final day. Muhammad proclaimed that the Koran existed outside of history.

For the Jews over their long history and for the Christians over their short history the search had been to know the mind of GOD. Muhammad declared an end to that search. He would do this by first proclaiming that we can never know the mind of GOD. Then, in the most precise terms he would define how each of us must live to please Him.

Muhammad was making these proclamations six hundred years after the death of Jesus of Nazareth. Jesus had already been proclaimed GOD incarnate by the early Roman Christian Church. The life and teaching of Jesus was for Christians more than just a window into of the mind of GOD, He was GOD. And He valued each and every human being regardless of who or what they were and how they were able to live according to the Mosaic Law. Moreover, He was a universal God, a God who said that as you show your love towards everyone, not just those of your own tribe or religion or family, you show your love for Me (God). He had even gone so far as to say we must *hate our mothers and fathers* in order to follow him, thus dismissing all religious family and tribal authority.

The Christian creeds and doctrines had already been formed by the Roman Catholic Church and were set in stone. The books to be included in the New Testament canon of authorized scripture had been decided. Other writings identifying Jesus of Nazareth in many other different ways, such as those coming from the Gnostic and Marcionite and Ebionite movements had been declared heretical by the early Church, leaving in their place one unified and exclusive Roman Catholic theology. Salvation was only available for those who entered the Roman Christian Catholic Church and accepted its definition of orthodoxy. Jesus was proclaimed the personal savior of those who joined the church and believed in him according to that Catholic orthodoxy.

One other part of Christianity just mentioned above presented a serious problem for Muhammad. In the fourth century the Roman Christian church under the Emperor Constantine had proclaimed that Jesus was one element in a Triune God made up of *the Father, the Son* and *the Holy Spirit.* Jesus was declared the son of God as a part of this complex formula. It was in fact a problem for many early Christians, those who had opposed these early Roman Bishops. How do you reconcile the two different images of God, the Hebraic Yahweh image and the Jesus image? Surely there could only be one God.

The Christian triune God was not the kind of God that the Angel Gabriel had described to Muhammad. The God described to Muhammad was a monotheistic God with one, not three natures. He was a God who agreed with some of the philosophical statements of Jesus, but rejected the idea of Jesus being GOD incarnate. Also, there was no place for the idea of a Holy Spirit in Muhammad's vision of God. The Holy Spirit was for Christians the replacement of Jesus on earth. It was a spirit that filled Christians, working in their lives bringing them closer to God. Muhammad rejected this idea of the transcendence of Jesus through the Holy Spirit. Muslims were to have no direct line to God through Jesus by way of the Holy Spirit. Allah wanted His followers to look to Muhammad himself as the intermediary.

The Christian idea of a Trinitarian God presumed both the divinity of Jesus and Jesus as having been the last Hebraic prophet. There would be no more. The final revelation had taken place. The very nature of GOD had been unfolded before human kind. How could Muhammad accept this and at the same time remain the greatest Prophet? Muhammad's answer was to refute the idea of the Trinitarian God and revert to the Hebraic monotheistic God, leaving Jesus as the second greatest Prophet after Muhammad himself. To make sure all of this was completely understood, the Angel Gabriel spoke to Muhammad saying that there is no God but Allah and he, Muhammad, is the Messenger of Allah.

If not the God of as defined by Jesus or the God as defined by the Jews, then who was this new God of the Muslim religion? One thing is certain. He was a God who demanded a heavy burden of compliance to a far greater extreme than the God of the Hebrew Bible. There was little room for individual choice. The Sharia Law dictated the way followers of Muhammad must live from dawn to dusk. Muslims were told not only to pray five times a day but also how to pray and in which direction to pray. The rules even dictated the specific movements and prostrations. And for those who did not comply or did not try hard enough to comply, eternal bliss could be withheld. At the time of final judgment Allah would examine every part of one's life, even as to the way he had prayed. Then there would be a final judgment. Everything about one's life was being recorded and placed in a Book of Records. Every last detail was being taken into account.

Islam was built upon fear of a distant powerful God, existent in some other place and time. It disallowed the Christian idea of any kind of direct forgiving and redemptive relationship between man and GOD through transcendent oneness with HIM.

Muhammad could not acknowledge the Christian message that we cannot be separated from GOD'S redemptive love, even in the face of all the rules of conduct and religious laws of the Hebrew Bible. He could not acknowledge, as the Apostle Paul had almost six hundred years before, that this love transcends all human weakness. Like the Jews who had rejected Christianity, for Muhammad, acknowledging this unconditional love of GOD would have meant seeing GOD not as a God to be feared, but as a God to be embraced. It also would have prevented Mohammad from laying down his own new set of rules based on the archaic rules of the Hebrew Bible.

He therefore chose the Hebraic vision of GOD. Essentially, the God of Islam remained a retributive Hebraic *eye for and eye* and a *tooth for a tooth* God, not a *turn the other cheek* Jesus God. He was a God who crushed the enemies of Islam as King David had crushed his enemies. He was the fearful ancient Hebrew Bible God of harsh judgment and retribution.

For Muhammad, the idea was to bring together all of the prophets, at least his own understanding of them, Jesus included, into one final and true revelation; however, he knew that this could not be done by a mere mortal like himself. There was the problem of credibility. He was just a common man and a mere merchant from Mecca. It could only be done by an angel speaking through Muhammad. There are only two angels mentioned by name in the Hebrew Bible. One is the Angel Gabriel. He appeared and spoke to Mary, as recorded in the Christian New Testament, when he gave the good news to her of the coming birth of Jesus. This was the principal angel—among others—who would speak to Muhammad.

Today, all worshiping Muslims believe that this is what happened, and the writings of the Koran given by the Angel Gabriel, as well as other angels without names, were from the mind of GOD. They believe the Koran to be the final and inerrant WORD of GOD. They believe that all Muslims, as well as certain Christians and Jews, will have the possibility on Judgment Day of entering Paradise. All others will be banished by GOD through eternity from any possibility to be with Him in Paradise.

Muhammad expected that the Jewish communities in and around Mecca and Medina would convert to Islam. He saw the synthesis with Islam as the ultimate revelation. To a casual observer, Islam can be looked upon as a variation of Orthodox Judaism with an added sprinkling of Christianity. As has been stated, the Koran is to a great extent a derivative of the Hebrew Bible. The religious practices of Muslims and orthodox Jews could be looked upon as being very similar. From the rules of conduct to the dietary rules, to the prayer requirements, there were many similarities. It appears that Muhammad thought the Jews around Mecca and Medina would see little difference and they would readily switch over to his Islam.

What he did not understand about the Jews was their historical stubbornness. Over 2000 years of Jewish history would make them stand fast. The Jewish people had been searching throughout this history to find deep and hidden meanings of their scriptures, which for them began with the very beginning of creation. It was an endless search that continues to this day. Suddenly, in the seventh century of the Common Era an illiterate—it is said Muhammad could not write— merchant from the city of Mecca claims that he is receiving messages from angels telling him that all of the ancient Hebrew scriptures were corrupted in the process of transmission, and that their Hebraic interpretations of them were also corrupted, and he alone is being given the ultimate truths about them. At the same time he was telling the Jews that they should convert to his new religion, Islam. The Jews showed no interest.

Muhammad was saying the same to the Christians. As has already been discussed, the doctrines of the Christian Church were firmly in place by the seventh century, including the doctrine of a Triune God. Jesus had been declared God Incarnate and a part of that Triune God. His blood was shed for the sins of the world. Salvation could only be achieved by professing belief in him as the son of God. So, for Christians, converting to Islam it was in many respects the same as going back to Judaism. Therefore, Christians showed no interest either.

There was a more far reaching problem for Christians. The way they were asked to respond to the presence of GOD in their lives differed from the way Muslims were asked to respond. God for Muslims was "out there". God for Christians was "within", at least through the Holy Spirit. Islam did not recognize the possibility of the transcendence of man in all of his weakness to be at one with God during his biological life. Muslims would have to wait for a final judgment day. This Christian presence came through the indwelling of the Holy Spirit—the presence of Jesus Christ—in the lives of Christians.

Islam, except for some fringe elements of mysticism (Sufism) that later emerged, rejected the possibility of any kind of union here and now in this life. Even with Sufism the objective was to connect more closely to GOD'S will, not to be at one with Him. The Koran, like the Hebrew Bible, said that we must wait for a Judgment Day when all who are living and all who have died will be judged, taking into account everything they have done or left undone in our lives. Only then will there be a possibility of being in GOD'S presence. (As discussed later in this book special dispensation was give to Muslims who died in the cause of Islam)

With the passing of years, the differences between Christianity and Islam became even greater. Christianity is a religion of revelation and change. Islam, like Orthodox Judaism is a Hebraic scriptural religion without change. Starting with the Apostle Paul and then with Great catholic philosopher/theologians like Augustine and Aquinas, enormous changes occurred in Christianity. Changes occurred on an even broader scale—than the observations of Aquinas—with the introduction of Renaissance classical Greek ideas and then Luther. Although the core belief in Jesus as the Christ and the Trinitarian view of God remained for most Christians inflexible, the search for deeper meanings of the life and death of Jesus continued. In the Renaissance, as early Greek thought was taking on importance, there was introduced a transcendental form of mysticism that we see today in much of Christianity. All this was never possible for Islam. For Muslims, the Koran is THE WORD OF GOD and Muhammad was GOD'S messenger.

As an example, for many modern day Christians the idea of a final Day of Judgment has lost its meaning, as has the parallel idea of a Second Coming of Jesus on that judgment day. These Christians question the biblical concept of time which is so much a part of the idea of a future Judgment Day. They look at time in modern relativistic terms as a construct of our perception of this earthly dimension, non-existent in the dimension of space and time that is GOD'S. They believe that the Christ—that is GOD— is with us in the presence of the Holy Spirit and that heaven is all around us at every moment of our lives. They believe that we are moving in the here and now—by how we think and live—either towards or away from a loving and non-judgmental God in a heavenly dimension that is both inside of us as well as outside of us.

Unlike Christianity, there is in Islam very little room for change. In the sense of the understanding that Christians and Jews have of religious fundamentalism, a large percentage of Muslims today are "fundamentalist". Muslims view the Koran in its entirety as the inerrant word of GOD. Viewing the Koran in this way is, in fact, a precondition for being a Muslim. All Muslims must believe that every word of the Koran is from Allah and therefore can not be changed. As we have seen, this is not the case with Christianity. Nor is it for Judaism, where only certain groups hold to the inerrancy of the Hebrew Bible.

As Islam rapidly spread, a need arose to bring its beliefs into a unified body of thought leading to a common code of conduct. Scholars, called Ulama, were appointed to do this. What they wrote was based on the Holy Book, the Koran (Qur'an), and on the life of the Prophet Muhammad, which had been recorded in the Sunna. This combination of the verses of the Koran and the life of Muhammad, the Sunna, was then brought together in what became known as the Shari'a. It was, in a sense, a codification of the Koran and the Sunna. The exercise was completed in the 11th century

This led to divisions within Islam. Well known examples of these are found today in the distinction between the Sunnis of Saudi Arabia and the Shi'a of Iran and southern Iraq. The core beliefs of all, however, remain very similar. Every Muslim is required to believe that the Koran was given to their prophet Muhammad by the Angel Gabriel, as well as other unnamed angels, that it is the true and only word of GOD and that all other scriptures from all other religions, Judaism and Christianity included, are corrupted.

Muhammad would use for his Koran, not the Jesus *love thy enemy* God or the evolving Jewish God asking Jews for *deeds of loving kindness,* but the ancient Hebraic Davidic warrior God. Like Alexander many years before him, Muhammad would choose to become a military conqueror first and a conduit for his ideas second. He would choose the Davidic model to achieve his purposes and he would take it to the extreme. Therein, lays our 21st century dilemma. .

If Muslims today lived in isolation from other parts of the world, as they existed over past millennia, there would be no problem with their way of thought. But this is not the case. The world is now an interdependent society of people who must live together in some form of harmony. The following section discusses what happened when this ancient militaristic religion, dormant for so many years, suddenly met with a 21st century secular western world, or to put the other way around what happened when a 21st century secular western world suddenly met a "sleeping giant", Islam.

Part II
Understanding the World Wide Threat of Islam

Waking a Sleeping Giant

The armies of Islam brought more than just conquest; they brought with them a new God. In the Levant the cries of those persecuted Christians and Jews were soon silenced by the Muslim invaders. It was the same for those from other religious traditions living as far away as India. Their religions too vanished under this new Davidic warrior God. People who had lived in these far off lands and had called them their home for thousands of years were told to abandon their Gods and accept Allah as the one and only true God. If they did not, the penalties for many were harsh; or at the very least those conquered were separately taxed and made to accept second class status. In time age old religious beliefs were extinguished.

Islam was reaching its Golden Age. Great wealth was being accumulated at its centers of power. In these centers Schools of philosophy and the sciences appeared. The military arts reach new heights. The expansion even spread to the European Continent. It crossed the Mediterranean into Spain where an intellectually sophisticated Moorish civilization flourished. Cordoba became Europe's most advanced center of learning.

Conversely, Europe was entering the dark period we now call the Middle Ages. Roman political institutions and centers of learning were slowly disintegrating and being replaced by the power of the Catholic Church. Wealth was being concentrated in the institution of Church. Advancement in the arts and sciences had come to a halt. Advancements in the military arts also were at a low point. As the stage was being set for the first of many future confrontations between Islam and Christianity, there was some doubt as to whether Christianity could survive the Islamic onslaught.

In 722 Spanish Moors crossed the Pyrenees and invaded Gothic Gaul (France), seizing several towns in the south of that country. Ten years later, in 732 the Moors launched what was to be their final bid to take over all of Western Europe. A massive army under the command of the Moorish governor of Spain began laying waste to large parts of southern Gothic France. He defeated the Goths at Garonne. The Goths were then forced to retreat into central France, carrying with them news of the frightful and merciless Moorish army.

Then came one of the most momentous battles in Islamic/Christian history. It was a battle that was to determine the fate of western civilization. Defeat of the Goth Christians would have meant that all of Western Europe would have fallen under the sway of Islam, and the mixed Muslim races from the East would have poured into continental Europe, even reaching as far as the British Isles. Had Islam won there would have been no British Empire, no America, no Christianity today as we know it today. In October of 732, the same year of the earlier Christian defeat at Garonne, the armies of the Goths (Christians), under Charles Martel and the army of the Moors (Muslims) under Abd ar Rahman, met between the towns of Tours and Potiers in Central France. The battle turned in favor of the Christians. The army of Abd ar Rahman was repulsed. The Muslims were forced back across the Pyrenees into Spain.

The pushing back of Islam, at least from Europe, continued. Christian re conquest of Spain over a period of five hundred years carried on in fits and starts. In a great battle fought on the plains of Toledo in July of 1212 the Muslims were again decisively defeated. They were then restricted to the southern parts of Spain. This gave the North time to recuperate and rebuild its strength. It was only with the rise of two great leaders, Isabella I, Queen of Castile, and Ferdinand V, King of Aragon, that the Moors were finally by the

16th century driven from Europe.

For the next five centuries, except for the fall of Constantinople in 1453, the map was set. The Giant lay dormant. The most powerful military/ political religion in the history of the world slept, frozen in time.

The thaw did not begin until after the First World War. It was brought about by the Christian West, and with a supreme naiveté. This was particularly true in the case of Great Britain where Christian evangelism had taken hold. The words of Jesus *to make disciples of all nations* played an important role. Great Britain's mandate was plain and simple. It was understood as the exercise of Christian anglophile manifest destiny.

To quote from Dexter Filkins in the NY Times as he reported from Baghdad in July 9, 2006: "Among the Ghosts: Heroes and Grand Plans":

"At the end of a long week, I went searching for her tomb…. In the quiet of a compound…, I found her. Gertrude Margaret Bell is interred in the Anglican Church's cemetery…Miss Bell, the British adventurer and diplomat, was as decisive in the creation of the modern Iraq state as any single person. She imagined it in the ruins of the Ottoman Empire, then ending its 600-year run. The First World War was over, and the Middle East seemed as blank as a sheet of paper. The borders of the new state would be long and straight like a ruler, cutting across deserts, tribes, and languages. It was a thrilling time to be alive. 'I feel at times like the Creator about the middle of the week ', Miss Bell said at the time. 'He must have wondered what it was all going to be like, as I do.'"

Gertrude Margaret Bell was part of a Christian mindset that led to the unbridled expansion of the Christian and Jewish western world into Muslim lands. It brought with it the degradation and humiliation of the Muslim people. There was no attempt to explore the higher values of Islam, to bring that religion into modern western societal consciousness. Muslim resentment and hatred, without recognition, was allowed to simmer and fester.

How do you wake a sleeping giant? You invade his territory. You torture and murder his children. You denigrate and abuse him. You make him angry. Without realizing it, that is exactly what Gertrude Margaret Bell and the many other Europeans, and in time many Americans like her, did. After the first world war, with the fall of the Ottoman Empire and the rush towards European colonial expansion, and then after the second world war with the strategic moves by the United States to prevent Soviet penetration of the Middle East, the Muslim countries in that part of the world witnessed one western territorial incursion after another. With each incursion came a flagrant violation of the religious beliefs of the Muslim population. This was done without any recognition of the human sensitivities that lay under the surface and the potentially violent and dangerous religion underlying these human sensitivities. The assumption was that the Crusades were over. Christianity had won. Islam had become an ancient and benign religion. It was an assumption that did not reflect reality.

The final blow came with the recognition by the United Nations of the State of Israel in 1948. With this Jewish territorial invasion of an Arab land and the immediate Palestinian as well as other Arab national resistance, the reality of the religion of Islam as a future threat to the western world began to surface. At the same time, as Great Britain withdrew from its involvement in the Middle East, America suddenly found itself deeply involved. Prior to 1948 American involvement had been closely connected to the development of oil reserves by American oil companies. In fact, from the first discovery of oil in Saudi Arabia the American oil companies had in effect acted as the American State Department.

Suddenly America found itself alone facing a problem that because of its insularity and limited colonial experience it was least able to understand. As the French had done in Indo China, the British all at once abandoned their Middle Eastern colonial problems. America filled the vacuum, once again as with Vietnam misjudging the dangers and complexities.

The sleeping giant was awakening. And, as he became aware of infidels all around him, he also found himself surrounded by petrodollars! Soon, Muslim terrorists were turning up in Israel, Lebanon and elsewhere. Then, in one moment of horror came the American—and western world—realization that it was facing a problem of enormous magnitude far beyond the previous minor—at least to the American and European public imagination—terrorist attacks. Just over half a century after Israel's independence, Muslim extremists engineered the single most invasive and destructive act in all American history by destroying the World Trade Center Towers in New York and a wing of the Pentagon. An awakened fundamentalist Islamic extremism was now presenting a serious danger not only to the Nation of Israel but to western civilization itself.

How did the two ways of Abrahamic thinking, one the 21st century liberal Judeo-Christian, and the other, Islam, grow so far apart? Can they ever come together? Can the three find common ground with each other? To answer this question, we must understand the roots of Muslim belief. But then, after we have done this, the question remains: What if we find that 21st century enlightened liberal Judeo-Christianity and Islam are not able to come together? What happens then?

The core of the problem is more than Islam simply seeing the image of the Abrahamic God in a different way; it is Islam envisioning all of society in a different way; in the way that Muhammad defined it. For Muslims; Western society is decadent, Islamic society has value. Like communists during the Soviet era, Muslims see human civilization through a different lens. Unlike world communism though, world Islam's view is grounded on a powerful all encompassing religious belief. The conviction is far stronger. This conviction has lasted for over a thousand years and could last for thousands more. Muslims see their society as superior to western society. They want to throw out western society, all of it. Most Muslims, not just al-Qaeda, want to replace western society with their own. This understanding of what Islam really is, beyond just "another of the great religions", as western politicians, including the US president have expressed it, is just now beginning to penetrate the consciousness of the western mind.

The West is now facing a dilemma far more complex than that faced under the threat of international communism. Its public finds itself unable to grasp the overall seriousness of this dilemma. Many political leaders are struggling to understand it. Important questions relating to it are: By what means beyond those employed today does Islam intend to go about replacing western society? How successful could it be? Can Islam be changed? How should the West counteract the Islamic threat to its existence? Will the rules of western civility prevent it from taking necessary action?

The battle lines are slowly being drawn. They are far more complex than those that were drawn in central France 732 years after the birth of Jesus of Nazareth. They revolve around a 21st century western secular society that, in the face of ecological and other challenges to future human existence, now has its own doubts about the validity of its own societal norms. They go far beyond the intransigence of Muslim clerics. They are being drawn against an Islamic world that, largely because of these clerics, will not back down from the words of its prophet Muhammad. There is an urgent need for each side to back away from historical failures and assumptions. Each is being called on to ask: How perfect is Judaism? How perfect is Christianity? How perfect is Islam? How perfect are the societies they have produced? Can we each learn from the other? Are there possibilities for compromise and accommodation? These questions go far beyond simplistic definitions of democracy and freedom as the solution to Middle Eastern or any other problems. They go far beyond all of past history. We—Jews, Christians and Muslims—must all together go back into our own religious and other histories to find their answers.

This book has up to this point explored the beginnings of Judaism and Christianity in an attempt to discover their weaknesses and their strengths. Now we will cast our light on Islam in the same critical manner.

In a remote city in the Arabian Desert 600 years after the death of Jesus, Muhammad framed his vision for the perfect society based on his observations of the spiritual and social depravity of the Pagan world around him. Then, it was a violent world under the control of desert codes of behavior that had existed for many centuries. Only a strong militaristic leader could change that behavior. It would not change by spreading the good news, as Christianity had done, but by brute force.

Muhammad would therefore model himself after the great Prophet Kings of the Hebrew Scriptures: David, Solomon, and especially Abraham. In these prophets he saw the hand of a powerful and protective warrior God, the kind of God who would lead Islam to victory in battle over all unbelievers. This was the God who would, through the Angel Gabriel, dictate to him the inerrant holy book of Islam, the Koran.

As we have seen in the first part of this discussion, Muhammad found his answers about the nature of the God who would become the God of Islam not in the Christian New Testament but in the Hebrew scriptures. The God of Jesus as the Christ would only be referred to where it suited Muhammad. His theology would be a revision of ancient Hebrew scripture. It would begin with the very beginning of man in the Garden of Eden. It would even borrow from Jewish scholar's interpretations, the Midrash.

The religion of Muhammad has not changed since it was formed. Islam sees all those of other beliefs as it did during its initial expansion when Muslim armies conquered the infidels wherever they went, subjugating those who were in disagreement. This Davidic God of conquest continues today as its model. 21st century Islam views the outside world in the same terms as it did 1400 years ago, as a world of pagan infidels. The thought patterns of Islam are the same as they were when the religion was formed. Muslims think this way because its clerics have kept them confined to a vision of GOD as He is defined in the Koran. Through fear of eternal punishment, Muslims cannot think of any other kind of God.

More frightening is the fact that Muslim clerics world wide in mosques and schools are teaching young Muslims that they have been given a mandate to repeat the Pagan, Christian, and Jewish conquests of the past and that Allah will favor them eternally if they devote their lives to this end.

Islamic thought has been calcified into a seventh century militaristic mold. As long as the Koran is considered the word of GOD, it cannot change. Islam cannot shake itself from its beliefs, because the Koran prevents Muslims from seeing the world in any other way than the way that the Koran describes it.

The social and economic progress throughout the world that has been carved out over the past 2000 years by men and women bowing down to a different kind of God, the one revealed by Jesus, cannot be acknowledged. Muslims cannot admit that for 2000 years this new vision of GOD and not the one described by Muhammad in the Koran has been a driving force behind world history leading to the advancement of human civilization. When Muhammad in the seventh century shut the door on the God revealed by Jesus, he isolated Islam into the singularity of his (Mohammad's) vision of the most negative aspects of the ancient God described in the Hebrew Scriptures. All that is left now for Islam is to hate the infidel Judeo-Christian secular West and resent it for the fruits of this new vision.

The hatred of Muslims towards the West is being waged against the backdrop of a secular western world that in the perception of Islam is fast losing its connection with the sacred. It sees the West as a consumer driven society that has strip-mined the mystery of life from the souls of its people. Rather than rigorously cultivating inner life according to the Koran and Sharia, it sees the West as obsessively pursuing mindless sensual pleasures that force attention towards the most mundane. Islam sees these distractions in western secular society as an impediment to a focus on the sacred; with the result being an inability to understand the complex higher values given by the Koran and Sharia law as Islam defines them. It sees those in the West as possessing little imagination, a shortened attention span and as unable to understand the beauty in the Arabic poetry of the Koran, unable to comprehend its deeper meanings. Islam sees the West as weak, superficial, and unable to prepare for the hard choices that must be made in order to follow the discipline of its one true religion.

Islam is both right and wrong in its blanket perception of the West; however, its clerics been blinded by a fundamentalist extremism which prevents them from seeing the positive aspects of western society. Many of their observations are, in fact, correct, but like all religious fundamentalists of all faiths, they cannot acknowledge the dynamism of a pluralistic open society and the human creative undercurrents that lie beyond their observation. They are held back by their doctrinaire religious beliefs from seeing the goodness and creativity of human beings living outside of Islam. They are unable to make such an acknowledgement for fear that their God will condemn them to eternal damnation. An open rational view of human behavior and a different view of their God would spell the end of Islam and of their very souls.

Beyond the human suffering that Islam has in the past and will inevitably in the future bring upon itself and others, there is a question as to whether Islamic intransigence really matters in a world moving as fast scientifically and socially as it is today. Those at the extremes always want to take control and often they do, but not for long. The recent history of the world has shown that it is the peacemakers, the pragmatic problem solvers, and those with new constructive ideas that in the long run make the difference. These are the people who take the talents their Creator has given them and use them for His purposes. They are the ones who clean up the pieces, set the broken bones, put back together the broken lives and open the future, after the extremists have become exhausted. They are the true sons and daughters of GOD. And, they are from all faiths. They are Jews, Christians, Muslims, Buddhists, Hindu…. Some have no faith in any particular creedal belief at all. They are recognized by the good that they do.

There is little that Islam can do to change itself. This is because Muhammad built his theology on two tragic errors. The first was that the Koran in its entirety is the inerrant word of God and therefore cannot be challenged. The other is that the God of the Koran was modeled after the militaristic negative side of the Hebraic God of the Old Testament, and not the New. It is this Hebraic image of God that has given rise to the view of Muslims that all who are not with us are our enemies who must be conquered and changed. They are the infidels who are living corrupted lives and are worshiping false Gods. This in turn has in recent years spawned 5th columns of terror throughout the world bent on destroying all who disagree with Islamic theology.

If Islam cannot move forward in its recognition of a different kind of God, can Orthodox Christianity and Judaism? Can the monotheistic ancient God of the Torah as well as the Triune father God of Christianity be seen in another way? Can a broad metaphysical interpretive view of God without the appendages from the past be acknowledged? The answer to these questions will determine the future of world history.

The future of Judaism, Christianity, and Islam as well as all other world religions lay in the validity of their perception of the Creator of the Universe.

There can only be one reality to our Creator. In time, whether that is one hundred years from now or ten thousand, the God that humans look to can be only one GOD, the one Creator of all. As in the past, religions that do not reflect the will of the one Creator of all will perish.

In time the way human beings deal with each other as well as with the physical world around them must be a reflection of the will of that one Creator. If it is not, the human species will cease to exist. Nothing is more important for the human species than to unravel the paradoxes of past religious belief and discover the will of the One Creator. There is only one nature to our Creator. We must not be held back by our perceptions of Gods constructed in ages past. We must not stop until we find the one GOD who will define our future.

Man from the beginning of time has been in search for the nature of his Creator. This quest did not come to an end with the Koran and Sharia or the last book of the Hebrew Bible or the authorized Canon of New Testament writings. It will go on regardless of how much effort is made by those at the extremes to hold it back. Man has shown that by his very nature he is willing to leave the comfort of the past for the uncertainty of the future.

We have a God given right to question the nature of the Creator as He was defined in ages past. His image is not something any Rabbi, Imam, Ayatollah, Pope, Priest, or Pastor can dictate. GOD gave each of us the intelligence to find out for ourselves.

Nor will man be content with placing GOD out there in some other place at a distance from himself. He will want to find GOD in the here and now within himself. This is not a new idea. It is the metaphysical meaning of the Christian sacrament of the Eucharist. The Eucharist is an act of acknowledging GOD within. It is the act of believing that GOD exists within me. He is a part of me. I am a part of Him. It is also an act that says we must invite Him in. We must take the initiative. We cannot grow, work miracles, and evolve unless we have become co-creators with a God who is a part of us, who is within. We, along with GOD, then become the co-authors of our own existence.

Scientific discoveries in the 20th and 21st century have presented a challenge to the picture of our nature as it was presented in the Hebrew Bible, Christian New Testament and Koran. Quantum Mechanics has uncovered a new and different level of reality against which all religions ideas about human identity must now be examined. These discoveries have shown us that matter is not what we perceive it to be and that we in our physical form exist only as pure energy. They show us that we have no physical form as we understand it. It may be that the ultimate definition and source of this energy—as well as ourselves—exists in some other dimension. We may in our essence be a reflection of something else. We may simultaneously exist in another dimension.

Islam has not caught on to this understanding. It is still living in its tribal past worshiping a fearful pagan God who exists far away in some other dimension. He is a God of obedience, not co-creation. He is a God away from Muslims, not a part of them.

The metaphysical vision of the 21st century God being described here is the vision that Jesus expressed to the writer of The Gospel of Thomas discovered in 1945 in Egypt at Nag Hammadi. This Nag Hammadi God is a God who beckons to Muslims asking them to enter His dimension not on a final judgment day at the *end of times* or today through martyrdom, but now here on earth. At the same time He calls upon them for servitude towards everyone on this earth. He asks them to cut out the bitterness from their minds towards those not of the Muslim faith and replace it with unconditional love towards all of humankind. He asks them to show their love towards Him, Allah, through these individual and collective acts of love and kindness, acts that become a reflection of the HIS presence in their life. He is saying to all Muslims: *Stop praying to me; start praying for the Jewish, Christian, Hindu and Muslim neighbor next to you.*

The ancient Abrahamic texts of the Hebrew Bible, The Christian New and Old Testaments and the Koran do not forcefully enough speak these words. Instead they keep turning us back to a pagan God of anger and retribution. As a result, it is now clear that the so called "fundamentalists" in the three religions of Abraham who hold on to this ancient God have set the entire world on a dangerous spiritual and ideological—as well as geopolitical—path by way of a dangerous miscalculation, one of confrontation that is having an adverse effect on human society. We are faced with a religious ideological war, a war that is slowly sapping our strength, one that may leave the Abrahamic experiment itself a footnote in history.

For this reason, it has never been more important for opposing voices to be heard. Never has it been more important for ideas and dreams to be thought about and discussed. Never has it been more important for dialogue to be fostered.

As for Islam, to the extent that a vocal religious Islamic orthodoxy is drowning out opposing voices of moderation and silencing them, this orthodoxy must now be vigorously challenged. Moderate Muslims can not do it alone. Those in the West, politicians, clergy, intellectuals, must speak out. It will be painful for some, the devout Christians and Jews who believe in their special covenantal relationship with their God. For others, those who are secular; they can no longer enjoy the comfort of remaining theologically illiterate. The West will never be able to understand the dangers that this seemingly foreign orthodoxy presents until we, each of us, are ready to confront the flaws built into the origins of the Abrahamic beliefs that formed our own society, those same beliefs on which Islam was built.

Changes we make in our thinking about the image of the God we choose to worship will determine not only the quality of our lives and the lives of all people in today's world and for future generations, but possibly even the survival of the human species as we know it.

This is the challenge today for the three religions of Abraham. Many Jews and Christians are already facing this challenge. Not all, but many are working through a redefinition of the Yahweh/Triune God. It is most unfortunate for human civilization that, except for very few, there is little evidence Islam has any desire to do the same with Allah.

Part III
Understanding the World Wide Threat of Islam

The Mind of Muhammad – The Mind of Michelangelo

Why did Muslim animosity towards Jews and Christians suddenly explode so violently in the 21st century? Was there a catalyst? No doubt the recognition of the State of Israel in 1948 by the United Nations with its sponsorship by the United States played an important part; but, was this the primary reason? After all, the land mass given to Israel, as the United Nations had originally configured it, was just a small piece of marginally productive soil surrounded by densely populated Muslim nations, many of them rich in oil and other resources. Few of them had shown any interest before 1948.

Israel was one more piece of dry wood placed on a smoldering fire. It was an important reason, but by itself it was not the primary one. The real reason was that the world around Islam had changed while Islam had remained in its seventh century form.

After World War I, with the downward spiral of Muslim society following the disintegration of the Ottoman Empire, the Islamic core belief in its religious superiority and its manifest destiny to dominate world society were being placed in doubt. It was not happening; in fact just the opposite.

We must begin our discussion in 1927 in order to understand the Muslim response. It is in this response where we find the cause of the frustrations and the violence that we are witnessing today.

Out of this Islamic despair emerged a prophet of hope for Islam. In its darkest hour there suddenly emerged a strong voice calling for change. It was calling for Muslims to abandon the secular and decadent western ideology that was destroying them and return to the purity of seventh century Islam. It was the voice of a highly gifted and charismatic individual, an Egyptian orator schoolteacher/clock repairer named Hassan al-Banna. He appeared out of nowhere on the streets corners of Cairo, as well as other cities, dressed in a flaming red robe and preaching his message. Like the early American Christian evangelists, he mesmerized his audiences with vivid descriptions of hell for those who had abandoned the purity of Islam. Like the American Christian evangelists he too warned of the Day of Judgment and Hell's torments.

There was, however, a difference between al-Banna and the Americans. Islam is a political/military religion. Muslims do not *render unto Caesar the things that are Caesars'*. Muhammad joined religion, governance and military conquest and made it one. Al-Banna's mission was to take over the Egyptian government and then the world. In 1928 he established the Society of Muslim Brothers. By the late 1940's the Muslim Brothers had some two thousand branches throughout Egypt and it was threatening the Egyptian government itself.

Its objectives were "individual moral purification and collective political and social regeneration through the establishment of a truly Islamic government in Egypt, as a springboard for universal expansion"; and as Banna described it, "until the entire world will chant the name of the Prophet (Muhammad), Allah's prayers and blessings be upon him". (see p 208-219 *Islamic Imperialism, A History* Efraim Karsh)

But there was a chilling side to these objectives. As Efraim Karsh further describes it in his book:

" In Banna's view, the Qur'an commanded its believers to love death as much as others love life. As long as Muslim society failed to abide by this sacred philosophy they were destined to remain in their current dismal position. 'There is no escape from death and it happens only once', he (Banna) claimed. 'Should death come down the path of Allah, it will be a gain in this world and a reward in the other.' This reasoning was duly incorporated into the Muslim Brother's Credo: 'Allah is our goal; the Qur'an is our constitution; the Prophet is our leader; Struggle is our way; and death in the path of Allah is our highest aspiration.'"

On February 12, 1949 Banna was murdered by Egyptian government agents, apparently in revenge for the assassination of Prime Minister Nuqrashi Oasha a few weeks earlier.

The scene was now set for the intellectual hero of all Islamic terrorists, Sayyid Qutb (pronounced KUH-tahb). From the agony and horror of an Egyptian prison he wrote his vast, many-volume commentary, *In the Shade of the Qur'an*. In 1966 Qutb was also executed by the Egyptian government, but by that time it was too late to stop the contagion that was to follow. His was a work that would inspire future generations of Muslim terrorists, including the wealthy Arabian, Osama bin Laden and his Egyptian deputy, Ayman al-Zawahiri. Cast under its spell, many thousands of young Muslims would accept Islam in the purest seventh century form, as Qutb had so defined it. Many more today continue to join their ranks.

The idea of a utopian society coming about by way of the righteous destroying the unrighteous was not a new one. It had existed throughout the Hebrew Bible and with Muhammad it became an important part of the Koran. An example of the Hebraic roots is found in a comment by the author John J. Collins in his book, *The Scepter and the Star: The Messiahs of the Dead Sea Scrolls and Other Ancient Literature*. He writes about the expectations in the Qumran community (140's B.C.– 68 A.D.) of the coming Messiah:

"He is the scepter who will smite the nations, slay the wicked with the breath of his lips, and restore the Davidic dynasty.... He is also the Messiah of righteousness, who will usher in an era of peace and justice."

The members of the Qumran community believed in a God who can be righteous on the one hand and a destroyer of the wicked on the other. This is both the Hebraic and Koranic interpretation of the nature of their Yahweh and Allah. The parallels to present day Muslim thought are obvious. Qutb believed in this kind of God. Allah would be the destroyer of the infidels. His loyal subjects would do the destroying. Those who participated and died for the cause would have fast entry into Paradise.

Qutb saw a world corrupted by Christianity and by Zionism. He would brush off Judaism as "a system of rigid and lifeless ritual." He saw Christianity as a two faced religion that had lost its direction. One part of it was secular and the other religious. Its biggest mistake according to Qutb lay in the words of Jesus when he said:

Render unto Caesar the things that are Caesars' and to God the things that are Gods'

Qutb, before his acceptance of al-Banna's credo, had visited the United States. In fact, biographers say he was not a devout Muslim as a young man. But at some moment upon his return to Cairo he must have decided that radical Islam was the only solution. Everything must to be rendered to Allah. How else could this perfect world come about? It would not be by way of Christianity. The Christian idea of a direct connection with a loving redemptive God made no sense. Under Christianity there was no way to make people subservient to a God who would *smite the nations, slay the wicked with the breath of his lips*. Besides, according to Qutb, Christianity had been polluted by Greek philosophy and all of its dangerous cultural creativity, personal freedom and creative introspection. Like Muhammad, he would choose his own distant and fearful Hebraic/Koranic God. Servitude to this God meant obedience. In order to please Allah, Muslims would live according to a system of mandated laws set down by the ancient Qur'an, Sunna and Shari'a. This would open the path to absolute purity for every human being willing to follow it.

Like the Apostle Paul many generations before him, Qutb saw the world overtaken by wanton sexual expression and undisciplined excess. Where Paul pointed his finger at Roman society, Qutb blamed the secular Christians and Zionists who had turned their backs on GOD for the pleasures of this world. He viewed western society as being consumed by its passions and therefore fallen. For Qutb, the western world had become a den of moral and ethical degeneration.

To bring about his New World, the Christian-Zionist world would be destroyed and replaced with an Islamic world. It would be a utopian world living by the revelations of the prophet Muhammad, the true messenger of GOD. It would be a world where every human being would live a Sharia life under Islamic law. The entire world would become an Islamic clerical state living in fear of Allah and the final Day of Judgment.

What Qutb and Banna could not face about this modern secular Judeo-Christian world is that it rested its belief on an enduring human strength built not on adherence to strict religious law, Islamic or any other, but upon the belief that every person on this earth regardless of religions belief is valued by GOD for his and her strengths and forgiven for their weaknesses. Qutb and Banna could not acknowledge this new God of Jesus, a God who had over a sometimes painful two thousand year history supplanted the Hebraic Yahweh. Allah would not allow them.

This new God had slowly spread His power through western civilization—Christian as well as non Christian. He had become a God who gives value to every individual, determined by how he or she lives in relationship to every other person. This new God had become a God who extends His love beyond the ability of any Jew, Christian or Muslim man—or woman—to please Him. This was a new God who says that for salvation humans must look not to Him in some other dimension but to his presence here on earth, a presence demonstrated through their lives as they individually and in unity contribute to the progress and dignity of fellow humans. The life and death of Jesus had become a metaphor for this new vision of God.

Many who were not Christian—and this may have included Muhammad—were quick to interpret this change from old to new as license for disobedience before the law. This was not so. Jesus did not give men and women an open permissive religion. His admonitions and parables placed deeply disturbing demands on them, far greater demands that those placed under Hebraic law, and six hundred years after his death under Islamic law too. Jesus made it very clear. Obedience to the law is of little value, nor is ritual. Change must come from within. Laws can only be outlines.

This new view God defined by Jesus had been the change agent behind western thought over its entire two thousand year formation. Jesus had redefined both the Hebraic nature of GOD as well as our relationship to HIM. He said we must focus our attention not on the vengeful God of the Torah, but on his (Jesus) God as defined by his (Jesus) life. By connecting men and women in all of their weakness to a loving and redemptive God, he had released them from fear of God. He said we must be "like I am", a person of unrequited love. He redefined God as being like himself, a power of pure love. He said to the world: You can only show you love of God in one way, by also being a power of "pure love".

Muhammad had rejected this Jesus idea of unrequited love. He could not release his subjects from fear of a vengeful Torah God. How else could he control them? In fact, his was not a problem only for Islam. Control too was a part of the early Christian church. Early on, the Roman church would not disavow belief in this Torah God. Even today Christian fundamentalists insist on worshiping the old pre Jesus God. He is the "father" part of their Trinity found in their Old Testament. He punishes. At the *end of times* he will cast into the fires of Hell those who do not accept Jesus as their personal savior.

But over time much of Christianity changed and the western world along with it. As these changes took place, Islam remained the same. To this day Islam continues to follow its ancient path, looking to a vengeful schizophrenic God, at one moment loving, the other punishing. Man—Islam is a man's religion with women being subservient—no matter how hard he tries, can never totally and completely please Allah; unless according to Qutb's interpretation, he were for the cause of Allah to die as a Jihadist suicidal bomber!

Qutb's was a philosophy of subservience to a punishing retributive God who would banish to eternal hell-fire those who did not follow Qutb's definitions as to what was and was not "pure" Islam. It closed life and forced an inflexibility of the human mind, and at the extreme through despair led to a lust for martyrdom; the philosophy of Jesus' was a philosophy of embracement of a loving God leading to a lust for life. Qutb's was a philosophy of fear of the unknown; Jesus' was a philosophy of liberation into the unknown. It is no wonder that this new vision of Jesus as the new form of the universal Christ, from the Renaissance onward, led to the greatest intellectual advancement human kind had ever seen.

This Jesus view of GOD and mans' relationship to Him opened new horizons for human civilization. The western world over its two thousand year period of development had chosen to place its faith in a God who did not restrain human kind but instead gave men and women the freedom to expand their vision into the unknown. In everyday terms; the father released the son and let him strike out on his own. In theological terms; Christianity moved away from the "Father" image of God in the Trinity and towards the "Son" image of God. It is understandable that for Qutb, Jesus and the world he produced would be an anathema. Given the freedom to think beyond the earth bound constraints set in place by his fearful Islamic God, Allah; the release of this new expansive, rebellious, energetic, creative, individualistic, curious, creative human consciousness represented a life or death threat to Islam.

As was just mentioned, Christianity was not always the religion of an itinerant first century Nazarene who said that *the meek shall inherit the earth* and that *we should turn the other cheek* and that *we should love our enemies*. It had gone through its dark period, turning its back on the authentic Jesus, looking to the same authoritative father God as Islam. Its history from its consolidation by the Roman Church in the fourth century to the Renaissance was not a pretty one. But once the Renaissance had begun, change began to occur and men like Aquinas, Giotto, Botticelli, Luther, Copernicus,

Michelangelo, da Vinci, Galileo and Descartes, to name only a few, literally exploded on to the scene.

This discussion would not be complete without mention of the enormous influence of early Greek classical thought on western civilization from the thirteenth century onward. It was this thought in combination with the revolutionary view of God by Jesus just described that enabled western civilization to advance so rapidly. This is the key to understanding the irreconcilable differences that exist today between Islam and the West. Over this period Islam as a religion and form of social organization was left in the dust bin of history. The resentment of many Muslims today can only be understood in the context of this combined western cultural advance.

A few very brief historical facts are in order. In 529 A.D. the Christian Emperor Justinian ordered the Platonic Academy in Athens, which was the last bastion of Greek thought in Christendom, closed—that year has often been used as a convenient date for the end of the classical period and the beginning of the Middle Ages. Greek classical thought was clearly at odds with much—but not all—of then Christian orthodoxy; although, a limited amount of Greek classical thought had in fact already been absorbed into Christianity by that time. With the closing of the school, seven of its teachers moved to Persia where they started a new school. This new school was later to serve as a way station for transfer of the Greek classics to Baghdad under the direction of the Abbasid Caliphate which was founded there in 750 A.D. The Abbasid Caliphate gradually moved all Islamic centers of learning to its capital, including Greek classical studies. Scholarship in these studies in Baghdad then became intense, even though most Islamic scholars rejected—except for mathematics and the sciences—Greek classical thought. About two centuries later, with Spain under Muslim control, Cordoba, the capital of Spain, began to vie with Baghdad as a center of Greek classical studies. Then, in the twelfth and thirteenth centuries, with the expulsion of the Moors from Spain, and with Spain now under Christian control; from Cordoba the Islamic translations and commentaries of Greek classical philosophy and science were transmitted across the Pyrenees to the newly founded universities in Paris, Bologna and Oxford. This sparked a revival of Greek classical scholarship in Medieval Europe. Soon after, largely as a result of this, the rigidity of Roman Catholic orthodoxy came under attack and the Renaissance in Europe had begun, marking a period of broadly based political, cultural, scientific and artistic creativity yet unknown in human history.

This cultural transformation in medieval Europe is very much a part of our western civilization today. It marks the difference between the West and Islam. Greek philosophers such as Xenophanes, Socrates, Pericles, Plato and Aristotle with their deeply penetrating observations about the human condition once again after a long period of European Continental dormancy once again showed themselves to be among the greatest thinkers the world had ever known. Their influence could be seen in every aspect of post medieval life. Their power was enormous, beyond all medieval institutional Catholic Christian imagination. Nothing could stop them. From Michelangelo's statue of David in Florence—a replication of the Greek—illustrating the perfection of the "new age man" to the soaring architecture of the Gothic cathedrals to Saint Peter's Basilica in Rome to the French Enlightenment philosophers to the western constitutional form of government; Greek classical influence was the underlying driving force releasing this new western creativity. The French philosopher Descartes articulated it in his epochal defining statement: *Cognito, ergo sum*—**I think, therefore I am**. All else was to be questioned, but not the thinker's self awareness. The power to form the future was being passed from the Roman Catholic Church to the individual, who now reigned supreme. The world would never be the same.

It is one of the great ironies of history that it was eastern Islamic scholars who were largely responsible for this western transformation when, as we have seen, during the Golden Age of Islam, they rediscovered the Greek classics at a time when medieval Europe had turned its back on them. Islamic scholars meticulously catalogued and translated these classics and studied then at great length, but they resisted accepting their humanistic ideas in the context of Islamic thought. Their Koran and record of the life of Muhammad would not allow them. These advances in thought forged a way of viewing human potential in a way that Islam at that time in history, as well as today, could not.

Author' Note:

℘

Greek Classical literature was also being preserved in other cities such as Constantinople. Some was also being preserved in the Christian monasteries, but only in the most rudimentary fashion. Throughout Christendom, the study of the Greek classics had virtually disappeared. The writings themselves had virtually disappeared. The Greek classical ideas introduced early on by Paul and by Augustine (both were students of the Greek classics) did, however, survive and they had become a part of Catholic Christian dogma. There is no question though that it was the Islamic scholars who preserved these classics by translation and study and that it was their scholarship that sparked the Renaissance. Western scholarship overall gives

91

little credit to this historical fact. This is the cause of much resentment among Muslim intellectuals today.

✌

For Banna and Qutb, as well as for their many terrorist followers, the fruits of this expansion of human potential would become the cause of enormous humiliation and resentment. They could reach only one conclusion. The enemies of Allah are not only the secular Christians and the Jews and all they stand for—and the secular Muslims who have been polluted by non Islamic values, but western civilization itself. Therefore, western civilization must be destroyed. This became their mission; destroy it. These radical Muslims would close themselves off to the new world, a world in which humans were, after so many years of darkness, now set to achieve their highest goals. They would revert to the seventh century words and life of Muhammad, their prophet.

Time is running out on Islam. In its present form, it has walled in the Muslim mind. It has done this through fear. Through fear of Allah's judgment, it has held Muslims back from participating in the solutions needed to face the challenges of our 21ˢᵗ century world. In its present form it has closed off the Muslim imagination. Its Jihadist fervor has released the deepest and most horrific impulses that can come from a human mind. Through separation from all others who have chosen alternative ways of life, it has isolated itself. Radical Islam, which is spawned by this Islamic thought, is like a spreading a cancer, bringing painful suffering and death throughout the world. Every day it citizens are forced to bear witness to the bloody body parts.

Islam has been betrayed not only by extremists like Banna and Qutb. It has been betrayed by medieval-minded clerics filled with anger toward a modernized democratic westernized way of life. It has been betrayed by Imams who spew out a message of hatred towards the West and are today protected by a powerful and elite wealthy class determined to continue its own privileged position. These monarchs, sheikhs, tribal elites, political leaders, business tycoons, and their followers live off the fat of the land, bullying and trampling on their subjects, forcing them to live on the periphery of world society. Banna and Qutb were correct. Muslim society had become decadent. But it was not the fault of western society. It was the fault of an archaic religion that had become a religion of the past unable to meet the challenges of the future.

92

If we were living during the Christian Crusades of the 12th century or the European Imperialism of the nineteenth and early twentieth or the Cold War of the mid and late twentieth, the mullahs might have an argument saying Muslims are being oppressed by infidel outsiders. This argument does not hold in today's world. The world economy and its political systems have rapidly moved past the last thousand years of its history. It is now a world crying out for new religious images—Jewish and Christian as well as Muslim—that will take it into the next thousand years, not those that tied it down to its dismal past.

Oil revenues over the last 50 years have provided many of the nations in the Middle East with a tremendous bounty. These nations have had ample time to assist their less fortunate Muslim neighbors, to take on reforms themselves and to enter the world economy. Today, these nations form the cradle of Muslim hatred towards the West.

Recent events have shown the religion of these nations to be:

<u>A religion of</u>—crazed terrorists with box cutters slitting the throats of defenseless airline stewardesses.

<u>A religion of</u>—human beings falling from the World Trade Towers in New York City.

<u>A religion of</u>—young people running from a horrific explosion in Bali that an Indonesia described in the following way: "It was sometimes hard to know whether the man who appeared to be running toward him through the flames was alive or already dead... Like you look at their face and you can't make anything out; there's nothing left ... People were missing ears, people were missing limbs, their skin was peeling off. There were blind people with glass in their eyes running around screaming that they couldn't see".

<u>A religion of</u>—sectarian violence in Baghdad with hundreds of Shiite and Sunni citizens each week being murdered in retaliation for each other's violence.

<u>A religion of</u>—carefully coordinated exploding bombs on commuter trains in Mumbai, India killing over 190 innocent commuters.

<u>A religion of</u>—teen-age Palestinians, Iranians, Saudis and Iraqis with explosives strapped to their bodies blowing themselves up in crowded disco clubs and pizza parlors, schools and shopping centers, sending pieces of steel in all directions, killing and maiming innocent people nearby.

A religion of—parents who rejoice at the martyrdom of their children as suicide bombers.

A religion of—silence among its leaders; who, if they were to criticize their Mullahs, would fear for their own safety.

A religion of—hatred towards all Jews and Gentiles driven by a festering jealously over what these people holding to faiths other than their own have made of their lives.

Not just those of the western religions but those in the entire world; Hindu, Sikh, Buddhists, Taoists, and all others of other beliefs are today asking the question: Is this all that Islam is? Is it a distorted and failed religion?

Is it only a religion of mind control leading to darkness and death? Is it only a religion of hatred? The constant stream of graphic pictures of carnage world wide is leading non Muslims to this conclusion.

Why is the Islamic response so tepid? Why is there so little discussion and debate within Islam? Why are Muslims unable to face these issues? What is holding them back? Fear is holding them back. Fear of challenging the Koran, the word of Allah, is holding them back. Fear of their clerics is holding them back. Islam is a religion built on fear.

Islam is locked into a seventh century theology built on the inerrancy of every word of the Koran. Every word must be believed as the word of Allah. Disbelief and disobedience is punishable by ostracism, physical punishment—even death—and at death eternal suffering. It is also built on the life of Muhammad. His life can not be questioned as he is believed to be God's intermediary on earth. These beliefs are holding Islam back from reformation, the same kind of reformation that took place and continues to take place in Judaism and Christianity.

How can we Jews and Christians begin to understand the fear that permeates modern Muslim thought and behavior? We must begin with the origins of our own belief. We must begin not just with Islam and its seventh century beginning but also with the other two religions of Abraham on which it was built, Judaism and Christianity. And, we must not just "understand" all three in parallel lines historically; we must dig deeply into each of them and expose the fault lines that began with their common formation.

For Muslims, central to the answers to the questions above is the question of whether Muhammad was just another spiritually gifted and even prophetic human being who interpreted the existing body of theological knowledge in his part of the world 1400 years ago in a way that would form a deeply spiritual and at the same time economic, social and politically binding religion in the context of conditions at that time and in that place.

If this was the case, how much of it then has application in the 21st century? How much impedes the free flow of political expression and ideas that serve to elevate human potential? How much is harmful in today's world? What parts of Islam are causing its followers to be held back in their economic and social development? These questions from the West are not new. Muslims for many years have rejected such inferences and termed them the Orientalist fallacy.

For a Muslim even to ask these questions is a sacrilege punishable by death. It is a defiance of acknowledgement that Muhammad is the prophet of God. It is a repudiation of the Koran as the word of God. It promises eternal punishment after death in hell. Unlike Judaism and Christianity, in Islam there can be no compromise or liberal interpretation. All of it must be accepted. To enter paradise a Muslim must accept every word of the Koran as the word of God. For Muslims the question of whether it is possible to live as Muslims in a harmonious relationship with other people of other religions can only be answered by the Koran. As we have discussed, Muslims believe that it is the destiny of Islam to be the one and only religion in the world. All nations are to become Holy Nations under Sharia Law. The stated goal according to the Koran is to accomplish this by any means possible, including war. Given the horror that is emerging from Islam under its present course, this is for the rest of the world, clearly a frightful utopian vision far detached from reality. In fact, for non Muslims the most pressing and at the same time perplexing question is: Can Islam even continue to exist at all as a viable means of religious expression in its present archaic fundamentalist form in the open, technocratic, pluralistic society of the 21st century? If it can survive at all, then in what form can it survive?

One way to approach this is to ask the questions: How much of the thought structure of the religion is based on an exclusiveness that leads to never ending conflict with people of other forms of religious and social organization? Does this exclusiveness prevent Muslims from seeing as equal others outside of its belief system? How much fulfills Muslim potential both inside as well as outside of Islam? Can parts of Islamic thought structure in any way be separated so that its followers are able to ignore its negative aspects?

These are, in fact, questions not only for Muslims, but also for all people of all religions who, like Muslims, consider themselves to be exclusive or chosen by God and use this to establish their feeling of superiority and identity through the denigration of those with other beliefs. This includes fundamentalist Christians and Jews. It includes all who feel that their religion entitles them to sit in judgment of others. The greater question for these extremists is whether the one CREATOR of our Universe and GOD of all humankind is making the same exclusionary choices that they are.

Muslims must understand that all of the language of their Koran is not from Allah, it is of the mind and hand of man. It is not revelation, nor can it be. It is simply an attempt at the truth or to be near the truth. It is an attempt made by mortal human beings that never totally reaches the truth.

The search for GOD'S revelation did not stop with Muhammad and his univocal understanding of God. It will carry on until the *end of times*. Until Muslims recognize this, there can only be stubbornness of thought leading to simmering hateful resentment towards a modern fast changing 21st century world in search for is meaning in the cosmos. Islam, along with its two counterparts, Judaism and Christianity, must acknowledge rebirth as a continuing process in this quest for understanding.

We were created by GOD to be open to His presence. We were created by GOD to reinvent ourselves and the world we live in through co-creation. Each generation is entrusted to carry on this search for HIS revelation. It is a never-ending search. The position of Islam that the search was over 1400 years ago is wrong.

IX

The God They Think They Know
The Torah God
The Triune God
The God of Jesus Christ

The God of the Torah began as more than just the Creator of the Universe and giver of the law. He had human emotions. And these human emotions were the same as those of His human creation, man. Like man, He had a dark and fearful side. But, He was not like any man. He was like a father. He was perceived in the eyes of His people as a small child looks with fear and respect at a powerful and protective father. Like a father, He could be loving, merciful, and kind, but then just as quickly He could be manipulative and punishing.

In the very beginning of man's appearance on the earth this God of the Torah would cast Adam out of the Garden of Eden for his disobedience, to live by the sweat of his brow. He would do the same with his mate, Eve. Years later, as a punishment for the disobedience of their offspring, He would bring a great flood upon the earth when all but His *Chosen* would perish. Years after the Flood, as a test of faith, He would call the first Jewish patriarch, Abraham, to kill his son Isaac.

He was the exclusive God of the Jewish people as well as their protector. In their Egyptian captivity 1000 years after Abraham had died, He would stand by as Pharaoh killed every first born child. He would allow Moses to survive, so that in later years Moses could lead the Children of Israel in their Exodus out of Egypt.

When He gave His law to the Nation of Israel, He made a covenant with its people. He said that as long as you obey Me, I will protect you. He said He would only punish them if they disobeyed Him. Later, when they did disobey, His anger was to be feared. His judgment could be severe. Then, He showed no mercy to the Nation of Israel.

He was also a warrior God who would bring victory in battle to the Nation of Israel. He was by David's side when David's army slew the

Philistines, the Moabites, the Syrians, the Edomites, the Ammonites, and the Amalekites. Their destruction was part of His plan. They were a threat to the reign of David and the future kings after his reign. The cause was always His cause. It was not to be questioned. The outcome was always connected to the continuity of the history of the Nation of Israel and the lessons learned from their obedience or disobedience. Their history was always about the God of Israel favoring His *Chosen* people. It was always about their special destiny as His *Chosen* people. Whatever happened, it was always assumed to be woven into His Covenant with His *Chosen* people.

None of the Kings of Israel were punished by their God for going to war and slaughtering their enemies. It was enemy blood, not Israelite blood. There was no mercy shown towards the vanquished. In the mind of the people of Israel, the victories in battle were always a part of His plan. They were of His will. He was their protector. Battles won against great odds were His miracles and they were rewarded as a part of His Covenant with their nation.

At times He performed miraculous acts. He separated the sea to allow the Jews to escape from Egypt. Joshua could not have brought down the walls of Jericho with a blast of a ram's horn if the God of Israel had not been there to aid him.

He was also a personal God who could give comfort to those overcome by pain and suffering. He brought them relief. He could be called upon to protect them against their enemies. He could strike down and plunge into a fiery furnace the enemies of those who believed in Him. He could give them vengeance. He could shield those who obeyed Him from their enemies. He could bless the righteous. He was their shelter and refuge. For those who believed in him, He could be the light of their salvation. There was nothing they needed to fear.

As time passed, He became a God of the law. It began as His law written in His hand. It defined the actions forbidden by the people of Israel. It passed out judgment on those who disobeyed it. The law started with just a few commandments, but as time passed and the Hebrew society became more complex, it became a law of many words and many interpretations. Even the interpretations remained His law, although they were now coming not from Him but from those who were interpreting what they thought He meant. Then it became necessary to devise subsets to the original law. These were rules and regulations related to every area of the lives of the people, such as how to eat, how to pray, how to worship, how to dress, how to marry, and how to bury the dead. They became necessary, not so much to please their God, but to assure that the people of Israel would continue to exist as a unified tribe and nation.

This was the Jewish peoples' understanding of the nature of their God and their law when Jesus, 2000 years after the death of Abraham, lived among them preaching about a new and radically different vision of God and the Hebrew scriptures. His was a vision that contradicted the Jewish view of the nature of God, as well as the body of laws and rules of behavior that had been woven around the original commandments. He did not dismiss the Hebrew Bible or the Mosaic Law. On the contrary, he rested his new theology on the prophecies of the Hebrew Bible and its law. But, the overall view of the nature of GOD and how humankind is to respond to Him was different.

It was a message that was to bring an end to Jewish History. Israel would no longer be a nation. Jews would no longer have an exclusive relationship with their God. There would be a new kind of covenantal relationship, this one between GOD and all of mankind. It would be a covenantal relationship that redefined the relationship between man and GOD and in doing so redefined the very nature of GOD Himself.

The God of Jesus was not an exclusive God, as the God of the Nation of Israel was. He was a God not of a nation but of the world. The God of Jesus was a God for everyone, no matter who they were. He valued every human being. In His eyes everyone was His child; the rich, the poor, those with hope, those who had lost hope. He was a God ready to show His love towards anyone who asked and even those who didn't.

He was not a God of divine retribution. Nor did He lead armies into battle. He gave those who followed Him not victory over other people or nations; He gave them victory over evil. He was a God who rejected the temptations of worldly power. He worked not with outward signs such as seas dividing or walls tumbling, but quietly in the hearts of people.

He did not punish those who did not obey Him. He did not cause pain and suffering to His people. He defined pain and suffering as a condition of life and then said He would help them to live with pain and suffering. He brought to those who followed Him a peace that passed all understanding, a peace that would overcome all pain and suffering. It was a peace that showed those who followed Him the path to His presence in eternity. It was a path that promised eternal life.

The coming of the Messiah had been prophesied in the Hebrew Bible. The fulfillment of this prophecy, for the Jews, was to reveal the Kingdom of GOD here on earth, at the end of time. Also, it was to reveal the true nature of GOD. The Jews at the time of Jesus assumed that this would incorporate the fulfillment of their idea of Israel as a powerful and influential nation.

This is how they interpreted the prophetic messianic vision in their Torah. But Jesus said this was not God's purpose. He said that fulfillment is to come from the inside of Jewish men and women, not come from the outside in terms of worldly power and influence. He invited Jewish men and women to enter GOD'S grace in the here and now and to leave all other ambition aside, including the ambition of nationhood.

Jesus presented a redefinition of the way Jews were to respond to GOD. The God of Jesus was a God who asked every person to turn his life over to Him so that His purpose in that life can be fulfilled. The Torah God did not require this. The Torah God was a God who required every Jew to engage in a life long study of the Torah so that he could live a Torah life in obedience to GOD.

There were other differences. The Torah God was a retributive God to be feared. The God of Jesus was a God who could not be feared, as He was a God of love incapable of retribution. The Torah God was a God who punished those who did not obey Him. The God of Jesus was a God who defined punishment as estrangement from GOD.

How did the Jews come upon their definition of the nature of their God? On what grounds was it challenged by Jesus? Can it be challenged using Genesis itself, using the very words that appeared there? The Jews believed that each word of the Torah was sacred and therefore could never be changed except by GOD Himself. Man could only interpret the Torah, not change it. Is it possible that Jesus went back to the very beginning and saw an error? We must go back to the very beginning of the Torah and try to find the answer.

As we examine a single line in the Book of Genesis, we find the source of two opposing interpretations of the nature of GOD, one the Hebraic interpretation and the other the interpretation that was given by Jesus. Genesis describes GOD'S creation of man as follows:

Let us make man in our image and likeness.

(Genesis 1:26)

The key words are *our image*. If man was originally made—before the fall—in GOD'S image, what was and is GOD'S image? The view of Jesus was that it is an image of love, perfection, and harmony. It is an image of enlightenment. It is a heavenly image.

The Hebraic interpretation of the nature of GOD was not the same. The Torah makes that unquestionably clear. It is based on a statement made later on by the serpent to Eve just before the temptation:

100

Then your eyes shall be opened, and ye shall be like Gods, knowing good and evil.

(Genesis 3:5)

The Tempter is telling Eve after she eats from the tree of *knowledge of good and evil,* she will become like a God. The Tempter then goes on to describe the definition of the nature of this God. It is a deity with knowledge of both good and evil.

The nature of the God of the Jews not previously defined in Genesis was for the first time being defined. The serpent (tempter) is making Him an anthropomorphic God. He is in effect giving GOD the same nature as that of you and me, a living creature having knowledge of both good and evil.

We must ask two questions:

- Who was defining GOD'S nature?
- Was it GOD HIMSELF?

A liar and a deceiver was defining GOD'S nature. The definition was not coming from GOD HIMSELF.

GOD was not defining HIMSELF. A deceiver was. The greater question then is why we should accept a deceiver's definition of the nature of our God.

This was the definition that would be accepted by the Jews. Their God would be like themselves. He would have an anthropomorphic nature. He would be like a father. He would be a powerful stern and protective man with a paternal love towards His children. Like a father; He could be angry; He could be vindictive; He could punish; He could be jealous; He could reward; and He could take away. He could even be a murderer of the enemies of the Nation of Israel.

This was to be the nature of the monotheistic God who would dominate the Hebrew Bible. The Jewish people would build their complex theology on this God. This would be the scriptural reference point for their thoughts and actions.

It was a definition that Jesus of Nazareth refused to acknowledge.

The question must be asked today, as Jesus asked two thousand years ago: Is this definition true? Is it what GOD is? Can this Hebrew vision of the nature of GOD that became the core definition from the beginning of its history be trusted?

This was not the picture of the God of Jesus. He tells the Pharisees in the

David Anderson

Gospel of John:

> *Your father is the devil, and you chose to carry out your father's desires. He was a murderer from the beginning, and he is not rooted in the truth; there is no truth in him. When he tells a lie, he is speaking his own language, for he is a liar and the father of lies.*

(John 8:44)

The difference between the God of Jesus and the God of the Jews becomes clear. We can see in the Book of Genesis that when GOD made man in His image, man had not yet sinned. He had not yet eaten of the tree of good and evil. He was not like we are. He was a different being. As he had no sin, he was pure and good. He was incapable of anything but love. Original man existed as a living human being in the image of a God of pure love. This was the picture of the God illuminated by the life and death of Jesus. It was not the picture of the Hebraic image of the nature of GOD.

Unlike the Torah and its commentaries, where the nature of the Jewish God was defined over the millennia by means of the oral and then written word, the nature of the God revealed by Jesus was beyond being revealed orally or in words. His was a God revealed by his life and death. His followers, based on first and second hand knowledge, wrote down, within the first 90 years after his death, stories that described that life and death. In their own imperfect way, these stories present Jesus as a reflection of the mind of a God of love and love only. They show his life opening a path to GOD not made possible by the Torah. It is a path leading to a perfect union with a perfect GOD, the same union that had first existed between GOD and man in the Garden of Eden before the fall of man. The life of Jesus revealed a way of thinking and living that would bring men and women into an eternal and perfect union, not with the God as defined in the Torah, but with the God as defined by Jesus, a God of pure love.

This was a picture not only at variance with the Hebraic description of the nature GOD, but also at variance with the Hebraic understanding of GOD'S will for our relationship to Him. The God of Jesus was a God who values every person on this earth, so much so that in an act that Jews could understand from their own biblical history—a father's sacrifice of his son—He sacrificed His own son as an symbol of His love. He revealed Himself as a God of forgiveness who does not require us to meet the demand for perfection that the God of the Hebrew Bible requires. By His mercy He offers forgiveness to those who make every effort to think and live as Jesus did. This is His only requirement.

Does this mean that the Hebrew image of GOD held throughout all of Jewish history, and also accepted by Islam, is not true? If so, from the beginning the theologies of Judaism as well as Islam have been flawed – and Triune Christianity too.

Why did the Jewish authorities 2000 years ago resist the message of Jesus so strongly? Why have the Jewish people over the following 2000 years resisted it so strongly? The answer is that Jesus challenged the vision of the God that had been the Torah vision from the beginning of Jewish history. This is the reason they rejected him.

Where did this new vision of GOD come from? Was it just from a reinterpretation of a few lines from Genesis? How do we know it was authentic? Out of nowhere there appeared a young Nazarene preaching about a different kind of God. He spoke as if he were speaking the very WORD of GOD itself. How did he know what he knew? On what authority did he say what he was saying? Most importantly for the Jews: Where could what he was saying be found in the Torah, the WORD of GOD? It was a vision of GOD and man's relationship to GOD in very many ways contrary to the vision encompassed in the Torah and the scholarly interpretations that had grown out of it over the course of Jewish history.

If Jesus had been a prominent temple priest who had taken on a new and radically different view of the nature of GOD and the relationship of all Jews to that GOD, no doubt he would, after a period of vigorous debate, have been rejected. These views would have been considered by the ruling orthodoxy a blasphemy against the WORD of GOD. But the family of Jesus was not a member of the priestly hierarchy. Nor was his father an intellectual. Joseph was only a carpenter. Jesus too was most likely a carpenter. His ministry, therefore, did not introduce these ideas at a high intellectual level. Jesus went directly to the people.

According the Christian New Testament he was first heard from at the age of 12 on what is thought to be his first trip to Jerusalem. He wandered off among the crowds and was separated from his parents, Joseph and Mary, for 3 days. When they finally found him, he was in a Temple discussing the Torah with the Temple Priests. It is noted in scripture that his knowledge of the Torah astounded the Priests at the Temple. There is no mention of any radical ideas, only of his superior knowledge.

Then his life becomes a blank for the next 18 years. There is no record of where he lived or what he did. All that is known is that his father, Joseph, was a carpenter, probably a scaffold builder, and there were other children. In fact, he may have had a twin brother. We are also told in the scriptures written long after his birth—and in some part disputed today—of his miraculous Virgin birth, of which he may or may not have been aware. Suddenly, at the age of 30 he reappeared on the scene.

The question of how this young Nazarene became what he became has been debated over the centuries, and not without a considerable amount of bias. For many Jews the influence was Hellenistic—from the spread of Greek philosophy throughout the area following the conquests of Alexander—and for many others the influence was from the eastern religions such as Buddhism. Jesus lived 500 years after Buddha. Buddhist, as well as Hellenistic thought, was known in Jesus' day throughout the Roman Empire.

For Christianity, over the centuries the very idea of any outside influence was considered an anathema. As a result of this, within Christianity, until recent years, there has been only limited Christian scholarship in this area, and this has been largely confined to academia.

Jesus may very well in fact have spent many of those 18 years working as a carpenter apprentice with his father in one or more of the towns in the local area. If so, he could have come into contact with educated and worldly Romans. One such town being rebuilt during that period was Sepphoris, a Roman city-town. It was located only four miles from Nazareth. There, we can assume that with his brilliant mind, by the age of 30, he may have mastered Latin and Greek, which were the languages of the time. He could also have been exposed to the Hellenistic ideas through theatre—Greek theatre may have existed in Sepphoris although we are not sure it did during his time—and debate, both associated with the Greek language. Highly skilled Roman engineers and architects were brought in as builders of Sepphoris, and he could have been exposed to their ideas. If Jesus did have contact with them, the conversations between this brilliant young Nazarene and these people, had they been recorded, would give us valuable insights today. These discussions in themselves would have changed history.

At the age of 30, Jesus began his ministry. To say it was a ministry that was built upon the philosophical streams of thought coming from the Roman Empire, as has been suggested, may be partially true, but this would be a very serious understatement. It was built on an altogether different foundation.

The foundation was Judaism. This was the understanding that man as a living creature has two natures, one good and the other evil. On the one hand, he is pure and good, on the other, he is evil, the opposite. No religion in the history of the human race had ever before defined man in such terms. The religions of the Egyptians and Sumerians did not. Greek and Buddhist thought, which developed in the same general time period as Judaism, did not address it. Judaism did. It represented a change from the way that man had looked at himself. For the first time in religious thought, the true nature of man was being revealed in very specific terms as a struggle between good and evil.

Jesus would reveal a new theology that would define the relationship of man in his imperfection to a God of perfection.

It can be concluded that as the answers to the most basic questions about the nature of GOD and man's relationship to GOD were revealed to Jesus, many influences may have been present. One thing is certain. He gave mankind a breakthrough into his predicament that no prior religion or philosophical discipline had ever done—including Judaism itself.

There are two questions that every monotheistic religion must address. Both the Nation of Israel and Jesus addressed these questions. They came up with different answers.

- What is the nature of the one GOD of the Universe?
- What must be the response of every human to that GOD?

We have already seen how Jews and Christians differ in the answer to the first question. They also differ with respect to the second. How GOD expects us to respond to Him differs between the God of Judaism and the God of Christianity.

Jews believe that the study of the Torah and its commentaries is the way to achieve the happiest and most fulfilling and observant way of life. Engaging one's intellect in the study of the Torah as the core of one's life is the highest attainable human activity. This is not just a matter of study. Life is to be lived in a process of trying to reach the perfection of the Torah. For Christians, studying the Hebrew Bible—Old Testament—is important for its insights into the teaching of Jesus, but not as important as being *born again* into a union with GOD. This calls for a conversion experience that in a sense serves to bring the person into the presence of GOD. This God is not the angry, fearful, yet merciful God of the Torah. The God of Christianity, as has been stated, is a God of pure love. This *born again* experience in and of itself is an experience that changes the person forever so that he or she can then be able to live life in the presence of GOD.

Christianity over the millennia has not always adopted this Christ centered view of GOD and the relationship of Christians to Him. Often, they accepted the Jewish one.

To understand why, we must address the following question:

Did the early Christian Church completely accept the vision of GOD defined by the life and death of Jesus? Did they abandon the God image of the Torah? Or, did they combine the two so that today they are responding to and worshiping the God of both Jesus and the God of the Torah?

Many early Christians combined the two. After all, they had been practicing Jews all of their lives. Christians today are under the general impression that early on the choice between Jesus as the Christ and Judaism was cut and dry. You were a Jew one day—or a pagan—and then suddenly you were born again into a new life in Jesus Christ. This may have been the case for some early Christians, but not all. The influence of the Torah and Jewish customs was always present. The message of Jesus was not always completely understood. During the first 300 years of the early Christian Church, the message of a radically different view of the nature of GOD as Jesus presented it was never allowed to stand completely on its own. The influence of the Hebraic vision of God was always present.

There were many serious doctrinal debates towards the end of this 300-year period. The council of Nicaea, which established the Nicene Creed, a creed that firmly put in place Christian Church doctrine, did not take place until the year 325 A.D. By then, the Roman Empire was in support of Christianity. The first Christian Roman Emperor, Constantine, lived from. 306 A.D to 337 A.D.

Was the message of Jesus so diffused over the first 300 years that it never really had a chance of being fully understood as Jesus would have wanted it to be understood? If this was the case, then what was the original message?

There is very little information available relating to the state of Christian Church doctrine from the time of the crucifixion up to the time when the Apostle Paul wrote his Epistles—from 50 A.D. to 68 A.D. Then, for the following years to 150 A.D. there are only fragments of information. What there is, however, tells us enough about the early church to say that it was in search of a common identity, an identity that would separate it from the Judaic influence of the Torah and Jewish customs and that it was not always able to make this separation.

The early domination of those with a Jewish background and bias shifted only slowly over the first 200 years to those with little or no Jewish biblical and life experience. The movement away from reliance on the Hebrew Bible and Jewish customs and toward autonomous reliance on the Gospel writings was a slow one. Often the leaders in the Christian Churches were Jews who were not about to give up all of their Jewish traditions and Jewish practices. So, there was from the very beginning a tension among Christians as to whether to follow the dictates of the Old Testament (Hebrew Bible) as well as Jewish Law and tradition or the varied and often contradictory sources of information they had about Jesus. This was not just a matter, as many church historians—until recent years—would have had everyone believe, of practices such as circumcision and dietary laws. The scriptural definitions of the nature of the God of the Old Testament and the way mankind is expected to respond to Him were often in conflict. There is evidence that this caused considerable strain and led to major disagreements within the early Church.

What parts of the Torah did Jesus challenge? Early on in the letter of the Apostle Paul to the Hebrews we see a broad spectrum of doubt as to the validity the Hebrew Bible itself. Paul says:

When in former times God spoke to our forefathers, he spoke in fragmentary and varied fashion through the prophets. But in this final age he has spoken to us in the Son ..., the stamp of GOD'S very being.

(Hebrews 1:1-3)

We must remember that the Jews at that time, as do many today, considered every word of the Hebrew Bible to be literally from the hand of GOD. Paul before his conversion was one of them. Orthodox Jews today believe this. The stories themselves and the meanings of the Hebrew words can within reason be interpreted, but they can not be changed. The fact that Paul was talking about the Hebrew Bible using the words *fragmentary* and *varied fashion* would for the Jewish authorities have been considered blasphemy.

Jesus set the stage for the clash between the Hebrew Bible and the New Testament. He would make statements such as *You have learned that they were told... But what I tell you is this....*

He was not just clarifying Hebrew scripture and its Hebraic interpretation; he was saying that it was incomplete and even wrong. As we have already seen, often he used the personal pronoun "I" when making statements to correct Hebrew scripture. This infuriated the Jewish authorities, as they believed that the words of the Hebrew Bible were from GOD and that only GOD could correct them by use of the personal pronoun "I". They saw Jesus as taking on the role of GOD Himself, and they considered this to be blasphemy.

Two cases where Jesus corrected scripture are worth mentioning as they point out the difference in interpretation of the Mosaic Law. They Follow:

You have learned that our forefathers were told, 'Do not commit murder; anyone who commits murder must be brought to judgment.' But what I tell you is this: Anyone who nurses anger against his brother must be brought to judgment.

(Matthew 5:21, 22)

107

You have learned that they were told, 'Do not commit adultery.' But what I tell you is this: If a man looks at a woman with a lustful eye, he has already committed adultery with her in his heart.

(Matthew 5:27, 28)

By taking the issue of obeying the commandments beyond the Mosaic Law and extending it into the way one thinks, Jesus was challenging the superficiality of the written Torah and the Law. He was casting aside all of the Jewish religious customs and practices and saying they are superficial and meaningless without the element of what would be called today in modern psychological terms "intention".

After the death of Jesus , is clear that there was a tension in the early Church that arose from a debate as to what to consider and not to consider from the Hebrew Bible as the Word of GOD and what to consider as the word of Jesus. Noteworthy in the early period are two records, one the letters of a Bishop named Ignatius and the other writings relating to the Gnostic movement.

The most recognizable evidence of this tension within the early church comes from the Letters of Bishop Ignatius who was one of the earliest Apostolic Fathers. He was the Bishop of Antioch in Syria and was arrested and sent to Rome around 110 A.D. where he was martyred. During the trip, like Paul only a few years before him, he wrote letters to various churches. These letters in large part addressed a problem in these churches, which was that some individuals in them were placing the authority of the Old Testament above that of the Gospels. These letters are important because they point out the problem many in the early Christian community had with their perception of the God of the Old Testament and the God as redefined by Jesus. Excerpts from some of his letters follow:

It is monstrous to talk of Jesus Christ and to practice Judaism. For Christianity did not base its faith on Judaism, but Judaism on Christianity, and every tongue believing in God was brought together in it.

(To the Magnesians 10.3)

Be not led astray by strange doctrines or old fables, which are profitless. For if we are living now according to Judaism, we confess that we have not received grace. For the divine prophets lived according to Jesus Christ. Therefore they were also persecuted, being inspired by his grace, to convince the obedient that there is one God, who manifested himself through Jesus Christ his son, who is his word.

(To the Magnesians 8.12)

Ignatius viewed the Old Testament only in terms of those areas that prophesied the coming of Jesus as the Christ and otherwise supported his teaching as the messenger—son—of GOD. He condemned those areas of scripture as well as Jewish law and tradition that did not, or detracted from His message. He left open the Old Testament as a valid document, but declared that only those parts that derived their authority directly by way of a connective link to the Gospel of Jesus Christ were true. For Ignatius there was no contradiction between the Old and New Testaments as long as this was the understanding. This is the view today of many progressive Christians who view the Old Testament as a source of knowledge as opposed to an authority for knowledge.

This challenge to the Old Testament was most pronounced in a religions movement called Gnosticism which flourished in the second and third centuries. Many of the Gnostics seem to have been full-fledged Gentiles who had little contact with real-life Judaism.

Although Gnostic beliefs—Gnosticism should not be defined as a single form of thought, but as many interconnected forms—were considered by the Roman Church to be heretical, and would be considered so by orthodox Christians today, some of its beliefs permeated early Christianity and have today become a part of progressive Christianity. Gnosticism emphasized the importance of the teachings of Jesus and opposed the doctrinaire ideas of the Hebrew Bible and Jewish law. It looked upon man in a way that would today be called metaphysical. For almost all of Gnosticism the idea of a final judgment day when souls will be separated was not a part of its theology. Rather, it looked at heaven as being all around us, with our essence passing at death into a heavenly dimension. Given the fact that the early Roman Christian church had thrown its lot in the direction of the concept of heaven being "up there" and a future and final apocalyptic judgment when Jesus would reappear, these Gnostic ideas were considered to be heretical, and they were fought tooth and nail.

The following passage by Justin Martyr gives an idea of the bitter feelings that existed against Gnosticism:

I made it clear to you that those who are Christian in name, but in reality are Godless and impious heretics, teach in all respects what is blasphemous and godless and foolish …. If you yourselves have ever met with some so-called Christians, who … dare to blaspheme the God of Abraham, and the God of Isaac, and the God of Jacob, and who say that there is no resurrection of the dead, but that their souls ascend to heaven at the very moment of their death—do not suppose that they are Christians …. But, all other entirely orthodox Christians, and I know that there will be a resurrection of the flesh, and also in a thousand years a Jerusalem built up and adorned and enlarged, as the prophets Ezekiel and Isaiah, and all the rest, acknowledged.

Justin Martyr, Dialogue with Trypho (circ. 80 A.D.— 160 A.D.)

This statement by a Christian not far removed in time from Bishop Ignatius illustrates the dissension that existed in early Christianity and the influence of the Hebrew Bible on early Christian thought. It is worth noting—as an example of overall Jewish influence—that it sounds very much the same as a Jewish judgmental quotation from the Mishnah:

These are they that have no share in the world to come: He that says that there is no resurrection of the dead prescribed in the law, and he that says the Law is not from heaven ....

(Sanhedrin 10:1)

Even though Jesus had contradicted the Hebrew Bible, it is now very clear that many of the leaders of the early Christian communities continued to believe every word of the Hebrew Bible—now called The Old Testament—was the WORD OF GOD. They did not give up the Hebrew image of the God described in the Hebrew Bible. For them He remained the same fearful, angry, judgmental and only sometimes merciful God that the Jews believed in. At the same time they accepted the God defined by the life and death of Jesus, even though He was a different kind of God. He was God of love. Can GOD be both? This is a question that has perplexed the Christian Church ever since.

To quote from the eminent Biblical scholar Oskar Skarsaune in his book, *In The Shadow Of The Temple:*

"It is quite clear that for the early Christians the distinction between orthodoxy and heresy amounted to something very simple and basic: Do you confess faith in the God of the Old Testament as the one and only God, Creator of heaven and earth, or do you not?"

By the end of the 3rd century the stage was set for a theology that would emerge under the name of Christianity. It would be a theology that would embrace writings about the God of the Old Testament and the God of the New Testament. The words of both would be without flaw. Every word of both was the WORD of GOD. The fact that the very nature of the God illuminated by Jesus Christ was clearly different was of no importance. GOD would be looked upon as being inscrutable. Any argument that challenged this duality and the challenges it imposed on a coherent theology would be considered heretical. The dogma was set in place for the next two millennia of Christianity.

How could God be the same? There were enormous differences between the two Bibles. The God of the Hebrew Bible was not in all respects the same as the God of Jesus. As has been stated, the God of the Hebrew Bible could be vengeful, he could be capricious, he could be angry, and he could only sometimes be merciful. This was not the same God as that described by Jesus.

After lengthy and considerable debate, an answer finally came. There would be in the Christian Church a Trinitarian God, a God with three faces or characters—described as three *persons*. There would be a Father, a Son and a Holy Spirit. The part of that Trinitarian God who would be the Father would be in non-specific terms the biblical reference Father God of the Old Testament. Jesus himself had often referred to "My Father." It would be assumed that Jesus was referring to this God of the Old Testament.

The God illuminated by Jesus as recorded in the New Testament would be a loving and forgiving God. He would be called the *Son*. There would be a separation of the natures of the two; the Father Hebrew God as presented in the Old Testament and the God of Jesus Christ as presented in the New Testament.

When punishment was required for Heretics who did not agree with church doctrine, the judgmental angry punishing Father God would be called upon and these Heretics would be put down or if need be burned at the stake. This would be the God who empowered the Catholic Church to have the Inquisition and to embark on the Crusades. He would be a God of judgment and of punishment. The God of the Old Testament would not tolerate blasphemy. He would show His wrath on those who disobeyed as He had done with the Nation of Israel whenever it disobeyed. Christianity could have it both ways.

There is no reference to a *Trinitarian God*—one God in three—in the Hebrew Bible. The Christian Church has for 2000 years been searching for a reference to this three part God in the Old Testament and not found a trace of scripture to support it. The nearest they can come is a reference to a plural God in Genesis where it says *Let us make man in our own image* (Genesis 1:26) and some other areas where GOD is referred to in plural form.

The Gospels do make a distinction between the Father, the Son, and the Holy Spirit, but do not speak of a Trinitarian God. The Apostle Paul in his letters written shortly after the death of Jesus did not refer to a Trinitarian God. He did, however, speak of each of the three in separate but synonymous terms. But then a question remains: Was Paul referring to the image of the

Father as the term was used in the Hebrew Bible or to the God as defined by the life and death of Jesus? The tone of his letters reveals both the personalities of the ancient Hebrew God and the personality of the God revealed by Jesus. We must remember, however, that Paul was also a Jew. He was one of those early Jewish Christians referred to above.

By the year A.D. 300 the debate among Christians had moved away from the influence of Judaism on Christianity to an acceptance of the definition of the nature of the *Father God* presented in the Hebrew Bible. The Old Testament in its literal form was accepted as the WORD of the Triune Father GOD.

The problem for the early Christian Church, as to how to position the three elements of the Trinity, was subjected to intensive debate and finally settled at the Council of Nicaea in 325 A.D. The creed that resulted is today a part of almost all Christian services. It makes the statement of belief in the Father, the Son, and the Holy Spirit, but it does not define with any specificity what they are, how they differ, how they relate or with their differences, how they connect to each other.

Christians intuitively know what the Jesus Christ part of the Godhead is. They are told that He sits on the right hand of GOD. They also, from their own life experiences, know what the Holy Spirit is. He is the spirit that has presence in their lives in place of Jesus. But do they have a clear definition in their minds of what the *GOD* part is? He is only referred to as the *Father*. Is it the Hebrew definition the *Father God* of the Hebrew Bible or is it the God revealed by the life and death of the *Incarnate* Jesus Christ?

We pattern our behavior after the God or Gods we worship. The persona of the God or Gods we worship underlies our thought processes and makes us think the way we do. It follows that it also governs the way we act. In the early Christian Church, as well as in the Christian Church of today, most Christians patterned their behavior after the God revealed by the life and death of Jesus. But, this was and is not always the case. Since the Trinitarian issue of definition was avoided from the very beginning and continues to be avoided, the God of the Old Testament often has taken the lead, and then behavior is patterned after the judgmental and punishing God of the Old Testament. As a result, looking back on the last 2000 years of Church history, we do not always see in the actions of Christians the God image of Jesus. Nor do we always see it in the Christian Church today.

This archaic God of anger and retribution became a part of Christianity. He still rules corners of the world and controls the actions of many extremist Jews and Christians. He also rules the religion of Islam. The God of Islam, which was constructed out of the archaic Hebraic vision of God, rules Muslims thought. The God of the Koran remains calcified in the ancient God image of the Hebrew Bible. The Hebrew Bible God of judgment, anger, fear, retribution, and only occasional mercy remains in control of the consciousness of Muslims and governs their actions.

It is clear that much of Christianity still remains in the grips of a frightful schizophrenic God, one with two often-contradictory natures. Because the early Christian church would not face the fact that in the Trinity the image of the Father is not that presented in the Hebrew Bible but a God of love and love only, Christians are left with an inscrutable Hebrew Bible God of the Trinity who, like a father, deals out mercy one time and then punishment the next.

As has been stated, this is not a description of the God Incarnate revealed in the person of Jesus. The God illuminated by Jesus is a God of love and love only. He is GOD in Genesis before the fall of man. He is not the God defined by the deceiver and accepted by the Jews.

To show the depth of HIS love for every person on this earth, in a final revelation of HIMSELF, HE made the ultimate sacrifice, using a symbolic act that all human beings of every belief could understand, the sacrifice by a father of his son. This message of GOD'S unconditional and unrelenting love did not reach all of Christianity, in fact only a small part of it. However, it continues slowly to penetrate thought and belief.

REFLECTION # 2

The Eleventh Commandment

For I the Lord thy God am a jealous God, visiting the iniquity of the fathers upon the children into the third and fourth generation of them that hate me.

(Exodus 20:5)

Following is an eleventh commandment suggested by this author for a reconstituted progressive Judaism, Islam and Christianity.

I have sent Jesus to give you the eleventh Commandment..

I want you to know that the Ten Commandments that I gave to Moses and the laws the Jews derived from them all in their written form did not truly reveal MY WORD.

I am not a jealous God nor am I an exclusive God for the Jewish people. I am God for all people. I am a God of love for every one. My love extends to every person on the earth. Nothing can separate anyone from my love. The words of Moses: that I will punish the sins of the third and fourth generations of those who hate me, are wrong. I am not a God who hates nor do I punish. Those who do not follow me punish themselves by their separation from me. Those who enter into my presence by following the path of love that I showed to all of mankind by the life and death of Jesus will be with me in eternity without punishment.

My eleventh commandment to you is this:

Honor all that I have given you. Love the earth that I have given you. Show your love and respect for everything that is a part of it. Love yourselves. Love your neighbor. Love all of man and woman kind. Do not confine or segregate your love. Make it unconditional.

As you have shown unconditional love to everyone, not just to those of your own tribe, nation or religion, you show your love for me.

Those who do not show this unconditional love exist separated from me. They will die separated from me.

Do we need an eleventh commandment? Yes, we do. The reason is that the definition of GOD'S nature and man's relationship to Him as described in the Hebrew Bible is in error.

X

A Revisionist View from a Gnostic Jesus Challenging All Three Religions Supported by Einstein's Theories of Space and Time

What you are looking for (heaven) has come, but you don't know it... It (heaven) will not come by watching for it. It will not be said, Look here look there! Rather, the father's kingdom is spread out upon the earth, and people don't see it.

The Gospel of Thomas

Unearthed in the Egyptian desert in 1945

1st or 2nd Century Christian Coptic Gospel text excluded

from the New Testament by the

Roman Church Bishops and ordered destroyed

The earliest evidence we have, going back into pre-human history, shows that from the very beginning of our awareness of a greater force outside of ourselves, there has been the question of whether that force exists somewhere in space and time away from our naturally known and experienced world, or whether it exists here in the present as a part of our world. According to the Gospel of Thomas, Jesus said the force is here present with us in our world, but we just don't see it.

As the books of the New Testament were being brought together by the early Church Fathers, those who subscribed to the argument that the Kingdom of God is somewhere outside of us, above the earth, won out. After all, theirs was a flat earth surrounded by the mystery of the heavens above. What explanations there were had come over the ages from the astrologers. So GOD was said to be *up above* in the heavens. When the Holy Spirit came to man, it *came down*. When Christ was baptized, GOD came from *above* to say, *This is my son in whom I am well pleased.* When Christ left this earth, he *ascended into heaven.*

115

The early Hebrew Biblical idea of a *final judgment* fell into line with this concept of a duality between heaven and earth as two separate places. This gave logic to the early Christian idea that Jesus would return from heaven, at which time the earth would end and there would be a separation between those predestined for heaven, the elect, and those who would descend to hell. The early Christians believed that this would occur during their lifetimes. To this day, Christians continue to make this distinction using the words in the Lord's Prayer, *Thy Kingdom come, thy Will be done on earth as it is in heaven.*

Early Christian Fathers, such as St. Augustine, saw the Universe as divided into two Cities, *The City of God* (heaven) and the *Earthly City*. The Earthly City was defined as a city of corruption, conflict, wars, and violence. Earth, including man and his physical desires, was looked upon as corrupt, and the things of heaven above were looked upon as pure and good.

As the end of the world did not come, over the passing years Christians gradually accepted the idea that the end would come not in their lifetimes but at some future point in time, and then there would be a separation made by GOD. Some people would go up to heaven, and the rest would go down to Hell. A new concept, that of Predestination or Election brought forth by the Apostle Paul gave a vague sense of definition as to who would be among the *Elect* or *Chosen*. Only those who were *Chosen* would pass on to heaven in the *Final Judgment*.

As time passed, the words of 27 books considered the *New Testament* firmly establishing all of these concepts. They were believed by most Christians without question to be the inerrant and true account of the teaching of Jesus. As Jesus was declared to be God Incarnate, they logically considered these approved writings to be sacred and to be the WORD of GOD. Most evangelical Christians today believe this to be the fact.

It is not surprising that these concepts were so readily accepted by the early Church Fathers. The world was far different from what it is today. Christianity was in its infancy, and it was struggling not only against alien religious ideas but also against radical factions within the movement itself.

But what if the early Church Fathers had it wrong? What if Thomas was right? What if we are living in a dimension right now that is both heaven and earth at the same time? What if we are walking in judgment every moment of our lives and not on some final day? What if there is no such thing as predestination or election and each of us is free to live within the love of GOD or outside of it? What if this applies to each and every person on this earth and there are no favored so-called *Elect*? What if we pass in and out of the earthly and the heavenly dimension every moment of our lives, as by our thoughts and actions we move towards and away from GOD? What if the natural beauty of our world and all its forms of life are not corrupt as St. Augustine—as well as the Apostle Paul—would have had it, but are a miraculous expression of GOD'S presence.

The answers to the above questions may have come to us in 1945 when twelve books hidden in a sealed jar were discovered by two peasant brothers near Nag Hammadi, Egypt. They were written in Coptic, a late Egyptian language using Greek letters. They are now preserved in the Coptic Museum in Cairo, Egypt. One of the books is now referred to as the Gospel of Thomas.

The four Gospels of the New Testament were brought together by the early Church Fathers long after the death of Jesus. The first is dated approximately 70 A.D. Scholars have always known that many other Gospels existed. In the Gospel of Luke, we are told that there were many Gospels written. This is recorded in Luke 1:1-4 where he states: *Inasmuch as many writers have undertaken to put together an account of the events that have been fulfilled among us.*

The question may now be asked: Why did the early Church Fathers not include the Gospel of Thomas from The New Testament? Why did they order it destroyed? The content of the Gospel itself was in most respects in line with the accounts of the teachings of Jesus found in the other Gospels. There was, however, a fundamental difference, and it was of far reaching magnitude.

The answer may have been that the Thomas Gospel was a challenge to the institutional validity and continuity of the Roman Church as it had defined itself four centuries after the death of Jesus. The Thomas Gospel called not for *joining* a church, but for *joining* GOD through an inner experience involving a thorough and penetrating inner search. It asked: Whose side are you on? And, it demanded the answer not be the Roman Catholic Church of the Emperor Constantine, but GOD.

Was this the reason for rejection of the Thomas Gospel by the Roman Church? Some scholars have concluded that it was. They have suggested that the reason may have been that there would have been less of a need for an organized church to, so to speak, *control the Gate*. If man were asked to look within himself for GOD and look around himself for heaven, the authority of the Church could not hold.

The power of the early church came from the fact that it had the keys to the Gate. To enter heaven, you had to pass through that Gate. As the church and its Christian doctrines developed, the rules for entry to heaven—passing through the Gate—became more complex and more onerous. In time they became so onerous that they sparked the Protestant Reformation.

David Anderson

By the time of the Protestant Reformation, the main doctrines of the Roman Christian Church had been established. The definitions of heaven, hell, and judgment were fixed. With a flurry of new ideas, Protestantism set out to put down its own rules as to who would and who would not enter the Kingdom of heaven on the Final Day of Judgment.

The *Reflections* that follow are an attempt to explore GOD'S presence in our lives, not in a heaven at some future moment in time, but in the here and now on this earth. They reinterpret the descriptions of Judgment and the time dimension of heaven given in the books of the New Testament and Roman Catholic doctrine. While they do not disagree with the idea of our capacity for evil and ensuing Judgment, they look at the human species not as the early Christian Church Fathers did, as being corrupt, weak and degenerate, but as being GOD centered, loving, and powerful. They see a world moving forward directed by a redemptive GOD in the midst of all people, a GOD at work in each and every life, not just in the lives of those who have passed through the *gate* of the Christian Church. They do, however, look at the teachings of Jesus given to us in the Gospel of Thomas as the presence of GOD guiding the world in its search.

REFLECTION # 3

A World Ceaselessly Seeking GOD

"… and you all my soul where you stand,

Surrounded, detached, in measureless oceans of space…

Ceaselessly seeking…

Till …the ductile anchor hold,

Till the gossamer thread you fling catch somewhere,

O my soul."

A Noiseless Patient Spider

Walt Whitman

1819–1891

For I am convinced that there is nothing in death or life, in the realm of spirits or superhuman powers, in the world as it is or the world as it shall be—nothing in all creation that can separate us from the love of God in Christ Jesus our Lord.

Romans 8:38-39

We sense the presence of GOD in the measureless oceans of space, but we cannot see GOD. Where is GOD? How can we know that we have found GOD? How can we know that GOD has found us? How can we be assured that even after we think we have found GOD, that the gossamer threads of hope we have cast out toward GOD have taken hold? How can we know that the anchor that we have set will not drag and then suddenly break loose to cast us adrift into the vast reaches of darkness in outer space?

Like Walt Whitman's noiseless patient spider, we too spend our lives launching forth filament after filament into the measureless oceans of space, although our search is not the same. Ours is both within ourselves and without, into the farthest reaches of our souls.

Also, like Whitman's spider, we too can sense when a filament we cast out takes hold. We can feel that there is something out there on the other end. But, we cannot be sure of what it is since we can only see the beginnings of our filaments; we can not see their ends. As we extend our filaments, sometimes in fear we ask ourselves: How can we be certain that we have found GOD?

119

David Anderson

How are we to know that we have found Him?

Jesus said GOD has given each of us a brief moment of time for our earthly existence and He wants us to use it to extend our filaments toward Him. Paul told us that those who search the endless oceans of space within and without of themselves, will find Him. The filaments will find a connection.

GOD gave life and a gift of time to the spider to extend its filaments. Jesus said GOD has given each of us life and a gift of time to extend ours. Jesus said that the choice is ours. We can use GOD'S gift of life in the process of extending our filaments toward HIM, or we can turn our backs on HIM.

Jesus warned us of what will happen if we do not search for HIM. He said that when we die, we will cease to exist. We will be as if we never were.

Paul told us that those who search for GOD'S presence will find HIM. He assured us that once we find HIM, the anchor will hold and we will not be cast adrift. He told us that as we reach out toward GOD, He will take hold of filament after filament and we will be drawn by HIM into His presence.

Paul said once the filaments are connected, they cannot be disconnected. Paul said once the anchor is set, it cannot break loose. He said that that nothing in all of creation can break the hold. Nothing can separate those who find Him from His love for them. Paul said *nothing in all creation … can separate us from the love of God in Christ Jesus our Lord.*

We wonder if Paul was right; if the connection is, after all, that permanent. Can we be so sure?

REFLECTION # 4

My Soul

For what shall it profit a man, if he shall gain the whole world, and lose his own soul? Or, what shall a man give in exchange for his soul?

(Mark 8:36-37)

circ. 70 A.D.

"The soul is the junction point between my physical self and my virtual self."

How To Know God

Deepak Chopra

2000 A.D.

I (Mary Magdalene) said to him (Jesus), 'Lord, how does he who sees the vision see it, through the soul or through the spirit?' The savior answered and said, 'He does not see through the soul nor through the spirit, but the mind which is between the two.'

The Gospel Of Mary

Discovered at Nag Hammadi

1945 A.D.

Date of origin unknown

What is the soul? Where does it exist?

Is my soul here with me now or is it something that will only come into existence after my death? If my soul is present now, what form does it take? Is my soul inside my physical being or does it exist outside of my body in some other dimension of space and time? Did my soul exist before my biological birth? Why in Christianity is the saving of souls so closely connected to escaping damnation? What happens to the soul in damnation?

The Hebrew Bible gave no exact definition of the soul. Most of the Christian definition has come to us from the early Church Fathers who were influenced by the Greek philosophers. As we examine all of this, we are left with an awareness of our souls in the here and now, an awareness of another *me* outside of my recognizable physical self. It is an awareness that has been common to many religions from the beginning of recorded religious history.

Today, modern Quantum Mechanics has taken this insight one step farther by showing us that our physical bodies are, in fact, no more than a soup of subatomic energy particles in motion separated 99.999% by space, and this energy is an interdependent part of an endless universal web of connectedness that exists throughout space and time in a dimension we can not comprehend.

Science deals with energy and matter, not with souls. It sets out equations that attempt to explain our universe and ourselves in mathematical terms. It does not concern itself with souls.

The message of the Gospel of Thomas coming from Nag Hammadi is that each individual by his own free will must examine his life in its greatest depth to find the *light within* in order to *save his soul*. For those who refuse this union, Jesus describes the soul's eternal existence as one of separation from GOD.

Modern writers such as Deepak Chopra have gone so far as to suggest that our brains may be the junction point between physical reality and virtual reality, the later defined as that which exists outside and beyond our perception of space and time. The suggestion here is that the brain is more than just gray matter collecting and storing electrical impulses. It is the connecting link between GOD and us.

Our souls are a real and recognizable part of us. We see and experience our souls as being at the same time both inside and outside of our bodies. We see our souls on the edge of GOD'S eternal dimension, but never in it. We sense that GOD and our souls are joining as we turn our lives over to him, but our souls remain within the confines of the comprehensible universe of our imagination. We long for our souls to be brought into GOD'S eternal dimension and for the time when our souls will no longer be separated from it, but will be at one with it.

REFLECTION # 5

The Unexamined Life

The unexamined life is not worth living
Socrates (470-399 B.C.E.)

When he finds, he will become troubled. When he becomes troubled, he will be astonished…..

(2)

Whoever has something in his hand will receive more, and whoever has nothing will be deprived of even the little that he has

(41)

The Gospel of Thomas

Is it important to find the inner self?

Often this takes the form of rituals that produce a euphoria transporting the person into another dimension. Many define religious experience in these terms. We find this approach throughout the three religions of Abraham.

It was different with both Socrates and the Jesus seen in the Thomas Gospel.

Socrates and Jesus criticized the superficiality of ritual. Rather, they emphasized a focus on an inner search.

They said there is no greater way for a person to affirm life. Both said that without pursuing this path to affirmation, a life is wasted.

David Anderson

REFLECTION # 6

Entering Heaven / Entering into the Presence of GOD

Make every effort (Strive) to enter through the narrow door, because many, I tell you, will try to enter and will not be able to....The lord will say; I don't know you or where you come from, Away from me.

(Luke 13:23-30)

Jesus said: 'Let him who seeks continue seeking until he finds. When he finds, he will become troubled. When he becomes troubled, he will be astonished and he will rule over all.'

(2)

The Gospel of Thomas

There is light within a man of light, and he lights up the whole world. If he does not shine, he is in darkness.

(24)

The Gospel of Thomas

Jesus is telling us that the door is narrow, and not all who try will enter. How can we be sure we will not be one of those excluded? Is it enough just to obey certain religious rules or to profess common creedal beliefs, or to go through certain rituals, or to say certain prayers? Or, is there more to it than that? Is something of even greater importance required of us?

In the Gospel of Thomas, Jesus says that we can find GOD, but only in one way. It is through a process that begins with our search for an understanding of who and what we really are. He says that before we can find GOD, we must embark on this search. He commands us to make every effort and warns us that it may be painful. He tells us that only through this search can we find GOD'S presence in our lives.

Where is this God Jesus talks about? In our search within how can we know we have found Him? How can we know He has found us? In the Gospel of Thomas, Jesus tells us that GOD is already within each of us. He has been there all the time.

Finding Him takes more than going through the superficial motions of religious belief. Jesus says we must dig deeply so that we can discover both

124

the evil and the good within ourselves. We must search to the depths of our very being to uncover the pride and arrogance that is holding us back from a knowledge of GOD. Only then will we find Him. Only then will He find us.

Jesus told us that we will know when we have found Him. Everyone will know. We will no longer be who we were. We will be different from what we were. We will become a light to the whole world.

XI

The Common Denominator on Which Jews, Christians and Muslims Must Judge Themselves: What is Happening in the Upper Room?

The number of names together were about a hundred and twenty... And when the day of the Pentecost was fully come, they were all with one accord in one place (The Upper Room of the Inn)...and suddenly there came a sound from heaven as of a mighty rushing wind... And they were all filled with the Holy Ghost, and began to speak in other tongues, other language.

Acts Of The Apostles

In the *Upper Room* of an Inn, by a sudden manifestation of His presence, GOD defined for the Disciples of Jesus their purpose and their future.

A group of individuals—followers of the newly proclaimed Messiah—were gathered. Their Prophet and savior had been crucified. He had reappeared to a few, but for most he had not. It seemed that the end of a dream had come. Then, suddenly everything was changed. Their lives took on a new and powerful dimension. The message of salvation through self-sacrifice, humility, and love of one's fellow man filled them with a new kind of hope. They were free from fear. They left the Upper Room eager to preach the Gospel of their Savior. In the following years many of them suffered extreme hardship and some even lost their lives.

The idea of having no boundaries or having and *Oceanic Feeling*—an expression used centuries later by Freud—has been common to other religions including the eastern religions. In many forms of religious belief, going into euphoric trances is common. There was far more to the experience of the Upper Room.

For the Disciples the experience was more than just a *feel good* or *euphoric* experience. It was GOD entering their entire being. It was the GOD that had been defined for them by their Messiah, Jesus the Christ, as they had observed him and listened to him. It was the GOD of universal love. It was the GOD of devoted service, not just to his or her own kind, but also to all of humankind. It was the GOD of humility. It was the GOD that said suffering is only temporary, and enlightenment is forever. It was the GOD of personal salvation.

This is the common denominator on which all religions claiming Freud's *Oceanic Feeling* must judge themselves. Any religious experience that does not meet the test of the Upper Room is not of GOD. It is of man.

REFLECTION # 7

The Enlightenment of the Upper Room

"The idea of two rooms is not new. For centuries spiritual directors in the church (like Augustine and Teresa of Alva) have been telling us of another place to be...the one the lord built for our souls where he waits ready to meet us."

The Safest Place on Earth

Larry Crabb

1999

"I can find nothing with which to compare the great beauty of the soul and its great capacity"

Teresa Of Avila

We have a Lower Room and an Upper Room.

In Our Lower Room

We are alone in our Lower Room. From birth we have poured into this room the daily experiences of our lives. Our Lower Room is filled with all of our past, the strife, anxiety, and anger as well as the joy and fulfillment from our successes. From this room we find our creative strength. The mental and physical energy we feel in this Lower Room at times can take hold of us, leaving us without control. Often this leads to poor judgment, which in turn leads to pain and suffering. Whenever this occurs, we attempt to fall back on discipline to bring our lives into balance. When we are not able to do this, we become frightened, depressed, and withdrawn. We lash out at others or even ourselves. This drains our energy and as we tire, often we reach out for help.

In Our Upper Room

In our Upper Room we receive a glimpse of the eternal. In this room we find ourselves facing GOD. We find that He is a God of love who accepts us as we are.

We find that the strains of the Lower Room disappear. We find an unlimited energy source, which quietly takes away the weariness of the Lower Room.

In our Upper Room we have:

- A new identity
- A knowledge and belief that in the eyes of GOD we have profound worth
- A passion to know His purpose in our lives
- An understanding of the love He has for us
- An eagerness to please Him and follow His word
- An understanding that each experience in the lower room, good as well as bad, is GOD'S gift to us for the purpose of bringing us closer to Him
- A peace that passes all understanding

Only saints spend all of their lives in the Upper Room. Many of us never visit the Upper Room. Others only visit the Upper Room when under the stress of the Lower Room.

The Upper Room is always there for us in good times and bad. Jesus said, *knock and the door will be opened, seek and you will find.* From the Upper Room GOD calls each of us saying; *come, spend more time where I am.*

David Anderson

REFLECTION # 8

The Temptations that Keep us Away
From the Upper Room

For forty days and forty nights he fasted...the Tempter approached him...but Jesus said: "Begone Satan!"

(Matthew 4:1-10)

GOD led Jesus into the desert where Jesus was tempted by the things of this world. Forty days later he left the desert. He began a ministry that ended shortly afterwards in his death. In that brief period of time he changed the world.

His was then and is now no secret. Through self-denial he became at one with GOD.

Can we become the same? Can we too in the solitude of our souls rise out of the desert and walk the earth with the power of GOD in us? Can we look to this same experience as Jesus to mold our own lives? Is the purity of GOD also available to us? Can we too change the world?

Yes, we can, but on one condition. We can not have it both ways. Those of all religions from the beginning have always thought that they could have it both ways. They could attach themselves to the power, the influence, the position, and to the material things of this world while at the same time living in oneness with GOD. We are born with this duality of thought.

But this duality will not suffice. GOD is saying to us—as He said to Jesus—I want all of you, not just a part. I want every thought, every action. Half measures are not enough. There are no compromises.

As it was with Jesus in the desert wilderness, it is the same for us. GOD is telling us that we too, if we want to change this world, must first separate ourselves from the things of this world.

XII

The Free Will to Make Our Own Choices

"Two roads diverged in a wood

And sorry I could not travel both....

Oh, I kept the first for another day!

Yet knowing how way leads on to way,

I doubted if I should ever come back".

The Road Not Taken

Robert Frost

1874–1963

Like the traveler in the poem facing a fork in the road, we too often must make choices that move us forward on new and uncharted roads, never to return where we started. Unlike the traveler in the poem, though, we often find that the choices are not always within our control. We find that we are on a road not by our own choice but by the choice of someone else, or by chance. The following Reflections explore these different kinds of choices. They explore the question of how much control we have over our future, and they explore what happens when we give up our attempts to control it.

Many of us have puzzled over the perplexing question: What if? We ask: What if I had done this instead of that? What if I had not done this or that? But, there is an even larger and more perplexing question. It is the question of whether I ever had any choice at all. At the split second of making choices, it is often hard to find the reason. Even those who think they have control over their futures know inside themselves that in the final analysis they made the choice because *they felt that it was the right thing to do*.

We do know that some choices are the wrong ones and some are the right ones. Some lead to bad outcomes and some lead to good outcomes. We know this from the outcomes of our choices, but then it becomes more complicated. There may be more than one choice involved, and some choices are prompted by past choices. If we make a choice, how far into the future will

131

the choice take us? At what point will this call for other choices? And, when will it be too late to reverse our course? At what point will we be forced to make choices we would not otherwise want to make? What if Robert Frost's traveler doesn't want to take either road? What if he doesn't even want to be in the woods?

Should we be making our own choices? Can we create our own future? What are the risks in making our own choices? Will our choices bring destruction, pain, and suffering to ourselves as well as to others? We know from our own personal experience that choices, which seemed at the time to be well thought out, can be the wrong ones. There is no guarantee of success when we make our own choices.

We also know that human beings have the capacity to make choices in their self-interest that are evil in that their choices can lead to painful consequences. Examples are the two great wars in the twentieth century as well as the present world terrorist conflict. On a personal level we can make self-destructive choices. Alcohol and drugs are self-destructive in that they destroy the capability of individuals to think and act clearly, which prevents them from realizing their full human potential. This shows what can happen when the human mind is given total freedom to make its own choices.

How can I make the right choices, not only the singular *I* as an individual, but the interdependent universal *We* as the whole human race?

To answer this question, we must look at our lives as having the possibility of following one of two diametrically opposed paradigms:

- One is the paradigm we construct for ourselves moment-by-moment from the time we are born and begin to discover our consciousness. We formulate this paradigm into our consciousness piece-by-piece. In it we carefully store each experience as if it were the only reality of our existence. Based on these experiences, we make our decisions and chose the direction of our lives. In this paradigm we rely 100% on ourselves to make our choices. Each choice, or most of them, is made in our self-interest. This is the paradigm that most people in the world follow.

- The other paradigm is the one that GOD has constructed for us. When we follow this paradigm, we let GOD make our choices.

The message of Jesus was a call to turn our lives over to GOD and break out of our own earthly formulated paradigm. He told us that our earthly paradigm is not in fact reality. He said another higher and eternal reality exists beyond our earthly perceptions and constructions. This reality transcends our own. It exists in GOD'S dimension.

Jesus said that each life on earth is precious in the sight of GOD. GOD loves each of us. But HE can only show HIS love for us if we turn ourselves over to HIS paradigm for our lives. GOD can only give to us if we give our lives to HIM. Jesus said that when this happens, we are reborn into a new dimension where all of our earthly requests, material as well as spiritual, will be met. But we will not be making our choices. They will not come from us. They will come from GOD.

The following Reflections show that there is a way to make these GOD directed choices. They show there is a way we can open up our futures by choosing the right road. This is the road that GOD has chosen for us. The famous Prayer of Jabez (I Chronicles 4: 9-10) discussed in Reflection # 9 answers the question, "How do I know which road to take?" This prayer shows how we can break out of the earthly paradigm that is of our own making and expand our future into the paradigm that is of GOD'S making.

REFLECTION # 9

Opening the Barriers of our Self-imposed Limitations

Oh, that you would bless me indeed, and enlarge my territory, that your hand would be with me, and that you would keep me from evil, that I may not cause pain.

(I Chronicles 4:9-10)

(Known as Prayer of Jabez)

"Live by your Bliss"

Joseph Campbell

Joseph Campbell tells us to "*live by your Bliss.*" The Jabez Prayer tells us to ask GOD to *enlarge my territory.* The question is: As we move forward into the unknown, how can we be sure that the path we take will not lead to our destruction? If we break through our self-imposed limitations, will we lose control? What will happen if we cannot turn back? If, as we attain new territory, we hurt others, is there an eternal risk to our souls? As we move toward our expanded goals, do we risk being sucked into a vortex of evil drawing us into eternal damnation?

Expanding ourselves beyond ourselves—enlarging our territories—without asking for the power of GOD to guide us can lead us to our own destruction and the destruction of others. There is no discipline in simply *following our bliss.*

If we think that we can be in charge of the territory we open, we deceive ourselves. We will be opening it to our own self-centered view of its unlimited expansion and then, by the time we have moved into the new and unknown territory, it may be too late to turn back. We deceive ourselves if we think we can always return. We may not have the power to return. We may lose our way and not know how to return.

We need the power of GOD to guide us. We need His presence in our lives to *lead us not into temptation.* As we break through our self-imposed limitations, we need to follow our *Bliss* but only as we place ourselves in

134

GOD'S hands. Only GOD can open our future for His purpose in our lives. Only GOD can protect us from our self-destruction. We are powerless by ourselves.

REFLECTION # 10

Be Careful What You Wish For

Ask, and you will be given what you ask for...

for everyone who asks receives.

If a child asks his father for a loaf of bread,

will he be given a stone?

If you give only good gifts to your children,

won't your father in heaven more certainly give good gifts to you?

(Matthew 7: 7-11)

How do we *ask*? What should we be asking for and what should we not be asking for?

Are we expected to take action to get what we have asked for, or will it just come to us?

If we do not receive what we have asked for, does this mean that we have not asked for it in the right way? Does it mean that GOD is not looking with favor on us?

There is a human dynamic that psychologists now recognize which they call *intentionality*. Its study examines the question: At what point does our vision of the future become reality, and how does this happen? At what point does our subconscious play an active role, so that we physically and mentally carve out the future? At what point does conscious wishful thinking become subconscious all out drive? At what point do our powerful inner forces take over, and what are those inner forces?

In this process of subconscious desire becoming all out drive, a question of enormous importance arises. This question is: As we unleash these cybernetic forces, is there any ethical or moral restraint built within us as a part of our brain function that will serve to hold us back from causing pain and destruction to ourselves as well as to others? The history of man has shown that to get what he wants, that is to achieve his goals, man's potential for harm, to others as well as himself, is unlimited.

We know that what we ask for may in the end not be what we really wanted. As the saying goes: "Be careful what you wish for; you may receive it."

Jesus is saying that we will not get everything we ask for. He is connecting GOD only with the *good gifts*. He is saying that requests must be in harmony with the future GOD has intended for us. The analogy of the parent and child is perfect. Out of love parents will only give their children what they think is in their best interests. GOD'S love for us is the same. He will only give us what is in our best interests.

We can also create a future that is not of GOD'S choosing. He gives us the freedom to make our own choices. He leaves it to us to exercise our own free will and to choose. As we open the territory in front of us and create the future out of our own self-interest, we must recognize that the landscape we are creating may not be of GOD'S design

We must examine our dreams and desires with care and ask GOD to guide us. We must be aware of the powerful forces of intentionality within us and not mistake them for GOD'S voice. We must recognize that without His guidance we risk not only harming ourselves and others in the here and now, but we may place at risk our very souls.

XIII

From Each According to His and Her Ability

"Half of my life is gone, and I have let

The years slip from me and have not fulfilled

The aspiration of my youth...

Though, halfway up the hill, I see the Past

Lying beneath me with its sounds and sights,

And hear above me on the autumnal blast

The cataract of Death far thundering from the heights."

Mezzo Cammin

Henry Wadsworth Longefellow

1807–1882

"Give the world the best you have, and it may never be enough; Give the world the best you've got anyway."

Mother Teresa

The Henry Wadsworth Longfellow poem is about a life that has suddenly reached the halfway mark. Sadly, the writer looks back and says: What have I accomplished? Like the writer, we too ask the question: Is it too late to make my mark before I reach the top and face *The cataract of Death far thundering from the heights.*

The Longfellow poem is a sad poem. It is a poem about a person who has not yet made his mark. He has not yet found his niche. He has not discovered himself. He has not made his contribution. It is a poem about a life that is being wasted. It is a poem about a person in despair.

The words of Mother Teresa are not sad. They are the words of joy and of action. They are the words of a person in search for a way to make a positive and constructive influence on the world.

Each of us was born with the ability to make a contribution. Each person, no matter how strong or weak, how dumb or smart, how able or disabled was given gifts by the Creator. Each was given the potential to fulfill a purpose. Each was given the ability to make a mark, to change the world by some small—or large—amount.

Any religion that does not encourage its followers to use their potential to its fullest to advance society, not just selectivity but in its broadest sense, is not a religion. It is no more than a mind controlling human activity. It is no more than an excuse to justify its own continued existence and to control its followers. This is true whether it is religion under the name of Christianity, Judaism, Islam, or any other.

The key word is *contribution*. The world today is the product of the contributions past and present of those from all backgrounds and religions who have realized their potential and made their contributions. It is not the product of those who have not. It is not the product of *False Prophets*. It is not the product of drug addicts, cheats, gangsters, terrorists and all others who are the parasites of society, who take as much as they can and contribute nothing. Nor is it the product of those, who because of material good fortune, choose not to contribute but to live in a somnolent state of luxury with their only purpose being to continue to maintain their level of opulence, and thereby satisfy their selfish desires.

The question comes down to what is and what is not a contribution. Jesus answered this question clearly. He said it is anything that:

- Shows love towards all members of society
- Helps to elevate the human mind to the level of GOD'S presence
- Helps to develop the *talents* of others
- Makes a contribution to the welfare of society
- Protects good people from those evil people who would seek to destroy

This is the message of Jesus for all people in our world. At least a part of it runs through every major religious tradition. It is a call for all persons on this earth, of all faiths and traditions, to question their religious convictions, asking: Is this what I in the deepest part of me believe? Jesus said that any part of any religious tradition that runs contrary to this message is false.

It is the message found in the Parable of the Talents, outlined in the following reflection, which is a parable directed to all of humankind. It says that in the eyes of GOD anyone who does not multiply his or her *talents* as best they can has wasted GOD'S gift of life.

REFLECTION # 11

Reaping Where He Has Not Sowed and Gathering Where He Has Not Strawed

---

The lord gave talents ... (A currency of the time)...to every man according to his abilities ... he that had received five talents ... made another five talents... and he that had received two talents another two, but he that had received the one talent went and hid it ... as he was afraid...and the lord said to him: Thou knowest that I reap where I have not sown and gather where I have not strawed... and the lord cast the unprofitable servant into outer darkness.

(Matthew 25:15-30)

In this parable Jesus is saying that GOD reaps where He has not sown and gathers where He has not strawed.

Is Jesus saying therefore that GOD'S purposes extend not only into the lives of those who have heard His Word, but also into the lives of all other people? Is Jesus telling us that every person, no matter what his or her belief, who uses as best he or she can the abilities that GOD has given them will enter the Kingdom of Heaven? Is he saying that GOD'S presence and redemption is not exclusive—as many religious believers of the three religions of Abraham separately hold—but is based solely on what each has contributed, given the talents that GOD has given to each?

Even today in the early spring to give new sprouts protection from the sun, rain, and wind, farmers will place straw over newly planted seeds. This gives them an advantage, so they will be protected as they begin to grow.

What about the seeds that are not protected and nurtured? Do they too have a chance? Jesus here says they do.

The servant has just told GOD that he feared Him and did not want to take the chance of failure with his talent, so he buried it. GOD is telling the servant that only He—GOD—can be the judge and would not have given him the talent if it could not be multiplied. The servant's only choice was to overcome his fear and multiply his talent.

Jesus is telling us in this parable that GOD'S presence extends to all of mankind. He is saying that every person on earth is a part of GOD'S plan. Each of us has abilities of which we are unaware. Only GOD can be the judge of our inherent worth. Only HE knows what we are capable of accomplishing. We are being asked to give up our fears and accept GOD'S judgment as to what we can accomplish.

XIV

Biblical Thoughts on Breaking Through to the Other Side

"Everything that we experience as material reality is born in an invisible realm beyond space and time, a realm revealed by science to consist of energy and information. This invisible source of all that exists is not an empty void but the womb of creation itself. Something creates and organizes this energy. It turns the chaos of quantum soup into stars, galaxies, rain forests, human beings, and our own thoughts, emotions, memories and desires."

How To Know GOD

Deepak Chopra

2000 A.D.

We are living in a tumultuous period of human history. Archaic religious beliefs are being challenged by new scientific discoveries. As this is occurring, we are seeing evidence that the two may not be contradictory. They may even be in support of each other.

We are discovering parallel meanings between our religious insights and our scientific discoveries. We are learning that there is a strong confluence of those ideas, which define both in religious and scientific terms, who and what we are in relation to our Universe and what lay beyond our perception of it. And, we are finding that the power of man to observe all of this extends far beyond the perceivable physical part of his senses. It extends beyond himself.

Not everyone agrees with this. As scientific inquiry has taken hold, for many it remains separate from religion. Today, for these individuals, the two are in conflict. They give two separate and irreconcilable viewpoints to the question of who and what we are.

Religion came first. It was the first to explore the unknown. It began its evolution at the very beginning of man's consciousness. It formed simultaneously among isolated groups of primitive man. In the beginning it took the form of man's primitive search for what lay beyond his earthly perception. It also recognized that man was unique and not like other living things in that he could perceive what other forms of life could not.

Scientific knowledge is a more recent phenomenon. It has only been with us for a few hundred years, but it has progressed at a much faster pace so that now it is challenging much of traditional religious thought.

As these searches moved forward and converged, they did not always find a smooth path. The observations of Galileo were condemned by the Roman Catholic Church. Even today, many of those who hold to the inerrancy of the Hebrew and Christian scriptures refuse to accept evolutionary scientific theory as it relates to life on the earth and the creation of the Universe itself.

For many of those who hold a metaphorical view of religious scripture, religious and scientific thought are seen as two codependent ways of looking at the same questions. The complexities of human metaphysical existence are seen as extending far beyond past religious doctrinal understanding.

Our vision of reality, from the smallest (Quantum Mechanics), to the largest (Cosmology), to ourselves (Biochemistry), is broadening at an exponential rate and bringing religion along with it. As these developments are occurring, we are becoming more and more certain that there is such a thing as direction in our Universe and in the other dimensions beyond it. Godless theories of chaos and randomness are no longer a choice. Like in a symphony, the underlying directing presence of an orchestrator becomes evident.

In 1905 and 1916 Albert Einstein made breakthroughs into our knowledge with his Special and General Theories of Relativity. This led to the Manhattan Project and the development of the atomic bomb. Further developments since then have led to a broader understanding of concepts relating to space and time. Since Einstein, we now have other theories that run from the String Theory describing the physical universe to Brane's law that says we ourselves are no more than the reflection of ourselves against the membrane of another dimension.

But we cannot see the things we are observing. We must rely on our advanced instruments of measurement and the language of mathematics to allow us to extend our vision. We are only limited by the level of advancement of these instruments and by the creative depths of our minds. It is only when we see in front of us the results of all of this new knowledge, such as the explosion of an atomic bomb, or the heat of a microwave oven, or any of the other practical applications of science, that we are convinced that our observations are real.

The combination of the advancement of scientific instruments and an understanding of the mathematical equations derived from their observations made possible most of the major discoveries of the 20th century. This was aided by the development of the computer. The fact that computers since they were first developed have obeyed what is known as Moore's Law—their speed and complexity double every twenty four months—tells us that this may just be the beginning of our exploration.

These scientific breakthroughs are allowing us to write in mathematical equations the language of GOD on this side of our perception of reality. As we develop and use this language, we are becoming aware of its limitations and the possibility that ours may be only one language being used to describe even another, a language we do not now know and never will, the other ultimate language of GOD.

Scientific developments of the 20th century presented entirely new kinds of challenges that would have shaken the very foundations of early Christianity. They not only challenged the inerrancy of biblical events such as the Creation Story in Genesis, but they challenged the inerrancy of biblical writings about the creation of man himself. In the past, organized Christianity only clashed with the scientific world when it was challenged in areas of scripture dealing with Cosmology. Galileo fought with the Roman Catholic Church over the relative positions in the heavens of the sun and the earth. But Galileo's science had not gone so far as to challenge the Creation Story itself.

As we begin to understand from these scientific developments more about the Universe and the evolution of man as a part of the Universe, we are seeing that much of the recorded message of Jesus is not in conflict. In fact his teachings support our scientific findings. It is largely in the historical/mythological events of the Hebrew Bible—The Old Testament—where the conflict exists. Jesus spoke in parables about the same dimension that science is speaking of today. He spoke at a time when science as we know it was unknown, yet he was able to define by the use of his words this other dimension.

The evolution of science and religion will continue like two lines approaching each other but never meeting. The distance between them will continue to be reduced but will always be more than zero. This means that they will never meet nor cross over. They will just get closer and closer. As this occurs, they will present stronger and stronger proof of each other's validity. But, there will always be an area where the answers will have to come from both.

As this near convergence takes place, we should be testing the inerrancy of past religions beliefs against the new scientific information we are receiving.

There is a harsh discipline to the forward motion of scientific ideas. They must be tested. This is not the case with religion. Proof is not necessary. Rather than retreat in fear, religions should look openly at undiscovered meanings in their scriptures that reveal ancient understandings of what is just now being proven.

The following Reflections examine what Jesus said about this dimension beyond our perception, and they examine what he said about how we, even as mortals, can approach this dimension. The path that he described is not always a *feel good* path or an easy path on which we can with little effort stroll. It is not a path where a sudden flash of light will appear and lift us up to heaven. Nor is it a path where we can just stand and wait for GOD to comedown to us.

It is a path that calls for self-directed and disciplined concentration. It is an upward path that calls for strength and courage.

REFLECTION # 12

Entering Into His Presence

Seek, and ye shall find; knock and it (the door) shall be opened to you…he that seeketh findeth; and to him that knocketh it shall be opened.

(Matthew 7:7-8)

Why is it so important? What does Jesus mean by saying that if we knock, the door will be opened for us? What happens then?

When we come to a door, we can just remain standing in front of it or we can knock on it. If it opens, we can remain standing and look to see what is inside, or we can step through to the other side. There are three separate decisions on our part, the first, deciding to knock on the door, the second, knocking on it, and then the third, walking through.

For the first—deciding to knock on it—we have to want to find out who or what is on the other side. For the second—knocking on the door—we have to take action. For the third, and this is the greatest of the three decisions—walking through the door—we have to take a risk. We have to step through and enter the unknown.

Using this imagery, Jesus is metaphorically describing for us our limited perception of our sense of reality in our earthly existence—outside of the door. He is reminding us that our minds can only comprehend the material world, and therefore we are unable to experience what lay beyond. But, he says; if we take the initiative and move towards the door leading to what lay beyond and we knock, the door will be opened for us. This is the door to another dimension. It is the dimension where GOD is. Then, if we step through, we will find ourselves not in the material world of our earthly perception but in the heavenly dimension beyond it.

We will find ourselves in the presence of GOD.

REFLECTION # 13

Submission to the Power of GOD

"Joy and happiness in this life come from remaining still and letting GOD speak to us. By turning our backs on the earthly things and their images that are pulling at us and taking over our minds, we can find this joy and happiness, and we can be nearer to GOD."

Meister Eckhart

1260–1327

How do we find GOD'S presence in our lives? Is it something that comes to us out of the blue? Or, do we have to work for it? Will it come to us from meditation and prayer? If so, how should we be praying? How do we meditate?

Jesus called on us to seek out GOD. His teachings were very clear as to how we should go about this. He said we must turn our attention away from the things of this world and to GOD.

Great teachers of the Gospels such as Meister Eckhart, a famous Dominican Monk of the 14th century, said that searching for GOD takes more than meditation, words and prayers. He said it calls for a disciplined redirection of our minds. It calls for a turning away from the material and emotional things of this world that distract us and prevent us from seeing GOD. He said we must empty our minds of the things of this world. He said only then will GOD speak to us.

Jesus told us that we must release the negative hold that the things of this world have on us. These are both emotional and material. We must turn our backs on emotions such as anger, hate, anxiety, and fear. We must also release the hold that our material desires have on us. We must turn from allowing the world to define our wants and desires and allow GOD to define our very being.

REFLECTION # 14

From the Least to the Greatest

The Kingdom of Heaven is like a grain of mustard seed, which a man took, and sowed in his field…which indeed is the least of all seeds, but when it is grown, it is the greatest among herbs.

(Matthew 13: 31-32)

Why did Jesus use the metaphor of a mustard seed to describe heaven? Why, when referring to our perception of the Kingdom of Heaven did he draw a distinction using the words *least* and *greatest*? Is it possible that there is a connecting linking between his words and our 21st century scientific understanding of the universe? Was Jesus giving us a clue to help us understand our personal relationship to the physical and observable universe?

First Explanation

The standard model of cosmology postulates that before the Big Bang our entire galaxy existed in a state of singularity in a Black Hole with all energy and matter compressed inside an area of near infinite compression. Some 15 billion years ago, from this near infinite compression came a singular event—the Big Bang—and the expansion of matter (energy) into space began, to become the universe as we observe it today. Just as life begins within the germ of a mustard seed, our universe began from the finite depths of a black hole. Both began as the least to become the greatest.

Second Explanation

We cannot see heaven around us. Like looking for a mustard seed, we have to make a strenuous effort and look very closely. When we do see it, we find that we have difficulty understanding its regenerative magnitude. We sense that the potential for life in a mustard seed is greater than anything we can perceive or understand.

Third Explanation

Just as life begins within the germ of a mustard seed and our universe began in the near infinite compression of a *black hole*, our lives began in near infinite smallness in the mind of GOD and, without nurturing, they will remain that way and at death pass on into nothingness; or, when we accept GOD in our lives, we will be born again into His presence. Then, our lives will take on another form. They will expand into the infinite dimension of heaven. Like a mustard seed, what began as the least will become the greatest.

Fourth Explanation

All three above.

REFLECTION # 15

Seeing Beyond the Prophets

For now I see through a glass, darkly; but then face to face. Now I know in part; but then I shall know even as also I am known.

(I Corinthians 13:12)

Will scripture tell us what lay on the other side of the *glass, darkly*?

We are conceived and born into a universe that covers us like a dark glass preventing us from seeing what is beyond. We can only know and experience what is here underneath. As we grow in knowledge and understanding, we become more aware of something more. But we are prevented from seeing it by a veil that presses upon us in its envelopment. It traps us in our earth bound understanding who and what we are. We strain to see the other side.

From the beginning of human history we have has been in search to find what lay beyond. From the words of the shamans and priests in the earliest years of human development, to the writings of the prophets of the Hebrew Bible, to the words of the New Testament, to the writings of the Eastern Religions, to the Arabic message of the Angel Gabriel in the Koran, we have searched for knowledge of the other side. Every piece of scripture ever written has been an attempt to penetrate the dark glass preventing us from seeing what lay beyond.

We must continue this search by studying the wisdom of all religious writings, but at the same time where they claim to be the word of GOD we must question their inerrancy. We must question what part came from GOD and what came from man. We must search these writings for GOD'S revelation, not man's. We must not blindly leave it to others in ages past to tell us how to see what is beyond the dark glass. We, each of us, must search for it ourselves.

XV

Biblical and Other References to The Other Dimension

> *While he (Paul) was still on the road to Damascus, suddenly a light flashed from the sky all around him. He fell to the ground and heard a voice saying, 'Saul, Saul, why do you persecute me?' .... He got up from the ground, but when he opened his eyes he could not see... He was blind for three days.*

(Acts 9: 3-9)

The story of Saul on the road to Damascus is a true story. It dates back to the earliest confirmed writings of Christianity. It was described in The New Testament in the Book of Acts and in Paul's letters. His life, which certainly can be proven, is in itself proof that it occurred.

This story tells us that our existence has a transcendental nature that goes beyond our perceived physical reality. It tells us that we can *break through* into something that is beyond our understanding.

What happened to Paul suddenly and dramatically altered the path in his life. On the Damascus road he was overcome by a power from a dimension beyond our understanding. After this transforming experience, he devoted the rest of his life to the spreading of the message of Jesus as the Christ throughout the then known world. It was a message that reflected a view of the Kingdom of GOD not only far different from, but in many respects opposed to the Hebraic one to which he had previously held fast and believed.

The story of Paul is not exclusive to Christianity. It has been repeated in many other forms of belief. For the religious person there is a sudden breakthrough to a heavenly dimension. This dimension is generally one where there is a bright light and a feeling of profound love. Then, there follows a change in the person's life.

As with Paul and for many others, there is a message that accompanies the experience. At the same time though, there is always confusion as to what really happened. The person generally finds it difficult to fully describe what he saw or felt except to describe it as a *bright light*. This is not so with the message which generally is clear and concise.

Only a few religions such as Islam can claim that the messenger receiving the light had a continuing and direct connection to GOD. But in Islam the message was given by Muhammad to individuals who recorded it. It was not written down by Muhammad himself. In Islam, it is claimed that the Angel Gabriel and other angels delivered the message.

In the case of Saul, he received a message from Jesus saying: *Saul, Saul, why are you persecuting me?* and then he went out to preach the message of Jesus Christ.

For most Christians the light takes a more subtle form. It comes from a belief in GOD'S dimension joining theirs through an understanding of the life and death of Jesus as the Christ. This takes place through the indwelling of the Holy Spirit. But the Holy Spirit is not a *light*. The life of Jesus, for Christians, is taken as the light. Jesus Christ is GOD in human form showing them the light.

We do not have to wait for another Saul to tell us about divine presence. In our world of today we hear stories of divine intercession repeated again and again. We have accounts of *after death* experiences where lives are changed. We have stories of healings where people healed feel a bright light moving through their bodies from head to toe, and healing both mental and physical occurs. In almost all cases the experience is the same. There is a pure light that moves through the person. Then, afterwards there is a feeling of love for all of mankind, and there is joy over the possibility of new life.

Except in the story of Jesus, where Christian belief claims that Jesus Christ was incarnate, the person is always overcome by the presence of the eternal, but remains a human being. In these cases, like Paul himself, it is a human being who sees the light and then interprets it in the context of his own understanding of what it meant, and he then lives the rest of his life on earth and in time biologically dies. A life is changed, but not biologically and not completely. The person remains a living functioning biological human being.

For Paul the underlying behavioral patterns did not change completely. Paul before his vision was a man burning inside to punish those who defied the law of the Hebrew Bible. After his experience on the road to Damascus, he showed this same intensity as he interpreted the message of Jesus Christ. He did not leave his past completely behind. He relied on his own past knowledge of Jewish law and traditions to reinforce his new and altered vision of redemption. Inside, he was still Saul of Tarsus. The experience of being shown the eternal opened up another dimension for him, but did not take him into it and leave him there. The visit is always short. We must always return to earth and face ourselves.

The meaning of being in the light is being in the presence of GOD. Most never experience this and for those who do, being in HIS presence never lasts long. Many expect a sudden *flash* like Paul experienced and are sadly disappointed.

The following Reflections will discuss some of these *glimpses of GOD* taken from Biblical scriptures and comment on their possible meanings.

REFLECTION # 16

The Meaning of the Light

The people that walked in darkness have seen a great light; they that dwell in the land of the shadow of death, upon them hath the light shined.

(Isaiah 9:2)

For God so loved the world that he gave his only begotten son, that whosoever believeth in him should not perish, but have everlasting life.

(John 3:16)

For GOD so loved all of His creation that He took the form of man in the person of Jesus of Nazareth, as prophesied by the Hebrew scriptures, to reveal Himself, not only to the Jewish people, but to all of mankind, so that whoever would think and live his or her life by the example of the life Jesus, would never be separated from GOD but would be reborn into the light of GOD'S presence here on earth and be in oneness with Him for all eternity.

An interpretation of *John 3:16*

by the author

What does it mean to be in the light?

The words of John 3:16 over the last two millennia have separated people. They have separated nations. The reason is that Christianity has not understood their original meaning.

For many Christians they amount to no more than a rhetorical belief in the reality of Jesus as the Jewish Messiah. Once that belief is affirmed, they can then say that they are living in the *light*.

But Jesus asked for more than just rhetorical belief. He asked us to live our lives in oneness with GOD. Acknowledging and even seeing the light does not assume accepting the light. The fact that a light shines on us does not mean that we are absorbing it. We can cover ourselves up.

John 3:16 has from the beginning of Christian history allowed many Christians to claim exclusivity in the matter of personal salvation based on a rhetorical belief in Jesus as the Christ. The message of Jesus went far deeper than that. It extended to whoever would think and live his or her life by the example given in his life. It is they who are reborn into the light of GOD'S presence to be in oneness with Him for all eternity. No one is excluded.

REFLECTION # 17

The light Within

(The Apostle Paul was being questioned by the Jews about his belief in Jesus Christ.)

How well the Holy Spirit spoke to your fathers through the prophet Isaiah when he said: ' Go to this people and say you may hear and hear, but you will never understand; you may look and look, but you will never see. For this people's mind has become gross; their ears are dulled, and their eyes are closed. Otherwise their eyes might see, their ears hear, and their minds understand. '

(Acts 28: 26, 27)

What did Paul mean; to hear but not to understand, to look but not to see?

The Jews Paul was addressing had not accepted Jesus as their Messiah. Paul was accusing them of hearing but not understanding, of looking but not seeing. Paul's statement must be viewed in this limited context.

The context is far broader. The words of Isaiah have a universal meaning. Today, they are directed at all Jews and Muslims, as well as all Christians. Isaiah said that the minds of the people had become gross, their ears dulled, their eyes closed. This describes our world today.

We try to escape the reality of the human dilemma by compartmentalizing our lives, by living with each feeling isolated from the others. We live like a king in a castle surrounded by high walls. Our minds are dulled. We choose not to comprehend the world around us. .

We think and act the same as those in Isaiah's time. We are no different. The people had taken cover by directing all of their attention to the consuming activities of their lives. We are the same. We compartmentalize our lives so we only see what we want to see and hear what we want to hear. Life is easier when we compartmentalize our lives. We can have one personality in the work place, another with our families, another in our competitive activities, and another at our place of worship. For the sake of our reputations and our own peace of mind, we can then go through the motions and give the appearance to others, as well as to ourselves, that we are what GOD wants us to be.

155

David Anderson

Our institutions are also at fault. Our political parties compartmentalize their agendas, supporting the ones that attract the most votes, leaving other agendas behind regardless of the human impact. Our organized religions do the same, placing reputation and the comfort of tradition ahead of principle.

The problem with this way of thinking and acting is that it blocks out the presence of GOD. He is there waiting for us, but we do not hear Him and see Him because we have isolated ourselves in our compartments. We pretend to hear Him, but we do not hear Him. We pretend to see Him, but we do not see Him. We pretend to think we understand his presence, but we do not understand His presence.

The words of Isaiah are as true today as they were then.

REFLECTION # 18

The Healing Power of the Light

"Dear Sigmund,

I admit that the techniques and insights that you and your followers have developed are vital to the treatment of troubled people. But there are questions of life, death, meaning and spirituality that you never touch.

Sincerely

Dr. Kenneth C Haugk"

(An imaginary letter to Dr. Sigmund Freud by the founder of the Stephen Ministry, an ecumenical ministry using Christian healing methods)

"I firmly believe there is a divine light in every human being ever born or to be born"

Malcom Muggeridge

1903–1990

Can the *light* heal? Does evil destroy?

A great mystery of our time is the question of why certain people are so good while others are so evil. An example is the life of Mother Teresa in contrast to the lives of Adolph Hitler and Joseph Stalin. In our own daily lives we see the same contrast. We observe in those around us acts of love among some and acts of selfishness and hatred among others.

In some cases there are conditional factors that have made a very large impact at a young age. Often these are used by psychologists to show that the destructive behavior is irreparable. But even under extreme conditions there isn't always a correlation. There are those who overcome negative influences early on. Also, there are those who break out of the mold later on in their lives and undergo transformations. And then there are those who, coming from apparently normal backgrounds, turn out to be demonic.

The question then becomes: Can the power of the *light* take away the demonic? Can it heal?

There is ample proof that it can. When it occurs, there is always something of great positive power that comes over the troubled or sick person, and then there is a change. The negative presence disappears. The positive power enters. We see this occurring both psychologically and physiologically. People are miraculously healed. We see this when people overcome drug and alcohol addictions. The transforming power of the Alcoholics Anonymous program is an example.

We are not just physical / mechanical / chemical / electrical forms of life. We are spiritual human beings, and our mental and physical health is derived from the presence of the power of GOD within us. As we move toward GOD, we move away from the destructive forces that are working to destroy us.

REFLECTION # 19

Guided by the Light

"I rob myself of life's richest possibilities when I stop with the human situation and do not press on to the divine solution".

"GOD may be waiting to show us the next step to take because we have not yet taken the last one he showed us".

"GOD may be working on levels far beyond my comparative analysis of success and failure".

"When GOD gives, man must be willing to accept".

The Back of God Signs of His Presence

Bill Austin

1980 A.D.

What place does GOD have in our lives? Is He there all of the time or does He just show up once in a while? If He is giving us messages as to which direction to take, how can we know what they are?

We think we can control our lives when deep inside we know that this is not the case. When things go wrong, we are suddenly reminded of how little control we have. At death we come upon the final realization of this.

In the time period between our birth and our death, we can view our lives in two different ways:

- We can see ourselves facing the world alone with the control of our lives in our own hands.

- We can open ourselves to GOD'S presence and trust in Him as we allow Him to work in our lives guiding every decision we make.

GOD is ever present in all of His creation. He is everywhere. He is both inside of us and outside of us. We live either alienated from Him or as a part of Him. He only works in lives that are open to Him and accept Him. When we open our lives to Him, they can then move far beyond our level of comprehension, in the direction of the divine, unfolding into the richest possibilities.

⊠

159

David Anderson

REFLECTION # 20

My Face You Can Not See

(GOD is asking Moses to lead the people)

Moses said to the lord, 'thou bidst me lead this people up, but thou hast not told me whom thou wilt send with me ....' The Lord answered, 'I will go with you in person and set your mind at rest' .... and Moses prayed, 'show me thy glory.' The Lord answered, 'I will make all my goodness pass before you ....' but he added, ' My face you cannot see, for no mortal man may see me and live ... take your stand on the rock, and when my glory passes by, I will put you in a crevice of the rock and cover you with my hand until I have passed by. Then I will take away my hand, and you shall see my back, but my face shall not be seen.'

(Exodus 33:12-23)

Like Moses, we all long to see GOD, not just to feel His presence, but also to meet Him face to face and to know Him. Why will He not let us see His face? Why does He remain a mystery to us? Why does He always step to the side of our perception of His reality?

If we could be face to face with GOD, we would not be mortal. We would not have to battle with the uncertainty of being human. We would be free from the stain of sin. We would be like GOD in His image, as we were in the original creation. We would be not in the image of mortal human beings but in the image of GOD. Our image would be His. We would be divine.

In Exodus we have this revelation not just to Moses, but also to all of mankind. GOD is saying that He is present in each of our lives; although, as we are mortals, we cannot see Him. He is telling us that He exists on the other side of our mortality.

But, GOD tells Moses that even though you cannot see Me, I will be with you. He tells Moses that Moses will see His presence, but only after GOD has passed through Moses' life. GOD'S message to Moses is His message to each of us. *I will make My goodness pass before you.*

Every moment of our lives GOD is watching us, waiting for us to take the next step. He wants us to take the next step, not by ourselves, but with Him. We never know what the direction will be. He asks us to trust the signs that He gives us. He asks us to listen and trust that He is working at levels we do not understand. Whichever direction our steps lead us, He asks us to accept what He gives us. All He demands is our faith in Him. It is a faith that says He will enable us to realize the full potential of what He has given us. This was His message to Moses.

As it was for Moses, it is for all of us. The real glory of GOD is not a momentary look at His face. It is; as we look back, seeing Him having passed through our lives. It is seeing GOD at work in our lives. It is being content with knowing that: *you shall see my back.*

David Anderson

REFLECTION # 21

Returning from the Light

Jesus took Peter, James and John ... up a mountain ... and in their presence he was transfigured; his face shown like the sun, and his clothes became white as the light ... and they saw Moses and Elijah appear.... Then Peter spoke: 'If you wish, I will make three shelters (Tabernacles) here....' While he was speaking, a bright light suddenly overshadowed them.... When they raised their eyes, they saw no one, but only Jesus. On the way down the mountain ... when they returned to the crowd ... a man ... fell on his knees before him ... and said, ' have pity on my son; he is an epileptic;' Jesus then spoke to the boy.... He was cured.

(Matthew 17:1-18)

Why did Jesus not encourage his disciples to build the three Tabernacles? Why did the light leave them as suddenly as it had appeared? Why was it that the first act of Jesus after he left the mountain was to cure an epileptic boy?

Peter, James, and John wanted the experience to last. They wanted to build three Tabernacles on the mountain. They wanted to remain in the presence of the light. But, Jesus did not want this. He knew that we can only be aware of GOD'S light for brief moments of time and then only when He has briefly entered and then passed through our lives. We must return to our mortality.

After the transfiguration, Jesus, Peter, James, and John went back down the mountain. Jesus had made it apparent to them that their place was not on the mountain; it was with the people. The first act of Jesus upon his return was to heal an epileptic.

The Christian experience is not meant to be one of lasting transcendence into the presence of GOD. That is an experience that can take place only temporarily. It is an experience that takes place in the here and now of this world. It takes place among and between people. Whenever a Christian is brought into GOD'S presence, he or she does not remain there, but is quickly returned to the real world with all of its pain and suffering. The Christianity of Jesus is a religion of people demonstrating the love of GOD among each other.

162

XVI

The Apostle Paul—A Pharisaic Jew Defines Christianity on His Own Terms

There is no question that Paul had a greater influence on the formation of Christianity than any other human being of his time, as well as since his time.

It is not possible to understand the way an evangelical Christian thinks unless one understands the way that the Apostle Paul thought. It is not possible to understand the way a Roman Catholic today thinks unless one understands the way the Apostle Paul thought. It is not possible to understand the stark differences between Christianity and Islam unless one understands the way the Apostle Paul thought. For this reason the author is including in this book his statement, in some respects controversial as it may be, on the Apostle Paul.

The Impact of Paul's Letters on Christian Thought

Twenty years after the death of Jesus, it was a pharisaic Jew from Tarsus schooled in the law of the Torah who would set in motion a theology that would establish the pattern for all future Christian thought. Three hundred years later, his letters, which were written to the struggling Christian churches throughout the Roman Empire, by interpreting the meaning of the life and crucifixion of Jesus, would form the theological foundation of Roman Catholicism. Another twelve hundred years later they would spark the Protestant Revolution.

The life and teachings of Paul were, from the moment of his conversion, surrounded by controversy. Not only the Romans, but also his fellow Jews and many of his fellow Christians were disturbed by much of what he wrote and said. As some of his statements are interpreted today in the light of 21st century secular values, the controversy continues.

163

Of one thing all Christians would agree. His life was suddenly transformed by the experience of the indwelling presence of Jesus of Nazareth. All of his thoughts and all of his actions were in a moment of revelation one day, as he traveled on the road to Damascus, changed. His brilliant mind and all of his physical being from that moment on became focused on one thing and one thing only: revealing to mankind what, according to his belief, had happened in the world 30 years before.

Unlike almost all other great writers and thinkers whose central philosophical themes run in understandable patterns and coherent fashion, Paul's writings often appeared as just the opposite. They often showed what could be described as bursts of brilliance separated by mundane observations, some of them inconsistent with his central theme. It is these *bursts of brilliance*, as they have given insight into the real Jesus and what his life and death meant for all of mankind, that have captivated Christian believers ever since.

Many of his statements show startling insights into the meaning of the Christian experience that are difficult to comprehend. This has not been helped as scholars and theologians over the years have attempted to interpret these meanings. The problem has been made the worse by inaccuracies in translation from the Greek language in which he wrote, as well as debate over which of his letters were actually by his hand.

His ideas not only reflected the impact of the every day Roman influences that surrounded him, but also his own temperament. Both physically and mentally he presents the picture of a driven human being. He worked under extreme pressure, some of it self-imposed and some not. Often he feared for his life. The strong influence of his Jewish educational and religious background is evident. At times he appeared to be boxed in by all of this: the Greco-Roman culture around him, the turbulent age in which he lived, his pharisaic religious upbringing, his fiery temperament.

Parts of his writings show insights of extreme depth and would appear clearly to be inspired not just by his knowledge of the teaching of Jesus but even by the spiritual presence of GOD within his very being. Other parts read more like a list of rules and regulations drawn up by a Rabbi for a Jewish sect. It is for this reason that any study of Paul should be limited to those parts of his letters that clearly may give insights into the Mind of GOD as it was revealed by Jesus.

His core belief, redemption of mankind through Jesus Christ, was not just a call for a rhetorical belief in the Prophet and his teachings; it was a call for a radical restructuring of human nature itself. It was a call for the turning over of one's life. And it was a call, not only to the Jews, but also to each and every individual on the face of the earth. It was a call for a faith in GOD like that of Jesus Christ. What this all truly means remains his message today. It is the reason that the writings of Paul continue to dominate Christian thought.

The Misplaced Emphasis on Paul as a Person

Because of the debate and controversy over Paul's writings, there has arisen in recent years a storm of criticism of him as a person. This has come from groups as divergent in outlook as liberal and middle of the road Christians critical of his views on sexuality, to Jews who see him as a traitor to his Hebraic religious traditions and biased by his Hellenistic Greek education and outlook.

Anything derogatory postulated about him as a person, now 2000 years after his death, can be no more than conjecture and therefore should be viewed with suspicion. What is most important about Paul and where the debate should be taking place is with the insightfulness of his ideas. Many of them offer Christianity's deepest and most far reaching understanding of the life and teaching of Jesus. As such, they offer penetrating insights into the mind of GOD as given by Jesus Christ. Therefore, focusing on Paul the individual often turns out to be no more than a futile effort by those with other agendas designed to discredit the message that he gave mankind, as well as Christianity as a religion. This does not mean to say that we should not closely examine the life of Saul of Tarsus and the times in which he lived.

If he was in fact a messenger, by way of Jesus Christ, of the WORD, how much of what he wrote came from GOD and how much from Paul himself as a vulnerable human being? How much was the result of his pharisaic training and how much came from the inspiration of the teachings of Jesus Christ? How much was a wrong interpretation of the message of Jesus Christ? How much possibly came from his own inner turmoil?

The Early life of Paul

It was not a disciple of Jesus who was to be the distinctive and dominant voice in Christianity throughout the ages, but a Jew born far away from Jerusalem in the town of Tarsus on the coast of what is today Turkey. He was from an influential Jewish family, which we can assume from the fact that they were Roman citizens. They were members of a pharisaic Jewish sect that strictly followed the law of the Torah. In Tarsus, Saul would have grown up surrounded by other pharisaic families, separated from the Greco-Roman community. He would, however, have been exposed from an early age to the outside world. In addition to his pharisaic religious education, his family would have had him educated in Greco-Roman philosophy and rhetoric. He spoke and wrote both Latin and Greek. We can assume that he also understood Hebrew and Aramaic.

He became the key figure in the change of Christianity from a sect of Judaism to a religion independent of Judaism. His writings date from approximately 50–68 A.D., which predates the synoptic Gospels, which are thought to have been written 70–90 A.D. The Gospel of John was written even later. Therefore, his letters can be viewed as the first widely recognized written record of the Christian experience.

He was a figure of controversy from the very beginning. As has been stated, his writings ran from pure brilliance into the deepest reaches of the meanings of the teaching of Jesus Christ to statements on issues that clearly had very little to do with those teachings. He was a person of deep passion who often seemed unable to escape from his pharisaic legalistic thinking. His personality was so powerful that he dominated all of those around him. His Letters strongly influenced the theological foundation of the early Roman Catholic Church and the dogma that followed. The power of one of his insights into the teachings of Jesus Christ, namely his observation relating to justification by faith, 1500 years after his death was so powerful that it sparked the writings of Martin Luther and the Protestant Reformation.

In recent years many of his ideas have been challenged as being of questionable insight, especially those dealing with election, predestination, and the roles of husbands and wives. This has led many Christians to question whether they should accept all that he wrote. It has led to the view among some Christians that he should be considered less a Saint and more a brilliant but fallible human being.

The State of the Roman Empire in His Time

It is not possible to begin to understand Paul's writing without an understanding of the age in which he wrote. When he was writing to the small Christian churches scattered throughout the Roman Empire, Nero was Emperor and the Empire was at the zenith of its military power and intellectual influence. It extended from the Atlantic to the Euphrates and from the North Sea to the African Desert. It controlled 120,000,000 people.

Christianity was just another of the many religious movements in the Empire, but for Rome it immediately presented a problem. Roman society was built on defined class distinctions among its citizens. Society was stratified into those who were recognized as privileged—Roman Citizens—and those less privileged—non-citizens. And then there were the slaves. Christianity was classless. All were equal in the mind of the savior, Jesus Christ. This egalitarian thought belief of Christianity was in direct opposition to the prevailing Roman societal ideas.

There were other problems. A major one dealt with sexual behavior. Many pagan sexual religious practices prevailed in the Empire. Some involved both female and male prostitution. It is reported that there were over 1000 prostitutes at the temple in Corinth alone. There was no sacredness to sex, outside of the elevating experience derived from the pure pleasure of the act. This was its purpose in the pagan rituals. Fertility Gods and Goddesses were worshiped for procreation. Pedophilia and bestiality were accepted practices. Abortion and even the killing of unwanted newborns were common. There was little respect for human life. This view of sexual behavior was in direct contrast to the Christian idea of fornication as a sin and the belief in the sacredness of human life.

Paul's Writing as a Response to Roman Society

The Christian communities were small isolated islands in a vast Roman ocean. From every direction came rejection and persecution.

As a response to this, Paul's concept that only Christians are elected or predestined by GOD was taken on as a core belief. As GOD'S Covenant had once been with the Nation of Israel, it was now with those who believed in Jesus Christ as the Messiah. All society outside of the Christian belief system, including those in Jewish society who did not accept Jesus Christ, was to be viewed as corrupted. All, except for Christians, were destined for damnation.

The idea of being *Chosen* was essential for the survival of the Christian communities. It enabled them to face up to the harsh conditions under which they had to practice their new religion. It therefore became one of the most important concepts on which Paul would build his Church. The concept was not new. It was one that had grown out of the early Hebrew experience and essentially for the same reasons. As we have seen in this book, it was introduced early on in the Torah going back as far as the story of Jacob and Esau. The messianic message from Jesus Christ, like the Torah message from Moses, was an exclusive message. It was available for everyone to hear, but offered no hope of salvation to those who did not accept it. For those who did not, there was only estrangement from the one true GOD. As with Esau, GOD would turn His back on them. In fact, as we see in one of the last books of the Hebrew Bible, in Malachi, he would *hate* them. It was an idea that continues to exist today with varying degrees of conviction in Judaism, Christianity, and Islam

Today, Christian evangelical fundamentalists view the outside world as Paul did. There is a parallel perception between Paul's view of Roman society and their view of 21st century society. The view of the depravity of all society outside of Christianity is much the same. Those outside the evangelical fundamentalist Christian communities are looked upon as being corrupted and therefore beyond salvation. All non-Christians are living in sin. There is no such thing as a *saved* person outside of the fundamentalist evangelical Christian community. Those outside are viewed as the enemy and a constant threat to the stability of those inside the community. Worshipers are told not to associate with those outside of the community.

All of this is largely based on a literal belief in the letters of Paul as the word of GOD. It should be noted that this way of viewing the world is not only found in Christian evangelical fundamentalism. It is also found in the fundamentalism of Judaism and Islam.

The Special Place of Judaism in the Life of Paul

In Paul's letters we often see a certain schizophrenia that shows him trying, but not quite being able to break away from the strictures of the Jewish law. He had been a pharisaic Jew and then one day he was a Christian. Could he in fact totally give up his Jewish way of thinking and looking at the world around him?

The Torah and its interpretations presented a special problem for Paul. He was schooled in the law of the Torah. The Torah and its interpretive written arguments had a comment on every aspect of human behavior. Paul's inclination, based on his early life, was to outline for the early Christians every aspect of their behavior. As a pharisaic Jew schooled in the Torah this is what one would expect him to do, but he was now a Christian. He was a believer in the indwelling transforming power of Jesus Christ. Christianity was a religion that freed mankind from the weight of the law. A life of love, humility, truthfulness—the message of Jesus Christ—would miraculously free one from the weight of the law. This was the reasoning that Jesus had used when he challenged the teachings of Judaism. He did not come like the writers of the Midrash to redefine the law in broad and penetrating legal arguments.

We see that Paul was not able to escape totally from his past. The Christian code of conduct set forth by Paul was in a mind set like the Midrashim commentaries that grew out of the Law of Moses. Paul gave a Christian interpretation of that law just as the Rabbis had used the Midrash to give it their own Hebraic interpretation. Paul's rules were to be the basis for human conduct under the command of a Christian view of GOD.

Paul's Clash with the Jews—Subjugation Under the Law

The clash between Paul and the Jewish community over the relevance of the Mosaic Law became an immediate source of friction. Over the years, the law had been extended further and further into the every day lives of the Jewish people. It went so far as to define every moment of daily existence for the individual Jew. What observant Jews could wear, the times of worship, with whom they could socialize, how they could eat, how they could marry, etc. became all important for a *Torah Life*. Disobeying the law was an act of disobedience that displeased GOD. Jews either obeyed their GOD or did not. It was that simple. It was a law that on the one hand clearly had certain practical benefits for tribal and religious continuity, but on the other was built on a fear of the wrath of GOD in the minds of those who transgressed it, even in the slightest detail. This fear gave tremendous power to the Temple Priests and Rabbis, a power that they would not relinquish.

It was this call to obedience through fear of displeasing GOD that had prompted Jesus to criticize the Jewish approach to the law and brand it as a pagan religious practice built on fear, a practice that demeaned Jewish worshipers in the sight of their GOD. He also criticized the Jewish authorities themselves, who held fast to the law and its interpretations. He criticized the authorities for the power they had assumed over the people through their insistence on adherence to all of the religious practices that had grown out of the law.

Paul ran up against the same form of resistance among the Jewish Rabbis and Temple Priests, as had Jesus 20 years before, even though he made it clear—as had Jesus—that his criticism was not against the Mosaic Law itself. In fact, Paul was in the process of building much of his argument on the moral and ethical foundation of the Mosaic Torah Law and the Bible prophecies.

His criticisms essentially took two forms, one dealing with the many rules that had grown around the law and the other with the obvious fact that human beings no matter how hard they try can never truly live up to the law. This argument had far reaching implications. It tied directly into his understanding of the cosmic meaning of the life and death of Jesus Christ. Paul believed that the crucifixion of Jesus was a message to humankind from GOD, a message that GOD'S love is absolute. This was demonstrated through an ultimate sacrifice, the sacrifice of His son, Jesus. From that moment on, for Paul the sins of mankind—including his own—were forgiven. Mankind was released from the fear of GOD'S displeasure. The slate was wiped clean. Man—and woman— became as they were before the fall, a perfect creation made in the image of GOD.

For the Jews, since Adam, man had been in sin and he would remain that way until the coming of the Messiah. This would occur at the *end of times*. The Torah God was a judgmental and punishing God who would at that time decide Himself who would be forgiven and who would not. There was no forgiveness now. Forgiveness would have to wait. For them, Jesus of Nazareth was not the Messiah. With their Midrashim logic arguing against Jesus being the Messiah, the Jewish authorities turned their backs on Christianity.

The Polarity of His Thinking

The interpretation of the Mosaic Law by Jesus had extended it past how one acts to how one thinks. This presented a challenge to the Jews for whom adherence to the letter of the law had become all-important. Also, it brought the Christian view of religion to the polar opposite of Roman understanding of the statist functionality of religious worship and belief.

Whether by actions or thoughts or both, Paul's letter to the Romans describes a Roman society existing in opposition to the Mosaic Law. In Romans 1:24-32 and 2:1-8 we can see from his word description as to how he viewed this society:

Vileness of their own desires

Degradation of their bodies

Shameful passions

Unnatural intercourse

Males behave indecently with males

Wickedness

Mischief

Rapacity

Malice

Murder

Envy

Rivalry

Treachery

Malevolence

Scandal-mongers

Hateful to God

Insolent

Arrogant

Boastful

No loyalty to parents

David Anderson

> No conscience
>
> No fidelity to pledged word
>
> Without natural affection
>
> Without pity

The Roman Empire had no need for Christian values. It had developed a social-political system that had allowed it to become the most powerful political and military power on earth. It had done so without Judaism or Christianity. Its one objective, the expansion and the security of the empire, overshadowed all else. Its success was evident everywhere, in its engineering, its military superiority, its law, its language, its arts and culture. The sanctity of the individual was defined only in terms of the practical use of the individual to the system and loyalty to the system. Allegiance to the state was given the highest value. The Roman society had prospered without the foreign values that Paul espoused. If the behaviors that Paul described in his letters were evil, it was of no matter. They were acceptable as long as they did not interfere with the objectives of the state.

When we look at the 21st century, we see, as do many evangelical fundamentalist Christians—as well as Muslim utopian radicals like Osama bin Laden—many of the same behaviors, and this might lead us to the conclusion that they are not only correct in their observations, but that our future will be as bleak as that of the Roman Empire. Many Christians—as well as non-Christians—hold to this point of view. Roman society was a secular society built on the pursuit of power. Ours is too. It worshiped Gods of its own choosing. We do the same. The Romans were often at the mercy of misguided minds. We often find ourselves at the mercy of the same. Its citizens exercised little or no control over their sexual passions. We have the same dilemma.

Even though we can see these many parallels, as we look more deeply, we know that our society and the Roman society are not the same. Too much history has passed with all of its pain and suffering as well as its creativity and enlightenment, and this has affected the way we think and the way we act. We know more about ourselves than they did 2000 years ago. We know more about why we as human beings think and act the way we do. We see every individual as a mix of Paul's good and bad.

Today, we face complex social challenges in our lives, which demand ethical choices that are far different from those in Roman times. It is true that the words Paul used are an accurate description of a part of human behavior, but the words do not take into consideration the fact that we are a combination of all of them to varying degrees at any moment in time. As absolutes they are an imperfect measure of our responses to life.

We see that Paul's categories of evil are too narrowly defined. Some have the potential to cause far-reaching harm, while others only cause harm to the self, if at all. Certainly murder cannot be equal to arrogance and boastfulness. Some are far too broad in scope. Shameful passions cover far too wide a range of human activity.

Paul was living and writing in a different age and at his own level of consciousness. As brilliant as he was, his knowledge of the world would be considered shallow today. He had no idea as to what makes up matter or what lay beyond the earth and the Sun. Sensitivities to the feelings and emotions of others that we take for granted today were unknown in his time. He used the word *love* as defined by Jesus Christ, but a reading of his letters shows that he did not extend it beyond his flock, and often not even that far. He comes across as a man in battle against all who would not conform to his rules and his point of view. There is no love left for those outside of his point of view. Words and concepts familiar to us today would have drawn a confused blank stare. He never heard Stravinsky's *Rite of Spring* nor would he have understood it; and if he did, he would have considered it an expression of evil primordial sexual desire, not a work of high art examining in musical form the regeneration of life. Likewise, Mahler's expressionistic *Sixth Symphony*, if he had been able to understand it, would have been equally disturbing to him. He was incapable of understanding that the dark inner passions of human nature are not all evil but can be the wellspring from which powerful inner forces can be summoned to bring forth human energy moving us towards creativity.

We have found that few if any can reach the utopian purity that lay on the other side of all of the character faults that Paul describes. At the same time, we have found that some individuals have a purity within themselves that is close to GOD. And, we have found to our surprise that some of those who appear to be close to perfection turn out to be far from perfect.

We have found that many of those who have reached Paul's level of *goodness* have not in fact been Christians, nor had they any more than a passing familiarity with Paul's dictums. We see people throughout the world of all religions who have witnessed by their lives and are witnessing every day GOD'S love for others as seen in the life and death of Jesus Christ.

Today we know more about the GOD revealed by Jesus. We have had time to look deeply into Paul's and other writings about the life of Jesus and to debate what the writings really mean. We have been able to sort out Paul's ideas and to draw the line between those that were his own and those that were from Jesus. We have found new material from archaeological discoveries such as the The Gospel of Thomas that places the teachings of Jesus in a new light. So, today we do not have to take Paul's word for it. We can study Jesus uncolored by Paul's pharisaic bias. We can look beyond the vision that was Paul's. When we do, we find a combination of the pure brilliance of Paul's insights into the teachings of Jesus and the sometimes-extreme biases and emotional turmoil of Paul as a human being.

Another criticism is that Paul does not choose to see the *good* people in Roman Society. No doubt, there were individuals who performed heroic acts of love and mercy. Their actions were grounded on the sophisticated philosophical thought that had come from Greek culture. Some of this thought was in fact borrowed by later Christianity. For Paul, those who were not part of his community were the enemy regardless of how they thought. This is understandable given the way he was treated personally, but it shows he had fallen into the same trap that many Christians today—as well as Jews and Muslims—fall into when they are confronted by those who oppose them. They look at everyone else as unspiritual and evil. This is especially true of modern day Christians and Muslims who think this way and have the view that those who do not believe exactly as they do are overcome by evil. All non-believers for them are doomed to eternal damnation.

The fact is people pass through various stages in their lives. GOD'S work in the lives of people is always a work in progress. It is through the experiences of our lives that we move closer to or farther away from GOD. So, the line between good and evil is not static and cannot be so easily drawn as Paul—and many modern day Christians, Muslims and Jews—would like it to be.

When we acknowledge this, we see GOD as powerful and redemptive, working every moment in the life of every human being on the face of the earth. We see Him as a GOD ready to forgive each of us for any and all of those sins that Paul writes about in his letter to the Romans.

The Theory of His Possible Homosexuality

Paul was single all of his life. His letters showed him wrestling with powerful inner emotions and bodily desires. Some even showed a fondness for other males. Under the Jewish law of the time homosexuality was punished by ostracism and even death by stoning. Therefore, it has been suggested that his conversion to Christianity may have been prompted by the sudden realization

174

that as a result of the sacrificial death of Jesus there was no separation for him from GOD'S love.

To understand this we must understand the purpose of the crucifixion for Paul. Paul had written in his letter to the Corinthians that *Jesus died for our sins according to the scriptures*. This was in fact the earliest attempt we have to ascribe purpose to the act of crucifixion. It was not the message of the Torah as it was interpreted by Judaism in Paul's time. There was no hope for the homosexuals in Torah. Sin was sin. God's love was withheld for those who did not obey the law. Certain kinds of aberrant behavior such as homosexual behavior were contrary to Jewish law. Therefore, the theory goes that Paul saw this release of sin as expiation for his own evil proclivity.

This narrow interpretation today has led to a form of homophobia on the part of many evangelical Christians who believe in the inerrancy of every word of the Christian Old Testament, the same inerrancy of every word of the New Testament and the statements in both relating to sexual behavior. These Christians join the words homosexuality and fornication as being one and the same. A closer look, however, at the Letters of Paul shows that the issue can not be so narrowly defined.

The interpretation of the word *fornication* taken from the original Greek language used by Paul refers to any kind of impure thought towards either the same or the opposite sex. It is not, therefore, confined narrowly to homosexual relations. It covers any and all impure thought.

The question then becomes: What is an *impure thought*. By Christian definition it is any thought that does not project pure love towards another. The next question then to ask is a rhetorical one: Does this mean that this love can only be expressed male to female and female to male?

An even more accurate interpretation of the word *fornication* from Greek in the way that Paul used it relates in a broad sense to what may be called *spiritual fornication*, that is thinking in any impure way outside of the purity of thought. During Roman times when Paul was writing, this would have applied to all of the impure thoughts and actions that were a part of the life style in the pagan society. All sexual acts outside of marriage were among those thoughts and actions.

This whole issue raises serious questions about accepted sexual behavior of human beings in 21st century society. The biggest question for Christians is whether they should blindly accept the premise of Paul relating to sexual behavior—as well as the very limited and confusing references in the

Torah—in its most narrow sense or look outside for a broader definition based on the broader message of Jesus. We know that Paul was strongly influenced both by the teachings of the Torah, the social behavior of the Pagan society around him, and even possibly his own sexuality. Therefore, this is an issue that calls for a thorough examination separated from the presumed inerrancy of ancient scripture and the apparent homophobic response of Paul himself.

Many Christians today, particularly those in the gay and lesbian community, would define acceptable sexual behavior in the eyes of GOD in far different terms than Paul did. They would define it as any relationship that is *pure and good* between any two people regardless of their biological sex. Purity of thought then would not be measured by the laws of the Torah dealing with sexual behavior or even by linguistic interpretations of the Greek meaning of the English word *fornication*, but by the overriding message of Jesus telling us how we should think and act towards each other. The qualities that Jesus instructed us to apply such as love, devotion, fidelity, respect, honor, and understanding can also be taken to apply to homosexual and lesbian relationships.

This broader message of Jesus is a far cry from the homophobic rhetoric that one hears today from parts of the Christian community. (It is interesting to note that the issue is far less important today among Jews) Homophobia nevertheless remains a part of Judaism, Christianity, and Islam today. These three religions need to face this issue and reexamine what Jesus said about how we should unconditionally love each other. It is this unconditional love that should be defining Christians, Jews and Muslims, not homophobic hatred.

GOD'S Final Revelation of HIMSELF in Jesus Christ

Paul believed that Jesus Christ was GOD'S final revelation of HIMSELF to all of mankind. The act of the crucifixion was an expression of the depth of His love for all of humanity. It was an act that the Jews of the time would know well from their scriptures, a father's sacrifice of his son, the ultimate act of sacrifice. GOD chose the crucifixion because it was the worst and according to Hebrew and Roman tradition the most debasing way a human being could be put to death. It was the ultimate form of societal rejection. Therefore, according to Paul, for GOD it was the ultimate sacrifice of GOD HIMSELF. In the crucifixion, GOD metaphorically showed both the depth of His sorrow for the transgressions of each of us and the extent of His love toward each of us. HIS was a love beyond the dimensions of our understanding.

The Jews of the time could not comprehend this idea. Their God was a God in some distant place who stood in judgment of them. He was a God of harsh judgment. He had given them laws, even telling them how to live their daily lives down to the last detail. Who should be rewarded except the most religious? Why should He care about a person who could not live up to all of His laws? Why have the laws at all if He is a God who loves even those who do not obey them?

Most human beings in the world then, as well as many today, could not fathom the idea that GOD is all loving. For them, GOD had to be both loving and punishing. He had to be a God of judgment and a retributive God of justice. For the Jews, their Hebraic scriptures as well as their life experience pointed to this description of GOD. Punishment and reward had been a part of their history and their individual life experience. This was not Paul's understanding. He, as well as many of the early Christians, saw a new and different vision of the nature of GOD revealed in the life and death of Jesus Christ.

With his conversion on the road to Damascus, it was this total understanding that drove Paul afterwards every moment of his life. Paul saw the crucifixion of Jesus Christ as the ultimate expression of GOD'S love for all of humankind and the final act of reconciliation that the Jewish people had waited for over their history. And it was for Paul an act of reconciliation offered to everyone, not only to the Jews. It included every person on the earth, even himself, a former persecutor of Christians and a man who had wanted to live by the Torah Law, but was unable to do so. There was a caveat though. One had to "believe" in Jesus as the Christ.

A New Interpretation of Pauline Theology—The Faith Experience

For Christians today the question then becomes: What does it mean to "believe" in Jesus as the Christ? And, how is one's life then changed?

In 1983, Richard B. Hays, a doctoral student, wrote a thesis entitled *The Faith of Jesus Christ*. It concentrated on several verses from Paul's Letter to the Galatians. His book quickly drew national attention among scholars because it reinterpreted several words from the ancient Greek in which Paul wrote. The new interpretation challenged the accepted belief among many Christians today that one's belief in Jesus Christ as his or her personal savior is all that is necessary for personal salvation. To quote directly from Hayes:

"I have grown increasingly convinced that the struggles of the church in our time are a result of its losing touch with its own gospel story. We have gotten 'off message' and therefore lost our way in a culture that tells us many other stories about who we are and where our hope lies. In both the evangelical and liberal wings of Protestantism, there is too much emphasis on individual faith-experience and not enough grounding of our theological discourse in the story of Jesus Christ."

Quoting from the introductory remarks by Luke Timothy Johnson in the Introduction to the second edition:

"Hayes invites us to read Galatians (and perhaps Paul's other letters) as a discourse that clarifies and corrects…. Paul does believe that humans are put into a right relationship with GOD … <u>through the faith of Jesus</u>." (author's underline)

And

"…faith is clearly a quality or power by the human person Jesus, not something directed to Jesus by others."

The value of scholarly religious works such as the one written by Hayes is in its formal academic process. It is a process that allows the author to zero in on a single issue taken from scripture. The strength of this is that the scholar can ferret out the stated truth of that scripture. The shortcoming is that this forces the scholar to tie his or her conclusions into a former period. Scholars are restricted to an interpretation linguistically of what was. The question we must ask in the 21st century is: Can we go beyond this? Can we take from the past and add to it? Are there things in scripture we must reexamine in the light of a new world reality? This is what Hayes has done.

The brilliance of many of Paul's words is that they reveal a message that cannot be explained solely through scholarship. They give us a universal message that takes us beyond scripture. It is a message not only for Christians, but also for Jews, Muslims, and those of all other religious beliefs. It is a message given by GOD to all of humanity.

This universal message is contained in the metaphorical meaning of the life and death of Jesus. What Hayes points to is that this is a message to all

178

of humankind that says all of us are being called on to accept the same power directing and controlling our lives that Jesus had accepted in his own life. We are being asked to bring into our own lives the same faith in GOD that Jesus had. And, as we do this, we are to let GOD shape our very existence—as Jesus allowed GOD to shape his. Faith, therefore, is not to be in Jesus—a point that Hayes from his scholarship makes very clear—but in GOD. It is a faith that calls for the same absolute connection to GOD that Jesus had. It is a connection that demands all of us, not just a part.

Connecting With GOD Through Jesus Christ

The God of the Hebrew Bible was not one within the individual. He was elsewhere beyond the individual, looking down, judging and only occasionally intervening. The God of Islam, as He was described in the Koran six hundred years after Jesus, was also a distant God. He was modeled after the Torah God, except now He was an interventionist God, directing every aspect of the Muslim's life. This was not Paul's God of Christianity. The God of Paul's Christianity was an active indwelling God working in the lives of Christians every moment of their lives. He was not somewhere out there. For Paul's Christians He was a God in the here and now to be absorbed within, *working in the lives* of every Christian.

Over the course of history we have seen that this *working in the lives* has not come about that easily. This is the important point Hayes makes in his interpretation of Paul's Letter to the Galatians. According to Hayes, many Christians today have gotten *off message*. Although he does not discuss it in his book, we can see that over history many never got the message. They did not understand then and they do not understand now that it is not their belief in Jesus Christ that matters but the example of the faith of Jesus in GOD that matters. This is what gave Jesus another dimension. It gave him a oneness with GOD. The Hayes interpretation says that during his life on this earth, Jesus was at one with GOD through his faith.

Many Christians are quick to argue that their faith in Jesus Christ is what connects them to GOD. Jesus is the connecting link. They even pray "through Jesus Christ". We can see, according to Hayes, it is not that simple a formula. It is more than faith as a rhetorical statement in the literary sense of the word or faith in an historical fact. It is a connection with Jesus Christ that can only be made by being like him.

How can we be like him? Paul says by grounding our lives on the life of Jesus Christ as his life was presented to us. In other words, we must think as Jesus thought. Paul tells us we must radically change our very being.

Paul believed that only by living and thinking about our lives like Jesus lived and thought about his can we be connected to GOD. A way of looking at this is to picture a two-way electrical wire connecting each of us to GOD. The wire is made of a material with a high resistance, so that very little current can pass through. For the resistance to be lowered and the current to flow, it must be connected through Jesus Christ. But, that in itself as a rhetorical statement of belief, will not make it flow, as the resistance caused by our preoccupation with all of the things of this world—our worship of other Gods—prevents the current from flowing freely. Its conductivity is dependent on our living our lives as Jesus lived his, so that we can become like him. To the extent we become like him, the resistance is lowered and a stronger current will then flow back and forth through the wire. As we live closer to the life of Jesus, the current will flow more freely both ways between GOD and ourselves. As this takes place, we will find GOD'S presence in our lives.

Unfortunately, most of us live lives swallowed up by the secular society in which we live. Many of us worship false Gods. The society and the false Gods we worship define who and what we are. We don't define ourselves in the model of Jesus. We let other influences define us. This keeps us from being like Jesus. We can make shallow statements about believing, and we can go through the motions by giving the appearance that we believe, but this in itself will not connect us to GOD. It will not free up the resistance in the wire just described. We will not have GOD within.

With a broad-brush stroke, Paul marked for exclusion all those who were not Christians. To him it was a *You are either with us or against us* issue. For him, non-believers in Jesus as the Christ could not be connected to GOD. It was a technical impossibility. Just over two centuries later, when the image of Jesus as the Christ and the meaning of belief in him was finally and irrevocably defined for all time by the early Roman Church bishops, a preordained description of Jesus of Nazareth became the institutional belief of all Roman Catholic Christendom. This was carried over into Protestantism in the 16th century, and so exists today throughout all of orthodox Christianity.

In today's 21st century world the Pauline issues are four:

1) For Christians, is simply professing a belief in Jesus Christ all that is necessary, or is there more to it than that? If so, what?

2) Is the description of Jesus proclaimed by Roman Catholic Christendom the real Jesus?

3) If a Jew, Muslim, Hindu, Buddhist, or a person of any other faith intellectually rejects the person of Jesus Christ as the reflection of GOD within, will that person then be rejected by GOD? Will salvation then be denied? Will salvation be given only to those who rhetorically profess a belief in Jesus Christ?

4) Can a person reflect GOD within in some other way? In our enlightened 21st century secular society, is it possible that there are many individuals, not believing in Jesus as the Christ—even atheists and agnostics—who are nevertheless living out their lives as Jesus of Nazareth did?

Paul's interpretation of the life and death of Jesus Christ amounted to a redefinition of the Hebraic nature of GOD. Disagreements with Paul and criticism of him, particularly among Jews but also among many Christians, have to a large extent been colored by disagreements over history, Hellenistic influence, and Roman Catholic doctrinal interpretations of Paul's words. Such disagreements should be over Paul's understanding of the redefinition of the nature of GOD given by Jesus. This is where the debate should begin.

This issue raised by Paul is as contentious today as it was during his time. It is where the debate should be. It is not being debated. It should.

Paul's Insights into the Mind of GOD Absent the Torah

When Paul started writing his letters to the churches, the death of Jesus was still a recent memory in the minds of those who knew him. Paul personally knew many of those who had followed Jesus. Through them he had an intimate knowledge of the teaching of Jesus. In many ways some of his insights penetrate deeper into the life of Jesus than the later purported eyewitness writings in the Gospels.

As with all ancient Christian texts, when reading Paul's letters, it is necessary to separate what was most likely authentically from Jesus from those ideas that were from Paul, the fallible human being. We must also take into account the age in which he wrote. Certainly, Paul's writings about

181

wives being subject to their husbands and man being the head of the woman (Ephesians 5:22), as well as slaves obeying their masters (Ephesians 6:5) in today's world are rules of conduct that are out of place. They show a lack of understanding of the complexity of the dynamics of human relationships as we now observe them in the 21st century. It is hard to imagine that these and many other similar ideas that came from Paul are truly from Jesus. It is only by an utmost stretch of the imagination that ideas such as these can be taken as the inerrant WORD of GOD.

Critics would argue that it is these inconsistencies that brand the Apostle Paul an imperfect messenger of the WORD of GOD. They are wrong. His main message for those willing to overlook Paul as a vulnerable human being has little to do with Pauline codes of conduct or the exclusiveness of those who "believe" in Jesus.

His is a message that overall speaks to the reality of Jesus of Nazareth. Paul devoted his life trying to get others to understand this reality as he saw it. He believed this reality to be the most important reality for all of us. He made the mistake of too closely defining this reality according to his own life experience. This was his tragic error. As we have seen from the Thomas Gospel discovered at Nag Hammadi, all of what Paul said could not in fact be what Jesus meant or said. Much of later Christian Catholicism and Protestantism compounded the error by taking Paul at face value. Nevertheless, all thinking people should put their skepticism aside and study Paul for the clues as to what Jesus really said.

In many ways the following Reflections show a different side of Paul from that held by orthodox Christianity.

They challenge all of us, including skeptical Jews and Muslims, to take the writing of Paul far more seriously than has been the case in the past by warning that:

You must work out you own salvation in fear and trembling; for it is GOD who works in you, inspiring both the will and the deed, for his own chosen purpose.

(Philippians 2:12-13)

REFLECTION # 22

Darkness

In their wickedness they are stifling truth... For all that may be known about God...lies plain before our eyes...they have refused to honor him as God ... hence all their thinking has ended in futility, and their misguided minds are plunged into darkness.

(Romans 1:19-22)

If the truth about GOD lies plain before our eyes, why do we not see it? Why do we choose to ignore Him? What happens when we ignore Him?

When we look for God in the trail of the consequences of our actions, we see Him both by His presence and by His absence. His absence we call darkness.

We do not need religious scriptures to tell us about the consequences of this darkness. If we look at the history of mankind, we can see them everywhere. From the rise and fall of ancient Greece, to the rise and fall of ancient Rome, to the rise and fall of Nazi Germany, to the rise and fall of the Soviet Union, everywhere in history, past and present, we see the consequences for mankind when he has defied GOD.

GOD is not present where evil is. He turns His back on evil. He is not with us when we defy Him. We can see this not only in history, but also in our own lives by observing the self-destructiveness of ourselves and those others who defy GOD.

We can see His presence in the lives of those who are a testament to His love for us. We see Him in the lives of powerful and influential people from all societies and all religions. We see Him in the lives of many who are not well known. We see Him in the inventiveness of scientists whose discoveries improve the lives of people. We see Him in the artists who let us reach into the depths of our human imagination. We see Him in the unnoticed everyday actions of people who help other people.

We also see Him in our physical world, in the beauty of nature and all forms of life. We see Him in the mathematical precision mixed with chaos

David Anderson

that forms our universe. We see Him in the complexity of the creation of the human mind and its intelligence to understand His creation.

Paul's message taken in the context of today's 21ˢᵗ century world is telling us that all we need to know of GOD lies plain before our eyes. We only need to open our eyes to see Him. He is telling us that HIS revelation of both HIS nature as well as the consequences of our defiance of HIM is evident all around us, and only those who live in darkness do not see Him.

REFLECTION # 23

Judge Not

For in judging your fellow man you condemn yourself.

(Romans 2:1)

Why did Paul raise this point with his fellow Christians? Why did they need his advice? Why suddenly, after accepting Jesus Christ, did they turn to judgment of those around them? Why do we see this taking place today? Why did Paul use the strong word *condemn*?

The early Christians as they were looking at the evil around them, not just in Roman society but also among their fellow Christians, were passing judgment. It made them feel good about themselves. It made them feel superior. They felt that they had made the right choice by following the teachings of Jesus and therefore they had a right to pass judgment on all others.

Paul was telling them that it is not for them to judge others. He was echoing the message of Jesus not to judge others but to look inward at one's own sinfulness.

Jesus said that only GOD knows our inner thoughts. Only He knows the desires that drive us. Only He knows who and what we are. Nothing is hidden from Him. Even we ourselves can only see our inner selves dimly.

Paul's is a message that turns us inward and demands our searching to the depths of our souls for our own weaknesses. Jesus said it is only after we have done this that we will find the path to our own personal redemption and to GOD.

Judging ourselves opens us to the presence of GOD. Judging others closes off His presence. Looking outward prevents us from looking inward. It is easy to look for faults in others. It is a way to disguise our own faults. It takes courage to judge oneself. It takes no courage to judge others. Judging others closes off having to face ourselves and GOD.

It is the coward's way.

David Anderson

REFLECTION # 24

The Weight of the Law on All Religions

No human being can be justified in the sight of God for having kept the law; law brings only the consciousness of sin ... for all alike have sinned, ... all are justified by GOD'S free grace alone, ...man is justified by faith quite apart from success in keeping the law.

(Romans 3:20-28)

Does GOD judge us by our adherence to religious law, or are we judged by some other means?

Whether it is the Hebrew Bible, the Koran or any other written religious set of rules, the belief is always the same. Our laws are from GOD. They must be followed. The words are GOD'S truth. Disobeying means estrangement from GOD. Our laws are the only true ones. Yours are incomplete and untrue.

Why does religion need laws? Would religion be the same if the laws were eliminated? Would there be a need for priests, rabbis, mullahs, and shamans? Would there be a need for structured institutional religion as we know it? Religious institutions and their leaders would lose their relevance. No longer would they have control over their people. These spiritual leaders have always held tightly to their laws. They have enlarged them, adding their own interpretations. It has always been in their interest to hold fast to the law. It is their justification for what they do. It gives them power and makes them feel important and necessary. It gives them control over their people.

Jesus centered his teaching on a way of thinking that transcended the Mosaic Law. He revealed a new and revolutionary paradigm, one based on a loving and redemptive relationship between GOD and man. In defining this relationship he did not eliminate the law but rather he dismissed the need for adherence to it as a way for man to justify himself before GOD. He dismissed the need to obey it as a precondition for salvation. He said that man was created with an imperfect nature and can never live up to the law. He said that GOD is looking at man in another way.

The very core of ancient Hebrew belief was being challenged. Jesus had redrawn the lines between GOD, Man, and the Mosaic Law. He was challenging the Jews then as he is challenging all of mankind today as to how we are to view religious law in relation to individual salvation.

REFLECTION # 25

Through Jesus Christ?

If God be for us, who can be against us? ... neither death, nor life, nor angels, nor principalities, nor powers, nor things present, nor things to come, nor height, nor depth, nor any other creature, shall be able to separate us from the love of God, which is in Christ Jesus our Lord.

(Romans 8:31-39

Likewise recon ye also yourselves to be dead ... unto sin, but alive unto GOD through Jesus Christ our Lord.

(Romans 6:11)

When Paul uses the words *through Jesus Christ our Lord,* does he mean that the *love of GOD* is reserved only for Christians? Is he saying that all others in the world who are not Christians are separated from *the love of GOD?*

Paul's message was that one must believe in Jesus Christ to be saved. It was a message that gave hope to the small and isolated Christian communities that were being besieged on all sides by both Roman society and traditional Judaism. The Jews and the Romans were actively persecuting Christians. Paul was therefore able to make a clear distinction between Christianity and all else. For Paul, those who rejected Jesus as their Messiah and their Savior were doomed.

It was a black or white issue. There are those with Christ dwelling within and those without Christ. Only those with Christ dwelling within can be saved.

This is the belief among many Christians today, and in particular evangelical Christians, who look at themselves as the early Christians did. They see themselves living in a wicked and corrupt world besieged by non-believers. They take Paul's words as fact. They look upon themselves as separate from the rest, as having been elected and predestined by GOD for eternal grace.

Was this what Jesus meant? Many scholars today say he did not infer this separation and exclusivity.

The unique conditions of the time had a profound influence on Paul's theology. As we view the world in the 21st century, we must recognize this and

187

break away from a literal interpretation of Paul's words. We must center our thoughts on the broader message of Jesus, who often spoke in other terms.

To have *the love of GOD, which is in Christ Jesus our Lord,* as understood by many non evangelical Christians today, is to live life thinking and acting in the same way that Jesus himself thought and acted. It is walking his path and having his faith.

Paul was wrong when he confined salvation exclusively to his Christian community. *The love of GOD* extends to anyone who walks his path toward GOD, Christians and non-Christians alike.

For Christians, as well as all others, nothing can separate the love of GOD from those who direct their lives along His path. These are the words of Paul that should hold our attention: *shall be able to separate us from the love of God, which is in Christ Jesus our Lord.*

But, they must walk His path! The path is the one Jesus showed the world. This is the message of Jesus for the 21st century. It is the real meaning in a 21st century context of Paul's words.

It is the message of Jesus to those of all religions and those with none at all.

REFLECTION # 26

Presenting Yourself to God

Offer your very selves to him ... a living sacrifice .... Adapt yourselves no longer to the pattern of this present world, but let your minds be remade and your whole nature thus be transformed.

(Romans 12:1, 2)

When Paul refers to our *whole* nature. does he mean both our physical nature as well as our spiritual nature? How do we remake our physical nature?

Yes, he also means our physical nature. We are to turn over our physical bodies as well as our spiritual being.

To understand the significance of this statement we must look to the beginning of the Hebrew Bible and examine the early Jewish concept of purity and impurity. It was this concept that Jesus challenged.

A detailed account of the Hebrew pure and the impure is found in the book of Leviticus where there is a description of impure animals and physically diseased persons. The impure is described in terms of those afflicted by diseases such as ulcers, sores, and leprosy that are any sort of disorder, *either loathsome or infectious.*

The distinctions between the pure and the impure were further developed throughout Jewish history and expanded to include foods for consumption. The reason was always a practical one that even today we can understand. The objective was to preserve the health and well being of the Jewish tribal unit.

When Jesus appeared—as many as 1000 years after the book of Leviticus—he refuted the mindset of the Jews regarding their interpretations of the Mosaic Law and the rules of conduct that had grown around it. At the same time, He challenged their definition of purity by giving the physical body a spiritual dimension that saw both the physical and the spiritual as having equally high value in the eyes of GOD, regardless of visible outward impurities and flaws. He demonstrated this when he healed the sick. He touched and healed impure untouchables such as lepers. He befriended impure unclean individuals such as prostitutes.

189

David Anderson

The Apostle Paul did not look upon this definition of purity of the body in the same way as Jesus. He looked upon mankind as being burdened by earthly unclean physical/spiritual desires. He looked at the body as weak and sinful. He took on the Jewish view. He saw the body only as a vessel to contain the soul.

Paul departed from the teaching of Jesus. He reached back into the ancient Hebrew texts using the concept of diseased persons with physically unclean bodies as a metaphor for the physical/spiritual condition of mankind. In his letters he even related this to the weaknesses of his own body.

Paul and Jesus looked at the human condition through two different lenses. Paul was an imperfect human being as well as a product of his own pharisaic religious training. This was his lens.

Paul's reasoning was correct in that the transformation of one's nature cannot take place without the abandonment of all physical attachment to the profanity of this world. The whole person; the physical body with its weaknesses, as well as the soul, *our whole nature*, must be transformed.

Jesus did not see the body as unclean but along with the spirit as the perfect unflawed metaphysical creation of GOD. He saw in both the body and the spirit the possibility of perfection. The idea of one's *whole nature* being transformed both physically and spiritually by turning one's life over to GOD was at the center of his teachings.

The distinctions between the teachings of Paul and Jesus are subtle, but of great importance. As Christianity developed, it took on Paul's view. It should have stayed with the view of Jesus.

REFLECTION # 27

A GOD of Anger and Love
or
A GOD Only of Love

Love your neighbor as yourself; ... the whole law is summed up in love.

(Romans 12:10)

Love is patient; love is kind and envies no one. Love is never boastful; nor conceited, nor rude; never selfish, not quick to take offence. Love keeps no score of wrongs; does not gloat over another man's sins, but delights in the truth.

(I Corinthians 13:4-7)

Must we love all others, even those who hurt us, who reject us? Will GOD be angry with us, withhold His love from us if we don't? Or, will He continue to love us? Does GOD Love everyone?

Throughout human history, in the early stages of all religious thought, it was common for man to personify the nature of GOD in terms of his own human emotions. The interpretation of the nature of GOD in the Hebrew Bible was no exception. The God of the Hebrew Bible was not always a God of love. He was a God of both anger and love. He acted like we act. He rewarded for obedience and He punished for disobedience. This is still the belief of Judaism today. Events such as the Holocaust are studied by Hebrew scholars with the question: Was it just another historical event in the long history of Jewish persecution or was GOD angry with the Jewish people, and if so, why?

The Apostle Paul takes us one step beyond the Hebrew Bible and its characterization of the duality of GOD, but not as far as he should.

In his letters he writes about GOD'S love, but unlike Jesus he makes it apply only to those within the Christian communities. He does not extend the idea of GOD'S love to all people in the then Roman world, both Christian and non-Christian. He paints those outside of the Christian communities with a broad-brush stroke as sinful people without love, respect, fidelity, trust, and honor. He does not affirm that the love of GOD extends to them.

Jesus affirmed that GOD'S love is a love that extends towards all of mankind: Christians, Jews, pagans. It is not, as Paul would have it, limited to

191

any special predestined or elected group of people.

By the death of Jesus GOD showed the world that He is not a God of anger as was portrayed in the Hebrew Bible but a God of unconditional love. He is not a God who chooses to punish and to reward.

The true message of Christianity is this: In the crucifixion, GOD revealed to mankind His meaning of what it means to *love*. He pulled us through the limits of our self centered earthly barrier into His own heavenly dimension and revealed His love for all of us by sacrificing, for our redemption, the life of His earthly son, a sacrifice He knew, we in our human way of understanding things, could comprehend as the ultimate sacrifice. He told us we are to respond to each other with this same depth of love. He said we must not limit our love only to those we favor. He said you must *love your neighbor as yourself*. Then, to make sure we understood, He defined the word *neighbor* in the parable of the Good Samaritan.

Finally, to make sure again that we understood the universality of His love, He said in the dying words of Jesus; *forgive them for they know not what they do.*

REFLECTION # 28

The Meaning of the Resurrection

He appeared to Cephas, and afterwards to the twelve. Then he appeared to over five hundred of our brothers at once, most of whom are still alive, though some have died. Then, he appeared to James, and afterwards to all the apostles. In the end he even appeared to me.

(I Corinthians 15:5-9)

What is the importance of the resurrection? How much proof do we have that it happened? Would Christianity be the same had it not happened?

Unlike the many phenomena extending very far back in biblical history recorded in the Torah such as the Creation of the Garden of Eden, Moses receiving the Ten Commandments and the Exodus from Egypt; the resurrection of Jesus is a claim that was recorded by eye witnesses during a recent time period. Therefore, it has limited but some historical credibility. When The Apostle Paul wrote his letters, many of those who were followers of Jesus were still alive to tell the story. Paul himself had witnessed the presence of Jesus when he heard him speak as Paul was traveling on the road to Damascus.

Beyond this there is an observation that gives strong credence to the argument. The Christian movement had been crushed by the crucifixion. Their Messiah had been brutally executed. Both the Jewish and the Roman authorities had turned against the followers of Jesus. Suddenly, their leader no longer existed. Dispirited and doubtful, they must have been left to wonder whether their Messiah had been just another of the many spiritual leaders who were suddenly to appear and then disappear to be forgotten in time.

But just as suddenly they were elevated and energized and took on a resolve that for many led to total ostracism within their families and communities. The risks in fact were so great that some lost their lives. Clearly, something unexplainable in human terms occurred shortly after the death of Jesus.

2000 years later, the resurrection story as told in scripture is debated as to historical fact, and there is ample evidence to suggest that it can be disputed as to the details of how it happened.

Was Jesus after his crucifixion physically real or did he just exist within the minds of those who saw him? Was his body laid in a tomb? Did the entrance stone roll away? One thing is certain. The arguments that he was not crucified and that he did not reappear are very thin. The first writing about his death and resurrection came from those who had witnessed this event. After his crucifixion, these writings state that as many as 500 witnessed his presence. Several years later, although he did not appear in person, he spoke to the Apostle Paul, totally transforming Paul's life.

The meaning of the message, metaphor or other, coming from the crucifixion of Jesus is authentic. It was 2000 years ago and is today a direct challenge to the definition of the nature of GOD as found in Judaism and Islam.

GOD came to men and women incarnate in the person of Jesus Christ. He told them to be like I am in Him. His message from the resurrection was that if we live our lives by the example of the resurrected Jesus, we too when we die physically like Jesus, will be resurrected metaphysically into GOD'S eternal dimension.

REFLECTION # 29

Christood Within

We too have put our faith in Jesus Christ in order that we might be justified through this faith, and not through deeds dictated by law; … The life I now live is not my life, but the life that Christ lives in me.

(Galatians 2:15-20)

How does Jesus come to live in a person? When he does, what happens to the person? Why is the law of the Torah—and the Koran—then unnecessary?

Unlike Judaism and Islam, Christianity is a religion that calls not only for a belief in GOD, but for a belief that GOD enters and then is present within the person. The Eucharist (Last Supper) is a material expression of this. The body and blood—in the form of wine and bread—of Jesus Christ is taken into the supplicant, and as this occurs, miraculously GOD in the form of Jesus Christ, comes into the person. Paul is explaining that when this happens, the law—the rules for conduct laid out in the Torah—are no longer relevant, since GOD Himself becomes the underlying determinant of the person's behavior.

Belief in this calls for an act of supreme faith. Christians must not only believe in the existence of GOD, as do Jews and Muslims, but also that GOD can enter their very being in the here and now. The need to comply with the law then becomes irrelevant. As God is within, there is no need for law.

Acceptance of this mystery cannot be conditional. There must be a willingness to risk everything, even our lives. We have seen many examples of this, and its results, in many individuals throughout history. Human self centeredness is overcome by GOD'S presence within.

Paul is saying that GOD in the form of Jesus Christ lives in him and that this is the controlling force behind his behavior, not his obedience to the man made law of the Torah. Paul is elevating GOD above the Torah as both the motivator/determiner and the judge and jury of his—Paul's—life.

195

David Anderson

REFLECTION # 30

Evil

For the fight is not against human foes, but against cosmic powers, against the superhuman forces of evil...

(Ephesians 6:12)

Is there such a thing as evil? If so, exactly what is it? Does it have power over our lives? On a broader scale, is it the cause of man's inhumanity to man? Using us as its surrogate, has the power of evil set out to destroy our world? Will it succeed?

Evil can be defined as a destructive dehumanizing force that denigrates and destroys the very act of human existence.

History can be interpreted in these terms. It can be seen as a war between the positive forces of good and the destructive dehumanizing forces of evil. The tendency of man to be driven by the forces of evil can be seen as the causal factor behind much of the past as well as present human degradation and suffering in our world. From the wars of the Middle Ages, to the German Holocaust, to the tribal genocide in Africa, to the present day Jihadist inspired terrorist suicidal acts, there is ample proof of man's eagerness to be taken over by the forces of evil.

Evil may be taking a new form unknown in the Apostle Paul's time. Man is denigrating the natural environment in which he lives. Our human species in recent years has become a determinant part of the denigration of our interdependent ecosystem. There is a question as to whether the planet can continue to support the human species.

We have ample evidence that the superhuman forces of evil to which Paul refers are real and that they exist both inside and outside of each of us. We fool ourselves if we brush this all off as an archaic religious idea. We should take heed of Paul's warnings about the power of evil. Its power is truly cosmic.

REFLECTION # 31

Your Own Salvation

You must work out your own salvation in fear and trembling; for it is God who works in you, inspiring both the will and the deed, for his own chosen purpose.

(Philippians 2:12, 13)

How hard is it to be saved? How does GOD work in us? What must be our role?

Most religions work under a simple formula. GOD is up there. We are down here. If we follow a certain set of rules, GOD up there will favor us. Then we will be saved.

Jesus said it does not work that way. It is different. His God was not in some far distant place. He is in the here and now. He is in the life of each of us. He is a universal GOD who works in the lives of everyone, not only Christians.

As GOD works in our lives, individual salvation takes the form not of compliance to law or ritual but as an inner struggle to find GOD'S purpose for our lives. It is a struggle that takes place between negative forces such as hatred and jealousy and envy and the positive force of love.

As this struggle takes place, GOD is always present. He is there to work in the lives of those who invite Him in. But He is not there to take over the struggle. He is only there to help in the struggle. It is up to each of us alone to enter into the struggle and fight against the negative forces that pull us away from GOD.

Jesus challenged every person in this world to work out his and her own salvation. Paul warned that it must be *with fear and trembling*. Jesus said there are no worldly intermediaries. There are no rituals, pilgrimages, daily prayers, sacred rites or holy shrines that can guarantee salvation. What happens must come from within. What takes place must take place from within, in the depths of one's self.

It is in these depths that GOD waits to be called.

REFLECTION # 32

Pressing Forward

Forgetting what is behind me, and reaching out for what lies ahead, I press towards the goal …..

(Philippians 3:13, 14)

How can we forget our past and reach out for what lies ahead?

Many of the experiences from our past hold us back, drag us down, and sap the energy from us. These experiences work against us mentally as well as physically by slowly grinding us down and keeping us from moving forward. In the extreme, they can lead to severe depression and even suicide.

To move forward with creative energy, we know that we must remove many of the past experiences from the control that they have over us. But how do we? These experiences are inside of us, influencing every thought, every move. Some have been so traumatic that they seem to be etched in the granite of our minds. We move throughout life carrying the weight of them.

Is it possible to wipe the slate clean? Jesus said that it is. He gave us hope not just of atonement, but a way to remove the past and remove it forever. He gave us the possibility of renewal.

Through the mystical experience of rebirth, we are reborn into the presence of GOD. With this rebirth, we give our lives to GOD, and by doing so accept His purpose for our lives. Then, we can no longer be held back by our past. All that is left is the possibility to move forward into the future that GOD has prepared for us.

Into what are we reborn? We are reborn into the presence of GOD by accepting the life of Jesus as the template for how we think and act. We are reborn into a person like Jesus. This is the mystical experience he gave us.

In this mystical experience the board is wiped clean and we become new people. We are recreated in a new form. WE become a person living here in this world as well as in the other, a person in union with GOD.

REFLECTION # 33

Have No Anxiety

Have no anxiety, but in everything make your requests known to God in prayer .... Then the peace of God, which is beyond our utmost understanding, will keep guard over your hearts and thoughts.

(Philippians 4: 6, 7)

Why must we block out all feelings of anxiety about the future in order to have a peace that passes all understanding?

To have anxiety is to fear for the future. To fear for the future is to sense that at any moment we may lose control over the future.

Just before an earthquake, animals become nervous and hide wherever they can to find shelter. They feel a sense of loss of control over their environment.

Like animals, we humans experience the same nervousness whenever conditions around them change. One reason is that in the past we have experienced unexpected outcomes. These unexpected outcomes have come suddenly at unexpected moments in time and from unexpected directions.

At birth there is no fear of the unexpected. In youth there is little of this sense. That is why the young will take risks that older people won't; however, as the years wear on, with the first negative experience and then more as time passes, fear of the unexpected becomes stronger. Ultimately it takes the form of anxiety towards the expected outcome of impending death.

Unlike animals, humans use self-confidence as pretence to hide the fear of the unexpected that lies underneath in the subconscious. Behind the surface of our self-confidence, though, is always the underlying thought that the unexpected may be just around the corner.

Jesus said that we must remove from our subconscious every vestige of fear for the future. He said we must have faith that GOD will take over our future. He said that this faith cannot be conditional; it must be total. It must have the same depth and conviction that he referred to when he used the expression, *If you have faith....* And it must even include fear of death.

It is only after we have taken this final leap of faith that we can experience the peace to which Paul refers.

199

REFLECTION # 34

The Higher Realm versus the Earthly Realm

Were you not raised to life with Christ? ... Then ... Let your thoughts dwell on the higher realm, not on this earthly life.

(Colossians 3: 2, 3)

What is the higher realm to which Paul refers? What is the difference between the higher and the lower realm? How do we connect to the higher realm?

All religion from the beginning of human consciousness has been an attempt to connect to the higher realm. Priests, shamans, healers have always staked their authority on being able to make this connection.

Jesus, in the Gospel of Thomas found at Nag Hammadi, defined the higher realm in terms of a parallel reality, a reality that coexists on earth and in heaven. He spoke of a heaven that is *all around you.* He introduced the idea that man in his physical, earthly form can live at the same time in this higher realm. He said that the higher realm transcends the earthly one.

The *Higher Realm* for Judaism had over its religious history been defined in terms of a separation between the material world and the mystery of GOD above. The same understanding was presented by Mohammad in the Koran.

Jesus introduced the idea to the Jewish people that they could live in the earthly realm and in the higher realm—heaven—at the same time. He told them that Heaven and Earth exist in both space and time. It exists in all dimensions.

REFLECTION # 35

Fragmented Through the Prophets.

When in former times God spoke to our forefathers, He spoke in fragmentary and varied fashion through the prophets. But in this final age he has spoken to us in the son... The stamp of GOD'S very being.

(Hebrews 1: 1-3)

If as Paul states, the messages of the prophets were fragmented and varied, how much of them can we believe? Are there dangers in looking at every word of the Hebrew scripture as the inerrant word of GOD? Will we be misled?

Paul is attempting to explain away the contradictions between the teachings of Jesus and the words of Hebrew scripture.

During Jesus' ministry he questioned Judaism on two fronts; one the Hebraic law that had grown out of the Hebrew Bible over the centuries, and the other the inerrancy of parts of the Hebrew Bible itself.

The teaching of Jesus relating to the nature of GOD was in many respects a contradiction of the definition of the nature of the God of the Hebrew Bible. He changed the definition that had been accepted by Judaism.

The Hebrew Bible set out the foundation for a Christian theology, but only as Paul states, in fragmented and varied form.

Paul did not realize it at the time, but it would not stop with him. We must examine all scripture that is man made, including the Hebrew Bible, Christian New testament and Koran. It is all from the hand of man. Only then, as Paul was attempting to do, can we move into their greater meanings. It is all *in fragmented and varied fashion.* Every word must be critically examined.

XVII

Emily Dickinson and The Christian Evangelicals Pride and Judgment in the Bog

"How dreary—to be somebody!

How public—like a frog

To tell one's name—the livelong June

To an admiring Bog!"

 # 288

EMILY DICKINSON

1830–1886

We see today two opposing branches of thought in each of the three religions of Abraham. There is a branch that holds to centrist thought, which can be defined as liberal and secular, and then to the extreme right there is fundamentalist thought. Fundamentalist thought in all cases rests its belief on the inerrancy of scripture and the infallibility of the dogma that has grown out of it. It holds to the belief that this scripture is the WORD OF GOD. At the extreme end of this fundamentalist thought we have clerics such as Muslim Ayatollahs, evangelical Christians Ministers, Orthodox Roman Catholic and Anglican Bishops, and Orthodox Jewish Rabbis.

It is their extremist view of their scripture that controls their religious belief. The possibility of their scripture being flawed in any way is an impossibility. The scriptures they follow represent the truth frozen in time.

Even though their individual belief systems differ, religious fundamentalists from the three religions of Abraham have many things in common. They all have a fear of the pervading values that come from the world outside of them. They look at these values as a threat to their own value system. They also believe that those people outside of their belief system, because they do not believe in what they believe, are doomed for all eternity.

Terrorism is an outcome of religious fundamentalist thought, although not all fundamentalists can be defined as terrorists, in fact very few. This should not, however, take focus away from those fundamentalists who do not actively engage in violent acts of terror. Fundamentalism can harm without the use of terror. It can harm if it isolates and denigrates those who are not in agreement. It can harm if it hurts other people. It can harm if it drives away from mainstream religious belief those who, because of the high profile of religious fundamentalism, only see religion as an aberrant form of extremism.

Fundamentalists rely on their literal scriptural interpretations as a way to fill themselves with a sense of self-importance. Like the frogs in Emily Dickinson's imaginary *bog*, they cluster together as a mutation from centrist mainstream religious thought. Like her frogs, with rhetorical gusto their spokesmen inflate their throats to croak the message. As the chorus among the followers of these spokesmen grows louder, the self-confidence of the group grows stronger. Theirs is the only true version of the message. They all shout: We in our *bog* are right and you outside of our *bog* are wrong. You outside our *bog* are doomed. We are the *Chosen* ones. If only you would hear us and believe what we have to say, then we would have a perfect world.

Religious fundamentalists cannot understand that the power of GOD is at work in the lives of each and every human being on Planet Earth—for those who will accept Him—and not exclusively in their lives and those of their fellow believers in their *bog*. Fundamentalists like Jerry Falwell and Osama bin laden do not believe this. To do so would diminish their power over their fellow believers in their *bog*. This is their big mistake. They mistake their power for GOD's power.

History has shown us that whenever those with extreme religious views have claimed a direct line to GOD'S power, human suffering has been the result. The word of GOD coming from man is always imperfect, because man is imperfect. The messengers who wrote the ancient scriptures were not gods, they were mortal. They recorded what they thought they heard or what they imagined their prophets said, but it was in their own words using their own frame of reference. The message always came from the hand of man.

Almost all religious fundamentalists in order to legitimize their message make the claim that divine intervention held the hand that wrote their scriptures. They proclaim that the foundation of their belief is the WORD OF GOD. Moses met GOD. The Angel Gabriel as an agent of GOD met Muhammad. For Christianity, the Jesus Christ of Roman Catholicism did not meet GOD, he was GOD! The two big questions for all become: Who wrote down the message? Can the messenger be trusted? Even with Jesus

Christ as GOD Incarnate, he himself did not write his message down. He, like Moses before him and Muhammad after him never wrote a word. The message has always come from the hand of mortal messengers.

There are common themes such as love and compassion that run through all of the religions of Abraham, but no matter how loving and compassionate the scriptural foundation, there are always to be found individuals intent only on preserving power within their own individually defined and fashioned institutional matrix, one created for themselves in order to preserve their power. Over history we have ample evidence that these individuals conveniently fashion religious scripture and dogma to fit their own specific goals and objectives. Early on these were tribal objectives. Today they are national and geopolitical. These individuals have always managed to pull out what they want from scripture and discard what does not suit them, whether they are Jews, Christians or Muslims.

Even after the scriptures and the dogma are cast in stone, they continue to slant them towards their own purposes. They pull out only what they need in order to give purpose to their belief. In doing so they leave out what does not fit their immediate needs.

Most religions hold to the belief that GOD is transcendent and represents what we call Higher Values, which are values such as the love of one's fellow man and compassion. In the mainstream of the three religions of Abraham there is, however, another idea. It is the idea that GOD made man in His own image and that in doing so He gave man the ability to comprehend these Higher Values.

Progressive Christianity takes this one step farther. It claims that when GOD gave man a mind, He did not just give him gray matter, He gave him an opening into HIS own presence. At the same time He obligated men—and women— to expand their knowledge in order to understand HIS purposes. Christians believe that in order to do this, men and women must use their minds to explore the ultimate truths about both their own existence and GOD'S.

We cannot do this if we confine our beliefs to the inerrancy of scripture. The reason is that the search for GOD is an ongoing process that demands exploration of the historical sources used for the construction of scripture, and it demands an understanding of the period conditions when the scripture was written. It also demands an understanding of the underlying mythological and legendary influence on scripture and the application of this to the revelation brought out in scripture. And finally, it demands a matching of underlying scriptural meanings to present day events, including the advances of science, and the current human sociological condition. It is only then that man can begin to understand the revelation of the nature of GOD and his relationship to GOD brought out in the scriptures.

All of this is impossible for the religious fundamentalist.

The world today is awash with religious controversy and flux—as well as dynamism—and religious change is likely to intensify in the coming decades. In the secular pluralistic world of the 21st century we will always have people who live and think differently.

There are moral/ethical/religious questions that every fundamentalist Jew, Christian and Muslim must address:

- Are my ideas and actions, or my complacency, hurting other people?
- Are my ideas and actions helping other people?

This is where the examination of the inerrancy of scripture and those who rest their case on it should begin.

David Anderson

REFLECTION # 36

Jerry Falwell and Osama bin Laden look at America

"I really believe that the pagans, and the abortionists, and the feminists, and the gays and lesbians who are actively trying to make that an alternative lifestyle, the A.C.L.U., People for the American Way—all of them who have tried to secularize America—I point the finger in their face and say; You helped this (9/11) happen."

The Late Jerry Falwell
September 2001

"Indeed, I'm a trustworthy adviser to you. I invite you to the happiness of this world and the hereafter and to escape your dry, miserable, materialistic life that is without soul. I invite you to Islam, that calls to follow of the path of Allah alone who has no partners, the path which calls for justice and forbids oppression and crimes."

Osama bin Laden after 9/11 from a cave in Afghanistan.

Both Jerry Falwell and Osama bin Laden had determined that GOD was angry with secular American society.

Both said the act of the suicidal Muslims was directed by GOD.

What does this say about their view of GOD? Where is the merciful and redemptive GOD of Jesus?

Falwell's fundamentalist extremism provided him with a sense of meaning for the events of 9/11. He viewed America as a disoriented and immoral society, except for those following his own belief in the inerrancy of the words of the Christian Old and New Testaments. As GOD had punished the Nation of Israel when it went astray, GOD was now punishing America.

Osama bin Laden's view of the nation was the same. Allah was the God of the same ancient Hebrew biblical texts. Allah was punishing America.

Both turned a blind eye to the evolving revelation of the nature of GOD as recorded in the message of Jesus. By avoiding this view, both fell into the same trap.

Like the Muslim terrorists, the self-righteous thinking of Falwell and his followers led them into an exhilarating sense of superiority over so called *non-believers*.

Falwell and bin Laden and those who follow them were wrong. Theirs' is a divisive message grounded on exclusiveness and pride. In a broad brush stroke they vilify all people who do not subscribe to their own form of belief. This leaves no room for interpretation and the exploration of deeper meanings. The mindset of the two is the opposite of the message of openness, non judgment, humility, individual repentance and forgiveness defined by the life of Jesus.

It casts aside into eternal damnation the vast numbers of people of all religious faiths who are making our world move in the direction of universal love and respect for the dignity of all human beings.

David Anderson

REFLECTION # 37

"Frogs" Bogged Down in the Muck of the "Bog"

Q. What do you think of Americans?

A. I do not like them at all because they are not Muslims I don't like non Muslims.

Q. How did you feel when you heard of the World Trade Center attacks?

A. It must be what GOD wanted.

Khashall Muhammad Runs target practice in Quetta satelite town. Born 70 years ago in Kabul.

2001 A.D.

*****

If anyone comes to me and does not hate his father and mother, his wife and children, his brothers and sisters…yes, even his own life…he can not be my disciple.

(Luke 14:26)

The statement of Khashall Muhammad has the appearance of being straight forward. He doesn't like Americans. But there is much more to it. There are deeper emotions at play. The statement of Jesus gives us a clue.

What is it about our father, mother, wife, and children, even ourselves that Jesus says we must hate in order to be born again into the presence of GOD? What would Khasall Muhammad have to do to be *born again*? If he were, what then would happen to him? Would his tribe and family still accept him?

Khashall Muhammad has subsumed his identity into the tribal religion of the social unit to which he belongs. His statement most likely is the same as we would hear from any other of his family members as well as others in his community. The grounding for the ideas of his social/tribal unit is the Muslim religion. It is within this interaction of ideas that he has found his identity.

When Jesus was confronting his fellow Jews with the idea of each individual being born into a new relationship with a God of all humanity, he was addressing a tribal people with deep religious roots extending back into

208

the earliest history of the Jewish tribe. Their loyalty then, as to a great extent it is even today, was to the Jewish tribal unit and the Jewish God. The idea of an individual Jew relating directly to a God of non Jews unattached to Jewish tribal and religious identity was not understood any more than it would be for Khashall Muhammad. Hating your family and even yourself was a way for Jesus to say that to accept the universal God of his teaching, every part of one's loyalty must be abandoned.

Loyalty to the tribal unit can be even stronger than religious ties. Even today in the 21st century it is common among Jews for a secular Jew or even a completely agnostic Jew to consider himself a Jew. This thinking applies today to almost all tribal groups. In parts of the Muslim world where loyalty to tribe and family goes back in time and calls for a total loyalty, even to the point of self sacrifice, as is currently occurring with Muslim terrorists, religion then just becomes a support mechanism for tribal loyalty.

2000 years ago in a world dominated by tribal, family, and religious loyalty, Jesus described how we must change in order to walk the path to GOD'S presence in our lives. He said we must reject all attachments that subsume us to all other loyalties. He pointed to the binding and exclusive traditions and beliefs of the Jewish people that separated them from finding GOD. As he spoke to the Jewish people 2000 years ago, he speaks to the world today. He said we can only have one loyalty. He said we can only have one identity. He said we must abandon all other loyalties and identities. We must become at one with the one GOD who extends His love not just to our own tribal, family, or religious group, but to all of humankind.

REFLECTION # 38

The Gift of Redemption Outside the "Bog"

(Some Galileans were killed by Pilate's soldiers while coming to the temple to offer sacrifice. Jesus was asked if God was punishing them for some great sin)

(Jesus replied)

Do you think that these Galileans were worse sinners than all the other Galileans because they suffered this way? I tell you, no! But unless you repent, you too will perish.

(Jesus then referred to other Galileans who had died previously when a building collapsed)

Or those eighteen who died when the tower of Siloam fell on them—do you think they were more guilty than the others living in Jerusalem? I tell you, no! But unless you repent, you too will perish.

(Luke 13: 1-5)

Does GOD punish here on earth those who are sinful? Does He rain retribution on whole nations that have gone astray and are living in sin? Did those who died in the World Trade Towers on September 11 die because GOD was displeased with our society? Did the Jews who died in the Holocaust die because GOD was displeased with the Jewish people?

What is the nature of the GOD defined in the Gospel of Luke by Jesus? Is it different from the GOD as defined in the Hebrew Bible? What is Jesus telling us about the nature of GOD?

The Jewish God, Yahweh, was and is today the God of Israel under an exclusive covenantal relationship. From the very beginning of their tribal existence, Yahweh has been seen as their protector in every crisis. It is Yahweh alone who is invoked to give victory and deliverance. Earth, stars, and rivers come to His battle. The forces of nature bow to Him. When Israel is good, He rewards and when Israel strays, He punishes. The God of Israel is a jealous God. He can be wrathful and angry. He has the same emotions as humans. He calls for good works and insists that the Jewish people follow His law.

Jesus revealed a universal GOD of love for every person, no matter how sinful or unworthy. He offered GOD'S forgiveness for transgression of the law. He elevated repentance as the central condition above all else, including good works, as the key to GOD'S acceptance. He said that the covenant is not exclusive to the Nation of Israel.

His revelation of the redemptive nature of GOD powered the development of Christianity. It led to Paul's conversion and his burning desire to spread this message throughout the then known civilized world. When the Roman Catholic Church diverted its attention from this idea and emphasized good works and church doctrine, it found itself faced with the Protestant Reformation.

The exchange of ideas shown in Luke 13 illustrates this fundamental difference between Jews, Christians and Muslims in their understanding of the nature of GOD. It is a fundamental difference that even exists today within Christianity where a large number confine their thought to the inerrancy of Old Testament texts and the God described in those texts. For many Jews of the time and for a large part of the world's population today, Jesus fulfilled a messianic hope. He brought to mankind a new understanding of GOD'S nature. Jewish writers of the Hebrew Bible wrote about a God of anger and retribution. Jesus showed mankind a universal God of love and forgiveness. These were contradictions in the definition of the nature of the Jewish God. For this reason, the Jewish Temple Priests and Pharisees rejected Jesus.

In the quotation above, those who questioned Jesus thought that GOD was punishing the Galileans. Hebrew scholars in the past would have interpreted it that way. Most Rabbis today would do the same. But, Jesus tells us that GOD does not cause buildings to fall or floods to occur as punishment for His people who have gone astray. Jesus turns us away from this kind of reasoning. Rather, he directs our attention to what is expected of each and every one of us by GOD. He says, *unless you repent, you too will all perish.*

His message penetrates our minds on a deep and personal level. It tells us that tragic events of this world are not from GOD nor is pain in our lives. All that matters is individual repentance.

☒

XVIII

Science, Evolution and the Hand of GOD

In the beginning God created the heaven and the earth

(Genesis 1:1)

Before I formed you in the womb I knew you for my own; before you were born, I consecrated you.

(Jeremiah 1:5)

"A legitimate conflict between science and religion cannot exist…. Science without religion is lame, religion without science is blind."

(Albert Einstein 1941)

Three and a half billion years ago as the surface of what we now call our earth began to cool, a highly complex DNA molecule emerged in its primordial oceans. In that molecule was the first set of instructions for human life. Over time as mutations altered and added instructions, the molecule became more and more complex. Today all human beings share this same DNA molecule. Only the most infinitesimal differences exist between any two molecules and therefore only infinitesimal differences exist between any two human beings. This original DNA molecule along with its mutations has connected every human being through human history including Abraham, Moses, David, Buddha, Jesus of Nazareth and Muhammad, to name just a few. The life of each shared the same original genetic instructions.

As millions of years passed, the information contained in the sequence of the molecule increased in complexity. Life as we know it was on the path of its evolutionary journey. It was not, however, a journey that would bring forth permanent lives fixed in time without an end. It brought forth lives that would only exist for brief moments in time. From the moment of conception to the moment of death, the duration of life was like a spark briefly shining in the night. However, by being able to replicate life through the miracle of the division of the DNA molecule into an almost perfect copy of itself, rebirth could continue to take place in like form through time. Without this

212

replication, our human species would not exist today. The possibility of its existence would have disappeared.

Our lives are like sparks of light in a vast cosmos blinking on, coming to life, and then blinking off in death. Each of us comes to life as a bundle of energy momentarily capturing the rays of light coming from our sun. Then we die and our bodies return to their inorganic lifeless composition. The light rays of our sun are converted into everything we need for sustenance. From the moment we are conceived in our mother's womb, our very existence is dependent on this energy. We feed off the organic matter produced by this energy all of our lives. Every apple, every pear, every piece of fish or meat is made possible by this energy.

Our physical bodies are no more than organic chemical factories under the control of our DNA, capturing the energy of our sun. At death this whole process comes to an abrupt halt—the chemical process that kept us alive stops. We, and the complex instructions in our DNA molecules that made us possible, break down and slowly disintegrate into the basic elements from which they came. In time there is no marker left that says who we were. Everything returns to the cosmos. We turn to *dust*.

The sun, which acts as our source of life, is surrounded by a solar system that is enveloped in vast reaches of space by total darkness. There are many solar systems like ours in our universe, which was brought into being over 13 billion years ago. There are great constellations of stars in vast reaches of space swirling like hurricanes. There are so many stars, possibly hundreds of billions, that we cannot comprehend the number. This space lying beyond us continues to expand into the darkness. The galaxies beyond ours continue to move away from us.

The possibility of a person's existence in this universe as a unique living thinking individual with his/her own inner spiritual identity defies all odds. From the moment of fertilization of a single egg through to the period of gestation, we develop an inner identity unlike any other. It is the *me* within the physical me. This identity emerged out of billions of years of mutation and replication of our DNA molecules, which was brought about in random moments of time as conception occurred between single sperms and single eggs.

Is our existence then just the result of a random selection of almost identical DNA? Are we just a momentary flash of energy in the seemingly endless space of the Universe? Do we cease to exist when the energy is spent and it is all over? Are we only a spark that gives light and then dies?

Or, is it possible that each of us is a unique form of creation that has

David Anderson

dimension beyond the one that we can scientifically measure by the observation of ourselves and our physical universe? Is it possible that the DNA molecular structure in each of us that evolved over billions of years through random selection has come into being as a unique creation in the mind of GOD, giving each of us the possibility during our brief period on this earth to be something beyond mere organic existence?

XIX

The Challenge for the Religions of Abraham in the 21st century and Beyond

Sometime in the dim past of human history, painters began the great painting. The first brush strokes were made. Cave walls suddenly became the backdrop for the deepest reaches of the human mind. The nature of God was being revealed.

At first this GOD was not as He later became, a God to be feared. He was not even a *He*. This GOD had no shape or form. This was a God with no gender or anthropomorphic identity. It was the GOD the cave painters had observed outside of the cave in the heavens and the earth filling everything with its greatness. Inside the cave and inside the minds of the painters and inside the minds of those who entered the cave with their torches to see the spectacle, this was a GOD of wonder, of awe.

Then, after tens of thousands of years, suddenly the brush strokes changed. A Hebrew tribe living in a barren desert looked at the canvas and reinterpreted the brush strokes from the past. A different view of God was revealed. He was now in human form and He had the same emotions as human beings. Also, He was now a God to be feared.

But the picture was not finished. Just as suddenly, fifteen hundred years later, the canvas changed again. A young man from Nazareth appeared reinterpreting the nature of the Hebrew God. He had no quarrel with the way his ancestors had defined the human predicament as a struggle between good and evil, but he did not agree with the way they had defined GOD'S view of man in relation to that predicament. So, he added new brush strokes to both the painting in the cave and to the Hebrew painting. He said that GOD was more than a God of wonder and awe. He was a God of pure love. He said that man was made in the image of a GOD of pure love. He also said that GOD was not a God to be feared, nor was HE a punishing God with a nature like that of a human being.

Six hundred years later there was another change. An illiterate merchant named Muhammad claimed that he was receiving messages from the Angel

Gabriel defining the one and only true nature of GOD. His God was copied from the Hebrew painting, but in many ways He was an even more demanding and fearful God—and more punishing.

The Hebrew Bible and the Koran were each written to set out for all time the Word of GOD. What was written could never be changed until the end of time. For the followers of these two religions the picture was finished.

This was not the case for the early followers of Jesus. After his crucifixion, Christians embarked upon a quest to know Him. For them, the painting was not yet finished. Three hundred years of debate only opened up new questions about the person claimed to be the Messiah prophesied in the Hebrew Scriptures, who He really was and what He really said. To settle the issues once and for all, a canon of writings was set out by the bishops of the newly formed Universal Christian (Catholic) Church. In a compromise these bishops decided to include in the Canon both the Hebrew picture of God from the Hebrew Bible and the one painted by Jesus Christ in the New Testament even though in many ways they contradicted each other.

All writings outside of this canon of Old and New Testament writings and all ideas opposing the creeds built upon them were then declared heretical. All heretical writings were ordered destroyed. The bishops too wanted to finish the picture.

But, questions remained. Many believers in Jesus as the Christ saw GOD calling upon them to continue to search for GOD'S revelation. For them, the picture was not finished. In fact, for them parts of it as set out by the bishops were flawed. The picture painted by the bishops did not have a purity of structure and form like that of the early cave painting, but distortions that gave rise to opposing and dissident elements of structure and form.

In a great painting there can only be one underlying truth that is revealed by its underlying structure and form. For GOD'S Great Painting this is the revelation of HIMSELF to us as well as the revelation of HIS demand on us. This is the two-part meaning of HIS canvas. This is what mankind has been trying to paint from the beginning of his consciousness.

Like any great painting GOD'S Great Painting has a structure and form that demands all of our attention. To begin to understand it we are called upon to commit all of ourselves to it. It cannot be understood by superficial observation. It can only be understood deep in the quietness of the mind. There can be no distraction. Meaning is not found on the surface, only beneath the surface.

Making up the unifying structure and form of all great paintings are the brush strokes. These brush strokes showing the human understanding of God first appeared on cave walls as colors and forms. With the development of language and writing, they jumped off the walls of caves and onto scrolls and the pages of books. The picture of GOD and our relationship to Him was now being painted in words. Words were being used to express ideas.

As each of the three religions of Abraham rushed to finish the painting, the words, and their meanings, became frozen in time. These words were looked upon as being from GOD and without error. The paint was allowed to harden on the canvas. Other words like *heresy* and *blasphemy* became a part of the language. Those who did not agree with the religious authorities were *damned* for all eternity.

Among those who came to see the first cave paintings the feeling of awe soon turned into another kind of feeling. The figures on the cave walls took on a power of their own. They became objects of belief. This switch from idea to object was not only confined to the earliest periods of human consciousness.

For Christianity the words from the scrolls and books that had expressed the original ideas became objects of belief. A religion that began with only two hieroglyphic icons, the cross and the fish, became a religion of majestic cathedrals lined with statuary, frightening demons rising out of an inferno, a human-like Sistine Chapel God of ferocious power, angels with wings, relics and mummified saints. Iconic images depicting the word meanings of Christian scriptures that began as ideas of belief had turned into a proliferation of objects of belief. It was easier to look at the original Christ images as objects of belief than to search inward for the ideas they had at one time represented.

But, for some Christians the picture nevertheless continued to change. The objects that had lost their meaning were cast aside. GOD cannot be hidden behind a facade. HE calls on us to go to the other side and search for HIS revelation. Discoveries in the present often contradict assumptions from the past. New assumptions replace old ones.

In a great painting one brush stroke is laid upon another, and in the chiaroscuro of the colors and tones, as errors are covered over, a new texture and shade emerges along with a new visual truth. The errors are hidden, never to be seen again. One true unifying artistic creation emerges. This has not been the case with the scriptures found in the Hebrew Bible or the Christian record of the life of Jesus or the Muslim Koran. For most of those who follow these religions, the words remain inerrant, frozen in time. Over the course of history, only the brave have come forward to challenge them.

The first stroke was made by the hand of the cave painter, not by the hand of GOD. Nor were the words creating what all three of the religions of Abraham defined as the Word of GOD made by the hand of GOD. The paints on the palette were always mans'. Some human beings claimed that GOD Himself was holding their hand and mixing the paints, but that was only their claim. What was interpreted to be the Word of GOD, and what passed for revelation was often no more than an expression of human wants, desires, emotions, and biases, conditioned by a changing world. In the end, individual views and interpretations as well as expediency often won out. No one has ever seen GOD face-to-face.

It could have been close to being finished, but it wasn't. Today, thousands of years after the first mark on the cave wall, GOD'S Great Painting is seen as a confusion of errors, contradictions, and omissions. Those brush strokes made in error over the ages were not covered up. Some brush strokes contradict others. Some stand out like a cacophony of thought challenging others. Some are hardly decipherable. This confusion draws our attention away from the underlying structure and form of GOD'S Great Painting. We miss HIS message.

We humans are proud and do not like to cover up old ideas and admit that we were wrong. It is hard for us to unlearn what we so confidently thought we knew, to shed the protective cover that for so long has been our protection. We fear that if we change one brush stroke, all of the others too will have to be changed. Then, like a painter forced to wipe the canvas clean we will have to start all over again. It is easier for us to keep the picture as it was. The canvas that we have painted revealing the nature of our Creator therefore appears as a confusion of many irreconcilable brushstrokes, laid not one on top of the other but side by side.

We cannot capture the meaning of HIS message if we concentrate our vision on each and every word and the dogma that has grown out of them. Nor can we begin to see the overall beauty and meaning of HIS message. We are prevented from understanding the underlying structure and form. We miss HIS truth.

Today, GOD is calling upon each of us to find and to cover up the past errors in the religions that came from Abraham. HE is asking us to fill in the omissions. HE gave us the intelligence to do this. HE endowed us at the very beginning of our creation with the ability to discern. This ability was not reserved for any special person or group of people; priests or pastors, popes or bishops, rabbis or mullahs, it was given to each of us, to each and every human being.

We are called on by GOD to search into the depths of our minds and

218

to paint over the brushstrokes made in error and to replace them with new brushstrokes taken from a new mixture of colors laid on a clean palette, new and different brushstrokes that will illuminate GOD'S real meaning. HE calls upon each of us to correct and to add to the picture. HE calls on each of us to finish the painting ourselves.

For those willing to open their minds to HIS presence, HE is ready to help them finish HIS Great Painting, a painting revealing HIS True Being. Those who do not let HIM help miss the revelation that HE wants them to have. They miss seeing HIS presence in the underlying structure and form of HIS great canvas. They miss seeing the subtle images arising out of the chiaroscuro.

They only see a confusion of brush strokes on the surface of a canvas painted in ages past, a canvas which in fear of a judgmental God, Himself created by these ancient brushstrokes, they have blindly accepted.

They see a canvas in which they have taken no part

Summary

The GOD OF ALL CREATION is testing the three world religions that sprang from the blood of Abraham. All are failing the test. GOD is saying to each of them:

I am not the God you think you know

Each declares: "I am right, you are wrong, I know GOD, you don't." Each bases its declaration on dogmatic appendages to ancient texts written down in ages past by the hand of man and declared the inerrant WORD OF GOD. Taking on the role of GOD Himself, each stands in judgment of the others. Each has created its own vision of GOD.

Christian Evangelists use their literal interpretation of New Testament texts to pass judgment on all those who do not profess a rhetorical belief in Jesus as the Christ. They see American society as perverted and adrift, overtaken by evil forces. They look forward to the end of the world as foretold in the Book of Revelation when GOD will destroy it; and they will then be separated from those who do not believe. The unbelievers destined for eternal damnation will include the likes of Gautama Buddha, Mohandas Gandhi and Dr. Jonas Salk, as well as those loving husbands and wives, fathers and sons, and mothers and daughters who perished in the World Trade Center Towers but were not professed *believers* in Jesus Christ. They refuse to acknowledge that GOD may be looking at each of us in a different way, with only the first clues to a deeper meaning as to our relationship with Him coming from scripture. They confine their inerrant view of Jesus to the fragments of scripture authorized by the Roman Church that were written down by the early Christian writers of the New Testament decades after his crucifixion.

Conservative and Orthodox Jews turn a blind eye to the message of Jesus, considering him irrelevant, even after having witnessed his transforming power as it challenged an inhumane pagan world of 2000 years ago and turned it into the 21st century enlightened western society in which we now live. They continue to worship the distant all-knowing, judgmental, powerful, fearful, inscrutable ancient God of their Torah, holding fast to their tribal insular religion, refusing to acknowledge a Christian God of love and a far broader covenant extending not only to their own Jewish people but to all of humankind.

Zionists declare the soil of Israel as having been given by Yahweh Himself to the self-proclaimed Nation of Israel and shed their blood for this cause. They stubbornly expand their territory, starting up settlements in Palestinian areas, believing it is their Judea, a land mandated to them by their God, knowing full well the universal Muslim hatred it is causing and the dangerous geopolitical forces it is unleashing. As the hatred intensifies, Israel turns its back on the teaching of Jesus to love even your enemies and as a national policy looks for its revenge for Palestinian atrocities to the biblical injunction from the Book of Leviticus:

Fracture for fracture, eye for eye, tooth for tooth, as he has caused disfigurement of a man, so shall it be done to him... For I am the Lord your God.

Muslims look at their Allah as a distant God of awe to be feared. They consider everyone outside of Islam as *infidel* and all Jewish and Christian scripture outside of the Koran to be *corrupted*. They say that only their Koran is the true Word of God. They look forward to an Islamic theocratic world under Islamic law. Brain washed by their mothers, fathers, and clerics into a euphoric religious frenzy, young Muslims use their bodies in ritual suicide to kill Jewish *infidels* in Israel by strapping on explosives filled with fragments of metal. They then blow themselves up, killing and maiming innocent bystanders, even those of their own belief, with the conviction that their suicide will transport them directly to the court of Allah where—for the young boys at least—there will be beautiful dark eyed virgins to greet them. This ritual suicide is now seen throughout the entire world. As the contagion of hatred spreads, fanatical Muslims from New York to Russia to Spain enter a Jihad against all non-Islamic nations, killing and maiming *unbelievers* by committing ritual acts of suicide, spurred on by the same dream of direct entry into eternal sexual paradise.

These are the extremists of the three religions and they have taken center stage. They preach that the only measure of certainty for eternal union with GOD is a blind belief in the inerrancy of their scriptures: the Torah for the Jews, The Old and New Testaments for the Christians, the Koran for the Muslims. They each consider themselves the only *elect* in the eyes of GOD with all others outside their own religious traditions, as well as inside who do not agree with them, destined for eternal pain and suffering. They drown out, even within their own traditions, any possibility for individual religious diversity by way of a liberal interpretation of scripture. They place their own fundamentalist stamp of approval on their own version of Christianity, Judaism and Islam for the entire world to see.

David Anderson

Is there a common thread of belief that runs through the three religions that can be studied as the underlying reason for all failing the test? When we study them closely, we see in each great truths with deeply positive meanings for humankind which certainly cannot be traced to the cause for failure. In the Christian New Testament the failing cannot be found in the Sermon on the Mount. In the Hebrew Bible it cannot be found in the Ten Commandments or the 23rd Psalm, which says: *The Lord is my shepherd, I shall not want.* It cannot be found in the rules of charity described in the Koran or the meaning of Ramadan.

But if we look more closely to the very beginning of the Torah, we see troubling signs. In Genesis after the thundering statement to Moses that *Thou shalt have no other Gods before me*, we see the heavy hand of a God who says:

He that smiteth a man, so that he die, shall be put to death.... He that stealeth a man and selleth him shall be put to death.... He that curseth his father and mother shall be put to death....

The rules continue to be laid down throughout the Hebrew Bible and over time become more and more demanding. Eventually there are over six hundred of them and they cover every aspect of the life of an observant Jew; from the *Tefillin* that one must wear on one's head to the making of *pilgrimages* to the Temple to the *uncleanliness* of *menstruous women* to the treatment of *lepers*.

The God of the Hebrew Bible over the course of Jewish history becomes a demanding God who asks for total obedience. He makes heavy demands on the individual Jew. In the Hebrew Bible and its interpretations He lays down rules that must be followed. When He says that you must *love* me, He implies that you must also obey me. Love and obedience join together as one. Their absence is expressed as fear, fear of a vengeful and vindictive God. If GOD is not obeyed, He becomes angry. Then, He punishes.

We see in the Hebrew Scriptures an all-powerful God whose anger is to be feared. In the 90th Psalm we read the words, *So we are brought to an end by the anger and silenced by the wrath... All our days go under the shadow of thy wrath... Who feels the power of thy anger, who feels thy wrath like those that fear thee?*

But, at the same time we see a God of compassion and of mercy. The twenty third Psalm says: *The Lord is my shepherd, I shall not want....* and *I will fear no evil, for thou are with me; thy rod and thy staff, they comfort me.*

Can these two sides to the nature of the Hebrew God be reconciled? How can we understand wrath and mercy at the same time? After the destruction of Jerusalem by the Babylonians, the prophet Jeremiah in his book of Lamentations struggles with this problem. He says that *the Lord had afflicted her (Israel) for the multitude of her transgressions* and that *He hath cut off in his fierce anger all the horn of Israel.* He says that God *has utterly rejected us; thou art very wroth against us.* Then he places GOD'S wrath in a personal dimension by saying that *God is surely against me.* Just as suddenly he changes the drift of the monologue and says: *Yet he will have compassion according to the multitude of his mercies.*

If GOD is *surely against* Jeremiah, how can He at the same time be *compassionate* and *merciful* toward him? How can GOD be a punishing God on the one hand and a merciful God on the other? Can He ever be pleased? How are we to know when in His *anger* He will come down and rain total destruction upon us? If it is because we have not pleased Him, how do we please Him? Is it by following all of the rules, or does He require more than that? Can we ever please Him enough?

The God that Jeremiah saw is the same as the God that Jews, Christians, and Muslims worship today, an incomprehensible schizophrenic God. This is the 21st century God of the Hebrew Bible, the Christian Old Testament—as well as parts of the New Testament—and the Koran. This is the God of many Jewish scholars who question whether GOD was punishing the Nation of Israel as a result of some form of disobedience by the horrible act of the Holocaust. This was the God of the late Jerry Falwell. He is the God of Kenneth Dobson and Pat Robertson and the other Christian Evangelicals who proclaimed that by the World Trade Center disaster God was punishing America for its wicked ways; just as He punished the Nation of Israel in ages past for its wicked ways. This is the God who permeates the consciousness of much of the world. It is the God whose worship today is patterning the behavior of many Jews, Christians, and Muslims towards each other. It is the God of Ariel Sharon, Yasser Arafat, Osama bin Laden—and American Presidents. It is the Torah God of the Hebrew Scriptures, the Koran and the Old Testament!

We must stop to ask ourselves the question: Are we worshiping a false image? Did this Hebraic definition of the nature of God come from the CREATOR OF OUR UNIVERSE or did it merely come from the hand of man? How much of His nature at the time it was defined was conditioned by the psyche of a tribal nation living in a barren desert surrounded by mortal enemies? Was this just another pagan God, pieced together by a desert tribe in search for a protector? Was the Nation of Israel only looking for a God who would assure its own survival? Why would the GOD of the Universe favor the Jewish tribe at the expense of their enemies? Why would He stand behind

David protecting him as he wantonly killed his enemies? The Psalms speak of vengeance and destruction of *my enemies*. How do we define the *enemy*? Is it possible that I could, at the same time, be their *enemy*? Should only I be protected? What of those who were destroyed? What of their loved ones? Did their lives have no meaning other than to be GOD'S sacrifice? Were they all irrelevant?

The idea that in GOD'S eyes everyone else is irrelevant remains strongly imbedded in our thought patterns to this day. For Jews this means all of those outside of their special covenantal relationship with GOD. For Christians it is those who do not *believe* in Jesus Christ. For Muslims it is all infidels. This is the underlying logic that justifies the thoughts and actions of religious extremists as well as the many millions who silently support them.

In the Hebrew Bible, we find a picture of a God who gradually grew out of the early Hebrew tribal experience and came into being as a reflection of the need for a God who could lead it through dangers as it developed into a religiously cohesive and unified nation. He was their protector from the dangers of living in a primitive world. He was their assurance of survival. Our Nations of the world face different challenges today. Should we look to the same kind of God? Can we rely on the same kind of God?

If the GOD OF ALL CREATION is testing the three world religions that sprung from the blood of Abraham, is this misunderstanding of His nature what is making them all fail the test? Can this failure be traced to this common view of GOD as expressed in the common source of all three religions, the Hebrew Bible? Can we find here the beginning of the answer to the riddle?

All religions, in their earliest stages, ascribe human qualities to their Gods. For the Jewish Tribes he took on the persona of a father. The Jewish nation was like a child looking up for protection to a father. In their scriptures he was even called "father." In the eyes of the young Nation of Israel, like a father he was protective but at the same time stern and disciplinary. Like a father he was seen as mighty and powerful, as vengeful, as capricious, as quick to anger, as judgmental, as unfathomable and as sometimes merciful. These were all human traits the Jewish people could understand as they gave shape and form to their God. And, as a father would do with a child, he made a covenant with them. Like a father, though, he remained the powerful figure in control of the covenant. If you do this, then I will reward you. If you disobey me, I will punish you. I will be the one to decide, not you.

As the early Jewish tribal society became more complex and as it developed into a nation, the nature of their God became more complex. It became a reflection of the experiences of their prophets, philosophers, and priests as they tried to reconcile the events of their daily existence with unknown and frightening forces beyond their comprehension. But their God remained essentially the same as he was from the very beginning; mighty and powerful, vengeful, capricious, quick to anger, judgmental, unfathomable, and only sometimes merciful. This was the God who filled the oral and then ultimately the written record of Hebrew existence. He became at first the God of the Oral Torah, then of the written Torah or Hebrew Bible, then the Christian Old Testament and then in the 7th century after Jesus, the Koran.

This was not the God of Jesus. The God of Jesus was more than sometimes merciful; He was always merciful. He was not vengeful. He was not capricious. He was not quick to anger. He did not punish. He said we punish ourselves when we turn our backs on Him, when we reject Him. He was however judgmental, but He made a clear distinction. He said we are not to judge nor even speculate how He is to judge; only He can judge. And, He was not unfathomable. His nature was shown in clear and certain terms by the life and death of Jesus.

It was this Hebrew concept of the nature of GOD, over 1500 years in the making, which Jesus of Nazareth challenged. But, it was not a concept easy to change. The Jews would not give up their concept of the nature of their God. He had become too much a part of their lives and their daily existence. To accept a God of a different nature would have meant changing the very foundation of their tribal culture. To change called for a totally different thought process. They would even have to give up their special covenantal relationship with their God. Nor could the change be made piece meal, it had to be total. One had to be *born again*. Jesus told them how far reaching the change would have to be when he said they would have to hate even their mothers and fathers in order to come to Him. He called for a complete break from the God of their tribal and personal identity.

As we have seen in this book, the early Christians too had a problem abandoning their image of the God of the Hebrew Bible. Even though they did become *born again* into this new vision of God presented by Jesus, they found it difficult to view differently the nature of the God they had believed in all of their lives. The reason for this was that they all had been devout Jews. Many, such as Paul and Peter, were intellectually gifted Jews. Others were common people. For all, before Jesus came into their lives, the God of the Hebrew Bible was the only God they had ever known. They were taught to believe that the words of their scriptures were inerrant, were from GOD Himself. At the same time these early Jewish Christians believed Jesus to be the Messiah foretold in their Hebrew scriptures. He was the fulfillment of those scriptures. In fact, for many of them it was those scriptures that gave Jesus validity. So they did what every society does when a new idea is introduced. They amalgamated the past concept of the Jewish God into the new concept given by Jesus.

But there were contradictions. How could they be reconciled? In time, an answer was found. After over 300 years of fierce debate and political maneuvering among Christians with differing interpretations of the meaning of the life of Jesus, the two concepts of the nature of GOD were incorporated into a formalized Roman Christian doctrine called The Trinity. The Jewish God and the Jesus God were incorporated as two separate Gods in a single Christian Trinitarian God (Father, Son and Holy Ghost); one God being the father God of the Old Testament—the Jewish Father God—the other God being the God as Jesus Christ—the Son of the Jewish Father God. But this did not entirely solve the problem. How could GOD be loving on the one hand and vengeful and capricious on the other? How could He be a merciful God on the one hand and a punishing God on the other? The debate goes on to this day. Over the years, the early Christian Church Fathers finally settled for an inscrutable God, one sometimes impossible to understand.

What does the Hebraic biblical concept of Yahweh, the Christian Trinitarian Old Testament concept of the Father, and the Koranic vision of Allah have to do with world conflict today? It has everything to do with it. This archaic concept of the nature of GOD is the motivating force behind the responses of those in the three religions towards fellow believers within their belief systems as well as non believers outside of them. Whether it is the eye for and eye retaliation of Israel, the world terrorism of Jihad against infidels, or the judgmental condemnation of homosexuals by evangelical Christianity, all can be traced to a personal identification with the archaic God of the Hebrew Bible.

This is not to say that the Hebrew Bible has not had a far-reaching and positive influence in our world. Its wisdom set the very foundation for the forward development of western society. It was the foundation for Christianity. It defined the human condition. It showed the predicament of man in the face of a perfect Creator. It pictured man as a creature quick to define evil but not always able to make the distinction between it and goodness.

What Jesus did was redefine the nature of the God of the Hebrew Bible. When Jesus would say: *The scripture of old says, but I say...*, it was a clarification of Hebrew scripture. He was pointing not just to the errors but also to the shades of gray. The God of Jesus was not in all aspects in conflict with the God of the Hebrew Bible. The conflict lay rather in the assertion by the

Jewish Temple Priests and the Pharisees of that time that the Hebrew Bible was inerrant, the laws must be followed to the letter and their interpretations were to be unquestioned.

We become like the God or Gods we worship. There is a dynamic motivating interaction that takes place. For those at the extremes of these three religions, it is the God of the Hebrew Bible who drives their thoughts and actions. The persona of this God they revere determines their behavior. For the others, those who are not the activists, it takes the form of silent agreement and compliance. If my God is vengeful, I can think vengeful thoughts and be vengeful. If my God is capricious, I can think capricious thoughts and be capricious. If my God is quick to anger, I can be angry and lash out with my anger. If my God is judgmental, I can think judgmental thoughts and be judgmental. If my God is unfathomable, I don't have to explain my actions, I too can be unfathomable. If my God is only sometimes merciful, I can withhold my love as I wish; I can be only sometimes merciful.

With Jesus the concept of the nature of GOD had changed. The final veil of the face of GOD had been lifted. But not all accepted it; not the Muslims, not the Jews, not even all of the Christians. Many Christians to this day have not abandoned the Hebrew God. Their bible studies center on the Old Testament. They consider the words of the Old Testament to be inerrant. Many others remain in the process of moving away from Him.

Western civilization broadly speaking has, however, moved away from this God. It has taken 2000 years to work through the last vestiges of a belief in a vengeful, unmerciful, powerful Old Testament God. For every St Francis of Assisi there was a Savonarola. But, the message of Jesus prevailed. The Father God of the Trinity became more like the Jesus God. Through all of the backsliding, the positive message of love and respect for human dignity still prevailed. It is the reason the western world moved forward. It is the reason we have an enlightened world today.

The Jews stayed with their Hebraic God until the enlightenment of the 19th Century in Europe when parts of Judaism began to integrate into Christian political and economic society. This movement has continued, particularly in the United States with the advent of Reformed Judaism. Under the influence of western European Liberalism, the Christian idea of social justice for all members of society in its broadest sense beyond the rabbinical community began to pull many Jews away from the enclosure of their rabbinical Orthodox biblical past and their definition of their Hebrew God. This movement continues. Many today have moved past their Christian brothers and sisters and hold to an even broader view of social justice. Many of these Jews are in effect teaching their Christian brothers and sisters how to love.

As we have seen in this book, this has not been the case with Islam. Over the course of the centuries it remained isolated and frozen in thought. There was no European Enlightenment. It remained calcified as to its understanding of the nature of the God taken by Muhammad from the Hebrew Scriptures.

For 1400 years, from the very beginning of Islam to the present day, this ancient religion remained frozen in time. Contact with the western world was limited As Islam spread outside of the European sphere of influence; the subjugation of those who did not convert to Islam was always a local affair. The cries of those persecuted Christians and Jews, as well as others as far away as India, living in the path of its conquests were not heard by the rest of the world. The brutal methods of warfare and subjugation remained largely unknown. Christianity and Judaism slowly disappeared from what is now called the Middle East. The Jewish Holy Land became Muslim Holy Land. Except for the brief—and failed—period of the Crusades, there was little interest on the part of Europe.

In recent history the first signs of conflict between Islam and the West came with the recognition of the State of Israel in 1948. From then on each year the reality of the meaning of Islamic belief for the West slowly began its penetration of western consciousness. Finally, by the enormity of its horror, the destruction of the World Trade Center Towers marked a turning point in world consciousness and an understanding of the dangers inherent in Islamic thinking. The non-Islamic world saw that fundamentalist Islamic extremism presents a serious danger to a pluralistic interdependent world that is moving quickly into the 21st century and beyond. Ironically it was the West's open and liberal view toward freedom of thought and freedom of religious belief that held it back from understanding this for so long—and continues to hold it back even today.

Islamic thought remains calcified in a 7th century mold. As long as the Koran is considered the word of GOD, Islam can not change. Islam can not shake itself from its beliefs, because the Koran prevents Muslims from seeing the world in any other way than the way that the Koran describes it. Islam sees the West as it did during its initial expansion when Muslim armies conquered infidels wherever they went, subjugating and slaughtering those who were in disagreement. The Davidic God of conquest remains its model. Islam today views the outside world in the same terms as it did 1400 years ago, as a world of pagan infidels. The thought patterns of Islam are the same as they were when the religion was formed. It thinks this way because its clerics have kept

Muslim thinking deterministically confined to their own vision of GOD as defined in the Koran. Through fear of eternal punishment, Muslims cannot think of any other kind of God.

More frightening is the fact that Muslim clerics world-wide in mosques and schools are teaching young Muslims that they have been given a mandate to repeat the Pagan, Christian, and Jewish conquests of the past and that Allah will favor them eternally if they devote their lives to this end.

The social and economic progress throughout the world that has been carved out over the past 2000 years by men and women bowing down to a different kind of God, the one revealed by Jesus, cannot be acknowledged. Muslims cannot admit that for 2000 years this new vision of GOD and not the one described by Muhammad in the Koran has been the great driving force behind world history leading to the advancement of human civilization. When Muhammad shut the door on the God revealed by Jesus, he isolated Islam into the singularity of the freightening side of ancient God described in the Hebrew Scriptures. All that is left now for Islam is to hate the infidel western world and resent it for the fruits of its new vision.

Beyond the human suffering that Islam has in the past and will inevitably in the future bring upon itself and others, there is a question as to whether Islamic intransigence really matters in a world moving as fast scientifically and socially as it is today. Those at the extremes always want to take control and often they do, but not for long. World history has shown that it is the peacemakers, the pragmatic problem solvers, and those with new constructive ideas that in the long run make the difference. These are the people who take the talents their Creator has given them and use them for His purposes. They are the ones who clean up the pieces, set the broken bones, put back together the broken lives and open the future, after the extremists have become exhausted. They are the true sons and daughters of GOD. And, they are from all faiths. They are Jews, Christians, Muslims, Buddhists, Hindus…. Some have no faith in any particular creedal belief at all. They are recognized by the good that they do.

There is little that Islam can do to change itself. This is because Muhammad built his theology on two tragic errors. The first was that the Koran in its entirety is the inerrant word of God and therefore cannot be changed. The other is that the God of the Koran was modeled after the Hebraic God of the Old Testament, and not the New. It is this Hebraic image of God that has given rise to the view of Muslims that all who are not with us are our enemies who must be conquered and changed. They are infidels who are living corrupt lives and are worshiping false Gods.

229

If Islam cannot move forward in its recognition of a different kind of God, can Judaism and Christianity? Can the angry, punishing God of the Torah and of triune Christianity be seen in another way? Can a broad metaphysical interpretive view of God as expressed in the life of Jesus, without the appendages of Roman Catholic and later then Protestant dogma, be acknowledged? The answer to these questions will determine the future of world history.

The future of Judaism, Christianity, and Islam as well as all other world religions lay in the validity of their perception of their God. There can only be one reality to our Creator. In time, whether that is one hundred years from now or ten thousand, the GOD that mankind looks to can be only the one GOD, the one Creator of all. As in the past, religions that do not reflect the will of the one Creator of all will perish.

In time the way human beings deal with each other as well as with the physical world around them must be a reflection of the will of that one Creator. If it is not, the human species will cease to be. Nothing is more important for the human species than to unravel the paradoxes of past religious belief and discover the will of that One Creator. There is only one nature to that Creator. We must not be held back by our perceptions of Gods constructed in ages past. We must not stop until we find GOD. Only HE and we working as one can define our future.

Man from the beginning of time has been in search for the nature of his Creator. This quest did not come to an end with the Koran or the Hebrew Bible or the authorized canon of the Christian New Testament. It will go on regardless of how much effort is made by those at the extremes to hold it back. Man has shown that by his very nature he is willing to leave the comfort of the past for the uncertainty of the future. Each of us has a right to leave this comfort and to question what has been written and said. The image of GOD is not something any Rabbi, Imam, Ayatollah, Pope, Priest, or Pastor can dictate.

These clerics have placed GOD out there in some other place and time at a distance so that we will not be able to find HIM. Jesus told Thomas in the gospel found at Nag Hammadi that GOD is not out there. HE is here all around us and within us. He is a part of me. I am a part of HIM. We, along with GOD, become the authors of our own existence.

Scientific discoveries in the 20th and 21st century have presented an additional challenge to the picture of the nature of the God presented in the Hebrew Bible. Quantum Mechanics has uncovered a new and different level of reality against which all religions must now be examined. These discoveries have shown us that we do not have physical form as we understand it. They have shown us that matter is not what we perceive it to be. We are nothing but energy. They have shown us that in our physical form we exist as energy in a multidimensional universe. The ultimate definition and source of this energy exists within this multi dimension.

These discoveries tell us what many have been telling us from the beginning of human consciousness; Vedic seers, Greek philosophers, Eastern mystics, Jesus of Nazareth; we are in the womb of GOD now, not at some future period of time and after some future judgment day, but now.

1000 Questions

As a guide for writing this book the author began by "framing" questions about Jewish, Christian and Muslim religious belief. Each dealt either directly or indirectly with the image of their God. Each explored how this image underlies and drives their behavior.

As the book was being written, the few hundred original questions grew. What follows is the current list as of this publication date. They now number well over 1000.

They were the "starting point" for the author's research and were written to question the validity of the God of Judaism, Christianity or Islam. They were also written to question the philosophical constructs that are used by atheists and agnostics trying to escape the Creator they deny; those people who declare there is no God, those who have no personal faith.

Following is a list of the questions that were "framed" by the author:

Absolution - Why did the early Roman Church design this concept? By confining the possibility of the remission of sin (Sacrament of Penance) exclusively through the office of the Roman Church, was this just a way for it to exercise and maintain control over the individual as well as group conscience of its members? How does this concept differ from the idea of personal responsibility to find God within—without the need for a Church—now revealed by The Gospel of Thomas found in 1945 at Nag Hammadi? Was this the reason the Roman Church would not include this Gospel in the New Testament Canon? To what extent does absolution open the path for the repetitive Christian— "Devil made me do it"—sinful behavior?

Abraham – Who was Abraham? Was Judaism formed in the desert outside of Egypt on its own or was it an outgrowth of Sumerian civilization? Is the story of Egyptian captivity true? Which Sumerian, as well as Egyptian myths and images were transposed? Which are as alive today as they were then? Are they destructive?

Adam - Given the differences between Judaism, Christianity and Islam, does it confuse our critical thinking about the three religions to call him the father of all three? How stark are the differences in these religions? What did

232

the story of his fall from grace tell us about the way Jews, Christians, and Muslims view self worth? What is the psychological effect of believing that we are sinful and cast off from GOD? What is the difference between this and the eastern religious idea of boundless Good?

Allah- In what ways was the Jewish Yahweh a template for the Muslim Allah? How much did Muhammad know about Yahweh? How much did he know about Christianity? What was the state of Judaism and Christianity at the time Muhammad was composing his Koran? From what sources did he receive his information? To what extent is the Koran Jewish; to what extent Christian?

Al-Qaida (Quaeda) - Is there any moral legitimacy to its Jihad? Can its evil be separated from any constructive anti secular arguments coming from its utopian dream? Is any part of its dream worth saving?

Angel

Gabriel – Did Muhammad hear Allah through the Angel Gabriel or was Muhammad only hearing voices within himself? What parts of the Koran appear to be from Muhammad as a fallible human being and what parts appear to be inspired by GOD? What kind of God was his Allah? Was He like the Jewish God or the God of Jesus Christ? Or, was he like some other God? Was he like a pagan God? Who and what was Allah?

Anthropomorphic - Were the Jews in Genesis deceived by the deceiver into constructing their Hebrew God after a stern, judgmental and protective anthropomorphic father God like man, like they themselves were, with knowledge of "good" and "evil"?

Anti-Semitism - The original Jewish response to the Jacob/Esau story was to believe that they as a Nation were "Chosen". Paul later adopted this idea of being "Chosen", but limited it to Christians. Today, many Christians think they are pre destined and "Chosen", and Jews in general still think they alone are "Chosen". Islam later adopted this concept for Muslims and interpreted it to mean "superior". Is this story the continuing foundational cause for anti-Semitism today? Are we deceiving ourselves to think that it only comes from second century bitter Pauline Christian feelings towards fellow Jews who would not accept Jesus as their Messiah?

Anthropology- Will the discoveries at Nag Hammadi chang world religious belief? What other discoveries are of significance?

Apocalypse - Is there a connection between this Abrahamic biblical belief and the environmental problems now coming from our disruption of the ecosystem? Why do biblical fundamentalists not care? Will the end of our species come about as a result of this?_

Apostle Paul - What was the impact of Pharisaic and Hellenistic influences on his thinking? How correct were his interpretations of the teachings of

233

David Anderson

Jesus? Could he have been homosexual and if he was, how could this have influenced his thinking? Could it have influenced his conversion? Could, as some suggest, the shame of Jewish homosexuality been the changing force?

Apostolic Fathers - Why wasn't Mary Magdalene included in the apostolic succession? Why were all of the women's movements crushed in the early church? Why did Christianity become a man's religion?

Apostolic Succession through Peter - Was it a only a doctrine designed to close off the early Christian debate? Are the words: *On this rock I will build my church* fact or fiction? Are they consistent with what Jesus would have said?

Archeological Discoveries - As the Nag Hammadi discovery and others begin to change interpretation of the the Old and New Testaments, why is religious belief not changing? Is this doing harm to our society? In what ways?

Aruis (fourth century Alexandrian Bishop) - Were his views really as "Gnostic" as Athanasius in 325 A.D. made them out to be? Was there a Roman political reason that Athanasius silenced him? What would Christianity be if Arius had not been silenced?

Assimilated Jews - Is this is a possibility or an oxymoron? Can a Jew be a Jew and also be a Christian? Would Roman Catholic creedal and other dogma and doctrine have to be discarded? What would have to be discarded? Why aren't Jewish scholars taking Jesus more seriously?

Athanasius (fourth century Bishop) - Did Constantine and Athanasius have a co dependent political agenda? If so, what was it? When will an unbiased study be done by the Roman Catholic Church?

Ayatollahs- Over the next century will their belief in the inerrancy of every word of the Koran prevent any meaningful accommodation of Islam with western secular democratic principles? Is the West fooling itself to think that Islam, like early Christianity, can in time mature and more importantly, does the world have time to wait? Are we headed for a bloody and final confrontation?

Baptists - In view of recent discoveries that question the inerrancy of parts of the Gospels, how long will it take before they are forced to re examine their literal interpretation of salvation passages such as John 3:16? During the Bush administration, were they a destructive force? In what ways are their beliefs contrary to the teachings of Jesus?

Biochemistry - How close are we emotionally to animals such as Dolphins, Apes and Elephants? Should we respect their feelings as we do our own? Do animals have souls? If not, why not?

Blood of Christ - Why is "blood" such a dominant Christian theme and not

234

a part of the eastern religions?

<u>Book of Genesis</u> - How much was borrowed from Sumerian myth, and how much is original? Was the Deceiver deceiving Eve when he defined the Torah God as a God having knowledge of both "good and evil"?

<u>Book of Records</u> - Christians believe in a Day of Judgment as does Islam. How can Christianity preach forgiveness while at the same time preaching about a Day of Judgment? Is God legalistic?

<u>Book of Revelation</u> - Why did the Roman Catholic Church insist on including it in the canon? Was John in his last years mad?

<u>Dan Brown</u> - Does the popularity of his cynical view of Christianity in the Da Vinci Code mark the beginning of a long lasting, self critical introspective Christian movement with the power of another Reformation

<u>Martin Buber</u> - What was holding him back from taking the next step and acknowledging the teaching of Jesus as the new Torah in place of the old? What holds back Jews today?

<u>Buddhism</u> - Could it have influenced Jesus as a young man? If so, from what source? In the teachings of Jesus, where does the thought of Buddha begin and where does it leave off?

<u>Joseph Campbell</u> - Without some form of inner guidance, what are the dangers of "Living by our Bliss"?

<u>Carbon Dating</u> - What is going on in the minds of the Creationists when they repudiate carbon dating and claim that this is all the work of the Devil? What do they mean by that?

<u>Lewis Carroll</u> - The metaphorical Humpty Dumpty (Dumpy) in Alice in Wonderland can not be put back together again. Can we? Can we be internally reborn?

<u>Deepak Chopra</u> - In *How To Know GOD*, is his characterization and criticism of the Hebrew Yahweh valid? Can we benefit from his eastern view?

<u>Chosen People</u> - What dangers to others go along with believing you are chosen?

<u>Christianity</u> - What are its major differences compared to Judaism and Islam? What are the similarities? With recent discoveries, will Christianity coalesce and then emerge in a new unified form or will it continue to splinter, and if it does, which core beliefs will prevail?

<u>Communism</u> - In what ways was the 19th and 20th century Jewish spiritual awakening a catalyst for the socialist movement and International Communism? Are the residual socialist elements left over today and accepted by the western world a product of the Torah, of Christianity, or of both?

Constantine (fourth century Roman Emperor) - Did he have other motives in becoming a Christian? If so, specifically what were they?

Covenant - Is it fiction? Was it self proclaimed and only to validate the Nation of Israel?

Larry Crabb - Does his Upper Room description in *The Safest Place on Earth* apply only to Christians? For those Christians who believe this, how solid is the foundation supporting their belief?

Creationism - Does this assume the parallel idea that GOD will also be the destroyer? Could belief in this lead to an extinction of the human species? Do recent studies on the role of intentionality indicate that this may be possible through man's "intention"?

Crucifixion - Based on recent historical biblical revisionism, how valid is each of the conflicting theories? How much of the movie, The Passion, is untrue? How much fiction?

Crusades - Did the crusaders have an historical claim to the Holy Land? Do the Jews today? Based on what logic? How far back should we let claims go? Who "owns" the Holy Land?

Darwin - What are the limits of his theory? Why has the creationist reaction been so violent? What does it say about those who hold fast to The Garden of Eden story in spite of all of its contradictions?

King David - Was he legend or reality?

Day of Yahweh - Why were Jews not able to understand Gnostic concept of judgment being in the here and now?

Desensitized World - Is there a way we as individuals can remove ourselves from it?

Emily Dickinson - Does an interpretation of # 288 accurately describe Jerry Falwell and his followers?

Discrimination of Women - As the Jewish, Christian and Muslim biblical origins are all essentially the same; what is the origin of their origin, and what does this say about the validity of the biblical passages that originated this attitude towards women?

DNA Molecule - Given the harsh environmental factors under which it had to exist, how could life have replicated itself from its beginning to now?

Kenneth Dobson - Beyond his façade of kindness, how judgmentally extremist are his personal views?

Eastern Religions - Did they have a significant influence on Jesus a young man?

Ebionites (first century) - Why were their writings destroyed? What would these tell us today about Jesus as the Jewish Messiah? What were the major differences between their beliefs and those established by the Roman church in the fourth century?

<u>Mesiter Eckhart</u> - As the early church turned its back on his view of Jesus then, is Catholic and Protestant fundamentalism doing the same today?

<u>Election</u> - How does the concept of Christian pre destination tie into the Jacob and Esau story?

<u>End of times</u> - How can the Hebraic religions use the word "end" with such certainty? Isn't this only a human construct? What if there was no beginning and will be no end? How then can they explain the Universe in which we live? Isn't this what is now being proven by modern science?

<u>Environment</u> - Is the Genesis story giving humans dominion over the earth and all creatures a flawed concept? Did the biblical injunction for man to "dominate" nature originate from a hedonistic desire to use it for his own selfish ends? Is this true today? Has belief in it allowed humans to embark on a form of evil not acknowledged in Genesis, that is the destruction of God's creation—nature— for his own selfish purposes. In modern terms can this be referred to as environmental terrorism? Will this Genesis belief lead to human extinction?

<u>End of times</u> - Will this orthodox Jewish, Christian and Islamic belief become reality, not by GOD'S intervention as believers predict, but by man as he alters and destroys the ecosystem? Are the real forces those of man's depraved "intentionality".

<u>Esau</u> - How can the story make sense? As Esau gave no cause, why did the Hebrew God nevertheless hate him? Why, for no reason, did this God love his brother Jacob? Does belief in this story remove believers from taking responsibility for their own thoughts and actions?

<u>Eucharist</u> - Does it take on new relevance in view of our knowledge of Quantum Mechanics?

<u>Euphoric Feeling</u> – Called "Religious Experience" How can we know when we are not being drawn in by false perceptions of GOD'S power into the self destructive forces of evil? How do we make the separation?

<u>European Social Democracy</u> - In our present-day industrial capitalist society was this in its humanist political application a real life synthesis of the teachings of Torah and Christ? When Soviet Communism fell, did the US "throw out the baby with the bath water"? Should the US now be building on this "liberal" framework? Is the New Orleans failure a living example?

<u>Eve, Her Creation and Temptation</u> - By making a woman secondary to man from the very beginning, this fueled the anti-feminism found in Judaism, Christianity and Islam. What does it say about the power other erroneous teachings of the Torah. How have these other erroneous teaching molding today's societal thinking?

David Anderson

<u>Evolution</u> - Has scientific theory today made the creationism position totally redundant, or does there remain some form of valid argument?
<u>Extinction of Human Species</u> - Are the scriptural apocalyptic prophesies from Judeo/Christian/ Islamic belief turning it into self-fulfilling prophesies?
<u>Eye for an eye</u> - Because this is their common religious belief, are both the Israelis and Palestinians being held under an archaic biblical spell?

<u>Jerry Falwell</u> - He said GOD was punishing America on 9/11. This is supported by Old Testament biblical passages. Are they all flawed? Is the Hebraic image of an angry God - Falwell's belief - , on which he bases his reasoning, flawed? Is his theology flawed?
<u>5th Gospel of Thomas</u> - Did it pre date the synoptic gospels and John? Will it re make the Christian World? Why do some scholars today still refuse to date its origins into the first century?
<u>Final Judgment Day</u> - Has this concept, which began as a way to give future hope in an ancient brutal world, for those who continue to believe in it today, turned into a form of religious vengeance towards non believers?
<u>Fornication</u> – Aren't we really just talking about those who are different physically? For many years Catholics believed left handed people were of the devil. In their homophobic furry, have Protestant fundamentalists missed the biblical meaning of fornication as it applies to aberrant thought? What is aberrant though? For example, is denying medical care to fifty million Americans aberrant thought?
<u>Robert Frost</u> - In his poem, *The Road Not Taken*, the traveler must make a choice. Can the power of GOD be present when making choices? As a determining factor, how relevant is the internalized image of the God or Gods we worship?
<u>Fundamentalism</u> - As knowledge rapidly expands, how long can those of the three religions of Abraham continue to hold on to a 5000 year old picture of GOD?

<u>Garden of Eden</u> - Given the pace of scientific discovery, how much longer can human beings continue to believe in a 5000 year old Sumerian myth?
<u>Gay Paul</u> - ? Is it possible that Paul was homosexual; and as a pharisaic Jew, that was the reason for his—and then the Roman Catholic Church and later Protestant—extreme position? Would a God of love not love all of those of every sexual orientation? Do ones' sexual feelings have any place at all in one's journey towards "oneness" with God? Is the judgmental rhetoric coming from the religious right in itself sinful? Should not religion open itself to 21st century scientific knowledge of natural biological and emotional sexual feelings?

Abraham Geiger - Did he move Judaism closer to or away from Christianity?

Mel Gibson - His movie depicts the depth of the love of GOD for all humanity through the suffering of Jesus. How does this square with the Roman Catholic Church Hebraic image of the father GOD in the three part Trinity? A sadistic father?

Gnosticism - By refuting the idea of gnosis - self discovery - did the early Roman Catholic Church miss the most important part of the message, the essential element, of the message of Jesus?

Gnostic Movement - Were there political reasons for the Roman Catholic Church using such a broad brush stroke to discredit it? If so, what were they? Did a more authentic Christianity give in to Rome? Did Christians end up with a Roman religion? Did Roman governance become the template? Has the world been paying a price ever since?

GOD -We subconsciously pattern our thoughts and behavior after the God or Gods we worship. What is holding back the political powers, the media, and academia from viewing world conflict and its solutions in terms of a discussion of the nature of the Gods of their religious belief? By hiding this debate, what dangers may we may face in the future?

Great Flood - Why would GOD, out of anger, destroy the life he had created?

Richard B Hayes - In his book, *The Faith of Jesus Christ*, does his revelation about being connected to GOD as opposed to having only a rhetorical belief in GOD give us an answer to the reasons for world conflict?

Heaven – The Pope today refers to heaven as being "up" and hell as being "down." In a multidimensional universe where there is no above or below, (Einstein's relativity) why does the biblical Heaven for the Abrahamic religions remain "up"?

Hebrew Bible - Why should those laws proven to be impractical in our modern world need to continue to be followed? i.e.pork

Hell - Is it no more than a separation from GOD, non-existence as if we never were? As a condition of eternal pain, what does this say about those who described it so?

Hellenism - Why do the Jews insist that the penetration of classical Greek thought into Christian thought by way of Paul was a bad thing? How much Hellenistic thought actually penetrated Judaism with the conquests of Alexander?

Heretic - In its zeal to crush heretics, did the early Roman Catholic Church at the same time crush emerging interpretations of Christs' teachings for which it and the world are paying the price today? Is this continuing to

239

take place throughout conservative and fundamentalist Christianity? What benefits can be derived from bringing back these discredited interpretations?

<u>Abraham Joshua Heschel</u> - Did he move Judaism closer to, or away from, Christianity?

<u>Holocaust</u> - As He often had done in history, was Yahweh punishing the Nation of Israel? If so, for what? Prior to the Holocaust, Judaism had in fact gone through one of the most enlightening periods in its history. If the Torah can give no explanation, what does this say about the validity of the Torah God?

<u>Homophobia</u> - Why does it exist in Judaism, Christianity and Islam and not in many other religions? Is it a form of self hatred?

<u>Holy Spirit</u> - Is this what Deepak Chopra is referring to when he talks about the human brain being a "junction point"?

<u>Humpty Dumpty</u> - (Dumpy) Unlike him, can we be "put back together again"? How then? Were we broken in the first place?

<u>Inerrancy of Scriptures</u> - What is the connection between this form of conviction and today's world conflict?

<u>Infidels</u> - Was the Koran's reference adopted from the idea of being "Chosen" as first presented in the Jacob/Esau Torah story?

<u>Inquisition</u> - Was its rational based on Old or New Testament references, or both?

<u>Irenaeus</u> (second century) - Why did he crush the feminist movement in Christianity? How long will it take for the Roman Catholic Church to admit that he was very wrong in this as well as in many of his statements about the heresy of early Christian ideas? How strong is his influence on Roman Catholic thought today?

<u>International Trade Union Movement</u> - Had it not grown out of 20th century Jewish thought, from where would it have come; Christianity?

<u>Intentionality</u> - Is there a determining force within ourselves that is stronger than anything we can understand?

<u>Islamic Fundamentalism</u> - How many Muslims are "Fundamentalists" in our understanding of the term? Is this the primary cause today of world conflict? What specific Koran references would support this? Which ones came from the Hebrew Bible?

<u>Islam</u> - Do any of its criticisms of secular western values have merit? Does its criticism of the Christian Trinitarian concept have merit? Which elements of the Koran have merit? Does its hatred stem from Allah being the same as Yahweh?

<u>Islam and Jesus</u> - How similar, how dissimilar, is Allah from the pre Nicene Jesus Christ? What are the parallels?

<u>Islamic Jihad</u> - Have there been the same Midrashim and/or Christian Biblical injunctions? What are they?

<u>Israel-Judea</u> - Who has first claim? Is it Israeli Holy Land or land expropriated from Muslims by way of the Balfour Declaration? Did Yahweh four thousand years ago give the land to the Jews—from the Nile River to the Euphrates including both the Sinai Peninsula and most of present day Syria? (Genesis 12:1-4 and 15:18) The Jews ruled this land only during the reigns of David and Solomon. The Muslims themselves were newcomers in the seventh century. Is this all worth a genocidal battle in the 21st? Are flaws in the religions of both the reason for all of the oncoming human tragedy? If so, what in specific terms are these flaws? How can we address them?

<u>Jacob</u> - He did not deserve any favor. Why then did GOD favor him? Does this story relieve us of responsibility for our thoughts and actions?

<u>Jacob and Esau</u> – In what ways has belief in this story been a curse on the West over the centuries?

<u>Jesus Christ God of</u> - How was the God of Jesus different from the God of the Jews?

<u>Jesus Christ Nag Hammadi</u> - Will the Nag Hammadi Library have over time an impact on a universal understanding of the real Jesus?

<u>Jesus Christ Lost Years</u> - Where was he for eighteen years?

<u>Jesus Christ Jewish Messiah</u> - On what biblical basis did the Jews disclaim Jesus of Nazareth?

<u>Jesus Seminar</u> - How much of accepted New Testament scripture is clearly unauthentic?

<u>Jews for Jesus</u> - Why don't they model themselves after the pre Nicene Ebionite Jesus? Why have they accepted the Christian evangelical form of Nicene Christianity?

<u>Jihad</u> - Can it be restrained without ending Muslim belief in the inerrancy of the Koran? Can its spell over all Muslims manifesting itself as a hatred of Jews, Christians and the secular West ever be broken? If so, how? Are there Muslims today willing to take the risk and come forward and defy this idea of purification, or will all Muslims universally be dragged down along with their radical brethren Jihadists?

<u>Gospel of John</u> - Was it only an honest expression by one second century Christian group of their understanding of what Jesus said? Why did it exclude other understandings? Where are its flaws?

<u>Judgment Day</u> - Fundamentalists can not see it as being among them in the present. They look to rewards at a future point in time. Why?

<u>Judaism</u> - Can Orthodox and Conservative Judaism have a purpose outside of the Synagogue over the coming millennia?

David Anderson

<u>Judeo/Christian Belief</u> - What does and doesn't it mean? What would Judeo/Christian/Islamic belief mean?

<u>Kingdom of GOD</u> - Did Jesus say it will come in the future or did he say it is here in the present? If he said the "present", what kind of immediate personal responsibility does it place on each human being?
<u>Koran</u> - Can it prevail over the millennia as the uncorrupted Word of GOD?
<u>Elizabeth Kubler-Ross</u> - Did she scientifically prove that there is an afterlife?

<u>Last Supper</u> - Is it only a metaphor for human beings being at one with GOD? Does it involve, in accordance with Roman Catholic belief, transubstantiation? Could science one day prove it to be both?
<u>Lesbianism</u> - Why was it not mentioned in the Hebrew Bible? Was it only because repressed lesbian Jewish women could express their feelings towards one another without the men being aware of it? Is it the same today? Also, does the same hold true for multi wife Muslim society? Does one's sexual orientation have any meaning in the (eye? mind?) of God? What was the pre Roman Catholic attitude of Jesus toward sexuality? How did the Judeo, Christian, Muslim attitude towards the body originate?
<u>Levitical Rabbinical Judaism</u> - Was it a positive or negative force for Judaism?
<u>Light Within</u> - Is it possible in religions other than Christianity?
<u>Henry Wadsworth Longfellow</u> - Where, in his *Mezzo Cammin*, is there hope?
<u>Gospel of Luke</u> - Which verses may not be from Jesus?
<u>Martin Luther</u> - Did his emphasis on "faith" - as opposed to "works" - open the first crack in the Roman Catholic Trinitarian Hebraic concept of GOD being judgmental and demanding?

<u>Marcion</u> (second century Bishop) - He declared that the God of Jesus Christ was not the God of the Hebrew Bible. He said there was a disjunction between the God of the Old and New Testaments. The Roman Catholic Church declared him a Heretic and destroyed all of his writings. Who was right? What were the implications for human behavior over the following centuries? What are they today?
<u>Mary Magdalene</u> -What was her relationship to Jesus? Should she have been recognized as an Apostle? In the lost Gospel of Mary why did Jesus kiss her? Was she excluded from the apostolic succession because she was a woman?
<u>Mecca</u> - How many ordinary Muslims in the US believe that one of their holy cities will become the future capital of a world Islamic Caliphate?

242

<u>Mesopotamian Area</u> - Beyond monotheism and the law, how were the Jews different? Eliminating the possibility of Divine Providence, what tribal/religious cohesive elements have allowed the Jews to survive? Is this the only reason they have survived? Are we seeing in the Israeli/Palestinian conflict two ancient tribes in conflict?

<u>Messiah</u> - Was Jesus the Jewish Messiah, the Messiah of the entire world, or both? Was early Hebraic biblical prophecy relevant to his universal purpose? Did the early Jewish believers simply construct their theology to prove to their fellow Jews that he was? Did Jesus exist outside of the Torah? Does he today? Should early Christianity have accepted him in this way? If it had, what would Christianity look like today?

<u>Messianic Age</u> - Is it already here?

<u>Metaphor</u> - Has much of organized religion missed the messages from the past by not seeing them as metaphor?

<u>Midrash</u> - Is it just a mind game, or more?

<u>Mohammad</u> - Was he not the messenger of GOD?

<u>Monotheism</u> - Why must GOD be a numeric "one"?

<u>Moore's Law</u> - As we turn ourselves into bio computers, will we lose our humanity? What are the religious implications if this is combined with mind altering drugs?

<u>Moral Majority</u> - Are some of their ideas immoral?

<u>Malcom Muggeridge</u> - Were his experiences living proof of another dimension?

<u>Mullahs</u> - Will they become an enduring impediment to the advancement of Islam?

<u>Muslim Brotherhood</u> - How long can its philosophy continue to prevail within Islam? Will it have multiple rebirths? Why does the American and Israeli strategy of "killing terrorists" only strengthen their resolve and encourage them to multiply?

<u>Muslims</u> - Do Muslims need Ayatollahs and Mullahs to tell them how to interpret the Koran?

<u>Nag Hammadi Discovery</u> - What value do the writings have towards an understanding of Jesus? What do they say about personal responsibility versus "I believe" rhetorical belief? Will they usher in a new form of metaphysical Christianity and serve as a bridge to mystical Judaism? Can they change the world?

<u>Nation of Islam</u> - Can it be split into Orthodox and secular?

<u>Nation of Israel</u> - Should American Jews be allowed to give their allegiance and support to a foreign nation, Israel? How much of the present danger of world terrorism in the United States has come from this foreign allegiance?

Are we seeing a repeat of the Hebrew 70 A.D. and 135 A.D. historical past being projected into the present and future?

<u>Neo Conservatives</u> - Their geopolitical philosophy dominated American foreign policy during the Bush era. Were its architects modeled it after an archaic Davidic view of the enemy? What are the implications? Does the Israeli conflict give us an example of what to expect in the future? What would be the view of Jesus? Would it work? If not, is there an entirely different approach that would?

<u>New Testament</u> - Can its exact words prevail over the millennia as the inerrant Word of GOD? What changes must take place?

<u>Council of Nicaea</u> - Why were Arius and other bishops excluded? What role did Constantine play?

<u>Nicene Creed</u> - How many Christians believe its words today?

<u>Noah</u> - Why would a God of unconditional love want to destroy the life he had created?

<u>Oceanic Feeling</u> - Many religions experience it. What are the dangers?

<u>Old Testament</u> - By accepting it in its entirety as the Word of GOD, does it give us a flawed theology?

<u>Oral Tradition</u> - What are the dangers of turning an oral tradition into a written one?

<u>Orthodoxy</u> - What, in specific terms, was the fourth century Roman Catholic definition?

<u>Elaine Pagels</u> - In *Beyond Belief*, she, as well as many other religious historians in their books, have opened the most direct challenge to Roman Catholic Orthodoxy in nineteen hundred years. Why has there been no response?

<u>Palestinian/Israeli conflict</u> - What religious changes, on the part of both Jews and Muslims, are needed to change attitudes and make it end?

<u>Particularity</u> - It was used to describe 20th century Jews. Were they "particular" then? Are they today?

<u>Island of Patmos</u> - What was the mental state of John as he lived out his life on the island? Was he delusional? Was The Revelation of John merely the product of an aging hallucinatory man?

<u>Passion</u> - Was the pain and blood of Jesus Christ necessary for human enlightenment? If "*The Passion*" is viewed metaphorically, does that make it understandable?

<u>Plato</u> - Has Judaism suffered or benefited by being largely able to insulate itself from Hellenistic thought?

<u>Pre Agricultural Civilization</u> - Did early humankind know something

about the world they lived in that we have forgotten and that, without our readopting it, will bring about our extinction?

Pre Agricultural Religions -What can they tell us about our own biblical inadequacies? Should we look to them for insights we have lost?

Predestination - How necessary was it for the Apostle Paul to co opt it from Hebrew scripture? Did he do it for expediency? How has the Nag Hammadi Library challenged the Pauline view?

Pre Emptive War - When American neo-conservatives designed this foreign policy concept, were subconscious Davidic biblical images at play? Was the image of the "enemy" the same as that held by David? What was the image of the "enemy" pronounced by Jesus? Can the neo-cons have it both ways? Can Christians have it both ways? How do they rationalize it? What are the beliefs of those who designed the policy? Was there a connection between their beliefs and their policies?

Prophesy - How much of biblical prophecy clearly came from man, how much may have come from GOD?

Protestant Reformation - Was it the last Christian groundswell? With the Nag Hammadi discovery will there be another?

Ptolemy (second century Christian Gnostic) - By insisting that resurrection is of the spirit not the flesh, is this idea, once rejected, now relevant given recent theoretical postulates of Quantum Mechanics?

Quantum Mechanics - Did Jesus of Nazareth intuitively sense the current observations being made relating to the nature of matter?

Sayyid Qutb - Did any part of his frustration over western non Islamic values have validity? If so, what were they? What parts of his frustration were caused by flaws in Islam itself? Why did he turn to hated and violence? What was the extent of his culpability for 9/11? How strong are his ideas today in the Muslim world? Are they continuing to spread? Has he become another Carl Marx? As with the Soviet ideology, will they evaporate, or will they gain steam?

Rabbinical Control of the Synagogue - Is this preventing Judaism from assuming its rightful role in the world?

Rabbinical Judaism - Why do Jews need Rabbis to tell them how to interpret Torah?

Religion - How important has the Hebraic anthropological image of a wrathful God been as a causal factor leading to aberrant war-like western human behavior?

Religious Fundamentalism - Is it the overriding negative geopolitical force in the world today?

<u>Pat Robertson</u> - Is he a saved Christian or a vicious judgmental demagogue? As a political force, is he a danger to society? If there is such a thing as evil, is he evil?

<u>Roman Catholic Church</u> - Why did the Bishops in the fourth century order all non-canonical texts destroyed? Will Roman Catholicism today re examine their actions? Can they? If they do not change, can Roman Catholicism survive through the next millennium?

<u>Roman Empire</u> - Did Constantine need Christianity more than it needed him?

<u>Eugen Rosenstock-Huessy</u> - Did he turn a blind eye on the purpose of the Synagogue?

<u>Franz Rosenzweig</u> - Why could he not become a Christian? Could he have become an Ebionite? What must a Jew give up to become a Christian?

<u>Savonarola</u> - Will Islam, too, in time rid itself of its Savonarolas' and become even tempered?

<u>Second Coming</u> - Why is there no need for a second coming of Jesus Christ?

<u>Sharia Law</u> -Will the world one day live under Sharia law? Are there elements of the law that have value?

<u>Schismatics</u> - Are they our new millennium liberators?

<u>Self-Discovery</u> - Wasn't this what Jesus was all about, not being told, but finding out for oneself - Gnosis?

<u>Sepphoris</u> – What was the religious/cultural state of this Roman town during the period of the "lost years" of Jesus?

<u>Sermon on the Mount</u> - Why did Jesus imply that we must reach the bottom before we can begin our climb to the top? What do we find at the bottom? Is this what the Gnostics were talking about?

<u>Sharia Law</u> - Can there ever be an accommodation with western legal concepts?

<u>Oskar Skarsaune</u> - Do all Jews remain in *The Shadow of the Temple*? Hasn't Reformed Judaism left the Temple over the last two centuries?

<u>Social Activism</u> - Was Jewish 20th century social activism a positive lasting force?

<u>Social Sciences</u> - In what ways is the gap between religion and science narrowing?

<u>Socrates</u> - How have Judaism, Christianity and Islam for so long insulated themselves from his method of inquiry? Why? What specific barriers have they put up to isolate themselves from other forms of thought? Is human civilization paying a price? What price?

<u>Soul</u> - How does each of the three Hebraic religions define it? How do

believers experience it? Do the eastern religions recognize it? How did Socrates define it? How does Chopra define it?

String Theory - Was this the other dimension to which Jesus referred? How did he describe Heaven? Does his description differ between The Gospel of Thomas and the others?

Subconscious - How deeply imbedded in the Western subconscious are the Hebraic biblical images of GOD?

Sumerian Mythology - How much did the Hebrew Bible rely on it?

Synagogue - What are the worship similarities between the Mosque and the Synagogue?

Talmud - How rigid is the power of this body of literature today, and how much room is there for future change?

Temple Sacrifices - Is the connection between Jesus as the "Lamb of GOD" and the temple sacrifices a valid one?

Mother Teresa - She showed her love to both Christians and to those who were not. By doing so, she was the prototype of the love Jesus talked about. Why can't Judaism and Islam show this same dimension of love outside of their own kind?

Terrorism - Where do its religious origins come from? What in religious belief makes it so?

Theist – Can one be a Christian without being a theist? Did Jesus challenge theism?

Gospel of Thomas - Why did the Roman Catholic Church exclude it from the Canon? Could this 5th Gospel change Christianity with the same force as the Protestant Reformation did?

Torah - In the face of a changing world, can it prevail over the millennia as the uncorrupted Word of GOD? How do the Jews rationalize its dark side as being from God?

Trinity - There were no biblical Old or New Testament origins. Why did the Roman Church devise this theory? Was it designed by the Roman Catholic Church only as an attempt to explain the incongruity between the New Testament son and the Old Testament father image of GOD?

Unified Theory - When we have it, will we find ourselves closer to GOD? Are attempts to find this theory bringing us closer to an understanding of God?

Unitarian Universalist Church - During the Revolutionary Period was it a legitimate reaction to institutionalized Christianity?

Unity - Does this church view of Jesus Christ have something to say to us?

David Anderson

<u>Vedic Verses</u> - Was Jesus in his youth influenced by them? Could he have heard of them from the Roman workers at Sepphoris? Was Rome exposed to eastern thought? In what ways? Are they meaningful today?

<u>Valentinus</u> (second century Christian Gnostic) - He said that people are saved first through an inner knowledge of who they really are. His ideas were rejected as inauthentic heresies. Will his idea of enlightened self responsibility through inner knowledge become the key for human survival over the coming millennia?

<u>Wahhabi Extremism</u> - Is it now a real threat to the House of Saud. Can 21st century Saudi Arabia survive it? What will become of Saudi Arabia if the Royal family is ousted? Will terrorists succeed in taking over? What would that mean for the west?

<u>Wahhabis</u> - Is Wahhabism at the core of the Islamic problem? Is there any possibility of change?

<u>World Islamic Terrorism</u> - Do Islamic origins of "vengeance" come to us by way of the Hebrew Bible? What elements of the Koran relating to vengeance are the same as the Torah? What elements relating to vengeance are different?

<u>West Bank Settlements</u> - Do the Israelis have an historical right to the land? Do they have a religious right? What are religious rights to land? Do American Indians have these rights?

<u>Walt Whitman</u> - How well does his, *A Noiseless Patient Spider*, describe the human condition?

<u>Wrath of GOD</u> - Did the Jews borrow this concept of wrath as they defined their God from their own life experiences?

<u>Yahweh</u> - In what ways is the Jewish definition of their God a direct contradiction of eastern thought? In what ways is He the same? How does He differ from the Christine Triune definition, the Muslim definition?

<u>Zionism</u> - In the '48 UN decision to grant Israel statehood, Secretary of State General George Marshall strongly opposed it for the two reasons we see coming true today; oil and Arab hostility. Had the '48 decision gone the other way, would this have changed the Muslim attitude towards the West? As a matter of principal, what right did the Palestinians have to Jerusalem? What right the Zionists? Looking at this more broadly, do people's rights to their Holy Ground supercede other rights? Muslims believe all of their land is Holy and that once they occupy land, it can never be returned. Can they change? How?

Comments on the Bibliography

This book deals with contemporary Jewish, Christian and Muslim religious issues which are important for an understanding of the underlying causes of present world conflict

The words and viewpoints are an interweaving of many ideas from many different sources. They have been brought together by the author as an expression of a single viewpoint, one considered as apostasy by many Jews, Christians and Muslims, nevertheless shared by many millions of people throughout the world. Because of this interweaving of ideas, their origins, with few exceptions, necessarily are presented without attribution to any one source. Therefore, this is not meant to be a PhD thesis with extensive footnotes. The reader is encouraged to refer to the bibliography below, read some of the books, articles and lecture outlines listed and then come to his or her own conclusions as to the truth about these vital issues of inquiry.

Wherever a quotation is used, the source is identified. All biblical quotations were taken either from the King James Bible or The New English Bible. Quotations from the Koran were taken from the electronic version of The Holy Qur'an, translated by M.H. Shakir and published by Tahrike Tarsile Qur'an, 1983, revised January 2000. The Lewis Carroll Humpty Dumpty (Dumpy) verse from *Alice in Wonderland* was taken from an Internet Lewis Carroll page. The poem from the dying Blackfoot Indian Chief is from an unknown source.

Direct quotations were only made where the author in his own judgment determined that they were from scholars considered to be among the most respected in their particular fields of study. In all cases the name of the scholar and book is given along with the quotation.

Although scholarship standards on religious matters in religious academic publications tend to be high, the author found that there exists a rigidity of belief grounded on the orthodoxy of the particular belief system. This is especially true of publications of scholars from religious colleges and universities. Contrarian voices within established religious belief systems are given very little freedom. As a result; Methodists extol Methodism; Catholics extol Catholicism; Baptists extol evangelical Baptist theology; Jews extol Judaism; Muslims extol Islam, etc. Religious writers are more likely to spend their energies supporting the view of their particular belief system than questioning it. For this reason, researching theological subjects necessitates trying to determine the bias in what one reads.

The author found that this is most pronounced in what can be called popular evangelical Christian literature, the largest segment of the American religious publishing industry today. A Christian fundamentalist bias to a large extent determines what is allowed into and what is excluded from this dominant segment of the publishing marketplace. The result is that Christianity is presented to the general public only in the most narrow Protestant fundamentalist sense.

There are, however, exceptions. Notable are the Christian academic authors published through The Westar Institute, most of whom have been contributors to *The Jesus Seminar*, a study group that set out to determine what Jesus most likely said and what he most likely did not say, Many academicians as fellows of Westar have been able on their own to break through this Christian publishing bias. It has not, however, been without some pain. There are examples of dismissals from Universities as well as the withholding of tenure. The author relied heavily on the writings of many of these authors.

The author found that in America there is a pervasive bias against religious criticism. This is not to say that there are no books critical of religion; but that these books are only published sporadically and generally are in atheistic form.

This bias also extends to the mass media. The author found that the level of commentator (talk show) understanding in the mass media is close to zero. There are no media personalities able to discuss religious subjects with any depth. A bias of *religious political correctness* combined with a lack of education beyond childhood prevents this. It is a pervasive bias against any kind of open constructive critical religious discussion contrary to predefined religious norms. Holding back any discussion is the fact that religious discussion in any depth is the "third rail" of social/political discourse. Though America prides itself on *freedom of religious expression*, there is in fact very little. Religion is looked upon as an internal private and personal matter not to be debated with anyone.

This religious political correctness does not exist equally in all religious discussion. For example, criticism of the religion of Islam is fair game. Criticism of Jewish religious practices and beliefs or the Torah (Hebrew Bible) or of Zionism is not. For any Jewish criticism, there is the constant risk of being labeled an anti-Semite. On the other hand, criticism of Roman Catholicism in recent years has become acceptable.

Although one might make the case that this filtering of religious discussion is "what the public wants", it would be naïve to dismiss the fact that the publishing industry and the media have a very strong influence on what is finally placed before the public and that the advertising industry has a strong influence on what reaches the public eye and what does not. Additionally, literary agents and publishing editors bring their own bias into the judgments they make. Each was influenced from their childhood by a Jewish, Christian or other cultural norms.

An example of this hidden bias became apparent with the pre publication advertising of one of the author's previous books which followed much the same theme as this one. Some of the most successful ads placed with a large internet advertiser speaking about similar violent images in the Torah and the Koran (As this book explains, to a large extent Muhammad used the Torah as a template for the Koran), after extremely successful responses by interested parties "clicking" into the bookstores, were suddenly stopped with the explanation that the advertiser had received complaints about the "potentially inflammatory nature of your ads." They explained that "users were offended by your ads, especially when displayed on general Keywords such as 'Koran' and 'Orthodox'".

The study of Judaism presented a special problem for the author. Almost all self criticism is internal and among and between Jewish scholars. It is in a sense hidden from the general public. The debate is very much confined to rabbinical academia and the Synagogue. Any cross-religious Christian or Hellenistic or eastern religious thought is absent and even denigrated. For example, within Judaism, any acknowledgement of the positive transforming power of Jesus on western civilization over the millennia is totally absent. The Hellenistic influence on the Apostle Paul for Jewish scholars is cause for a total disregard of his letters.

Evolution in Jewish thought is kept within Judaism as an internal affair. External philosophical ideas are looked upon with suspicion and arouse a defensive stand. This is not the case in the Christian dialogue which not only recognizes the importance of the Jewish historical experience—Christian Old Testament—but also to some extent over its history has been open to other influences such as the influence of Hellenistic (Greek philosophical) and even eastern religious thought. This is now being accelerated by the Westar kind of inquiry mentioned above.

David Anderson

Islam presented an even far greater problem for the author than did Judaism. In Islam there is the same kind of stubborn resistance to any kind of cross religious influence. It is a religion that exists with far greater restraint than Judaism, principally because it is more rigidly tied into the Koran and it has not been exposed to the secular western world as has Judaism. By definition it is a static religion. The Koran cannot be challenged. Islam by its very nature is not a religion of self-criticism either internally or externally. The penalty for criticism by a Muslim of the Koran under the Sharia law is death and eternal damnation.

Writers in the West generally view Islam as if it exists in a time warp out of the past. This view is largely filtered through the eyes of western intellectuals. Positive aspects of Islam are largely ignored. Criticisms of Islam coming from the West, therefore, generally are harsh. There is no end of books critical of Islam. The writer of this book faced these constraints when researching material relating to Islam. Hopefully, the book will stimulate an intellectual response from moderate Muslims in defense of their belief system. Islam has made a stand against western secularism. It is time for it to present a unified discourse through dialogue. In spite of the paucity of positive information, the author in his study of Islam came upon many aspects that, in his own judgment, could be viewed as being very beneficial for secular western society. Given the current world religious crisis and the association of world terrorism with Islamic belief, such a unified dialogue from Muslims would be constructive and beneficial for all.

Such a dialogue should first center on the identification of all references to hatred and violence not only in the Koran, but also in Jewish and Christian religious texts. This would mean standing up to fundamentalist extremism in all three religious beliefs. A quick study of the Koran by the author showed that there is sufficient ambiguity to enable Muslims to move forward with a pacifist view of violent behavior. The same applies to Christian and Jewish sacred texts and interpretive writings.

With regard to the sciences, the author found that in America the only perceptible bias is coming from evangelical Christianity based on its non-evolutionary creationist stand, a stand that neatly dovetails into its—and Orthodox Jews as well as all Muslims—apocalyptic argument saying that GOD will destroy the world. The scientific arguments in this book, which are opposed to this creationist and apocalyptic stand, are based on the biographical sources listed. The author carefully reviewed these sources and determined that they are considered by the scientific community to be current and authoritative.

252

Lectures at Florida Atlantic University are presented without outlines. This is not the case with those of The Teaching Company where extensive outlines and bibliographies are furnished. Lectures are available from The Teaching Company in audio and video form. They cover a broad range of religious thought presented by some of the most prominent academicians in their field. Reference is not made by footnote; however, individual lectures that were of particular importance in drawing conclusions are enumerated in the bibliography. The author encourages readers to listen to these lectures, read the source material and draw their own conclusions.

QuickVerse Essentials Version 6 (Parsons, 11640, Arbor St., Suite 201. Omaha, Nebraska 68144) was used extensively for calling up biblical scripture and researching both Orthodox Christian commentary as well as traditional scholarly commentary on biblical subject matter. Examples are the author's research done to answer questions such as: whether Jesus regarded himself as the Messiah, the origins of the Doctrine of the Trinity, how Jewish belief in future life developed, and the Jewish concept of the *Day of Yahweh*— day of judgment (Isaiah 2:12). For further study of these and other subjects, it is suggested that readers conduct their own similar research through sources such as QuickVerse.

Examining the role of religious belief as a cause of world conflict over two millennia without including an examination of the contraposition of the teachings of Jesus as the Christ is inescapable. The question of how those who followed Jesus caused conflict then and continue to do so now, becomes all-important since his was a ministry of peace and non-conflict. To find answers the author examined the conflict producing shortcomings of institutional Christianity against the backdrop of a questionable rightful or wrongful historical interpretation of the life and teachings of Jesus, as presented in the canon of writings authorized by the Roman Church in the fourth century A.D.

It is now an accepted fact—although largely confined to the world Christian non seminarian academic community—that the early Roman Catholic Church stifled the ideas of at least half of early Christianity and then, with Eusebius' 10 volume *Ecclesiastical History*, rewrote early Christian history to support their inclusive view of Jesus Christ. In doing so, the Church systematically defamed the leading intellectuals in all of the early opposition movements, calling them *Heretics*. They then ordered all of their writings destroyed. It has only been in recent years that the ideas of movements such as the Ebionites, Valentian Gnostics, and Marcionites, to name only a few, have been painstakingly rediscovered. This was well documented in Walter Bauer's

1934 ground breaking book entitled *Rechtgläubigkeit und ketzerei im altesten Christentum*; translated into English as *Orthodoxy and Heresy in Earliest Christianity* 1971—preceeded as far back as Hermannn Samuel Reimarus (1694-1768), the first critical scholar of the Gospels who observed that who Jesus said he was and what he did may have differed from the New Testament Roman Catholic and Protestant reports of what he said and did.

Many of these other views of Jesus show a radically different Christianity from the one that is commonly accepted today by mainline Protestants and Catholics. Since Bauer's book, scholarship in this area has been intense. That fact remains though that these revisionist ideas have not penetrated modern Christianity and certainly not general public thought. In fact, organized institutional Christianity—including the Roman Catholic Church—has to a large degree succeeded in fighting them tooth and nail. The chapter in this book on the naming of Benedict XVI as the new Pope bears this out.

In recent years, writers such as Elaine Pagles, Bishop Shelby Spong, and Robert Funk, all associates with *The Jesus Seminar*, the institute discussed above, have begun to chip away at the preconceived institutionalized ideas of who Jesus of Nazareth was and what he said, and more importantly what he did not say. This ground swell of deconstruction of the God (s) of Christianity—and by implication the God of Judaism and the God Islam—was begun by writers such as Dietrick Bonhoeffer, Paul Tillich and John Robinson, to name only a few. The audience, however, always remained small in relative terms. Only occasionally has a writer broken into the best seller lists, as Elaine Pagels did with her book, *Beyond Belief: The Secret Gospel of Thomas* published in 2003 by Random House.

The publishing power of evangelical Christianity (see above comments) and Roman Catholicism world wide remains enormous by comparison. Furthermore, Christian evangelical publishing houses in recent years have extended abroad into areas such as African and South America. Equally, the power of Jewish and Roman Catholic literature world wide has continued to remain a force against the introduction of self criticism and new religious ideas.

Unfortunately there is no central theatre where new religious ideas can come together as a singular form of worship, thereby enabling the "new" reconstructed Christian believer or modern Jew to congregate with others of his or her same mind. There is even some doubt among scholars as to whether a new form of worship is even possible, since by definition deconstruction of a theology does not necessarily imply there can be a reconstructing of a set of theological statements in its place. Two, protestant denominations do, however, come close to providing a solution. They are the Unity Church and the Universalist Unitarian Fellowship church. On the Jewish side there is Kabbalah and the liberal extremes of American Reformed Judaism. All of this presented a problem for the author in defining what is today loosely termed the "New Christianity" or the "New Judaism.". Christian scholars are presently using terms such as "Panentheism", "Non-Realism", and "Religious Naturalism", but none give the kind of definition that the general public can firmly hold on to.

It is the author's sense that we may be living in the very early stages of the formation of a new world religion that will encompass the thought of many historical world religions that will replace the orthodoxy of the three religions of Abraham. A vocabulary has yet to be invented for this, but it could. This book has attempted to capture a view of the form this new religion may take.

A writer with considerable influence on early Roman Catholicism and by default Reformation Protestant Christianity was the Apostle Paul. The author therefore included a study of his role in the formation of the early Church and an interpretation of what is now considered orthodox Christian belief. This included an examination of the outside influences on his life that may have affected his writings, influences to include his pharisaic background as well as his possible homosexuality.

Every attempt was made to leave open to readers their own conclusions as to who Jesus of Nazareth really was and whether in fact he has been over history and is today being rightly or wrongly interpreted. Whether it involves the Nag Hammadi Library findings or the letters of the Apostle Paul, it is left up to the reader to decide what is authentic and what is not.

The reader should know at this point that the author of this book is a Christian and that his bias is towards the Nag Hammadi Jesus. The ideas expressed therefore lean towards this reconstructed view of Jesus. Those who read the book will, however, agree that at least in their orthodox forms, the criticisms of Christianity are as numerous as those of Judaism and Islam. It is the author's hope that Jews and Muslims will look at their own religious beliefs in the same critical way he has looked at his.

The central idea that archaic religious beliefs in each of the traditions to one degree or another must bear much of the blame for present world conflict and ecological and social degradation is the overriding theme. It is the rigidity of all of our belief systems that goes to the core of the problem. The author has concluded in his own mind that the anthropomorphic judgmental, fearful, yet merciful father God found in the Torah, Hebrew Bible (Christian Old Testament), much of the Christian New Testament, and the Koran is the patterning force behind the behavior of those believing in this God. This underlying image manifests itself as a sub conscious force of enormous strength driving our aberrant behavior towards each other. We pattern our thoughts and behavior after the God or Gods we worship.

Are the three religions based on the Torah flawed? Is the Torah definition of God not GOD? Were the early Jews deceived? Have Christians and Muslims, who adopted this God/Image from the Torah also been deceived? The author asks the reader to decide these questions for him or her self. Each of us must face the question of whether his or her beliefs taken from the past are false or are true.

Unfortunately, the answers to these questions, because of the strong general bias in religious information referred to above, are not being broadly debated. They should be. As the 21ˢᵗ century moves forward, many of the answers can no longer wait.

For the human species, the moment of physical existence from its beginning to the present has been only a flicker in the infinite dimension of time and space. There is no guarantee that this human species will continue to exist even through the next millennia.

For each of us individually, our moment of physical existence is only a fraction in cosmic time. During this time on the planet earth, we are offered the possibility to become something beyond mere organic existence, something beyond our physical selves that can bring not just each of us individually, but the whole human species closer to GOD'S purpose for it here on this earth, closer to that dimension that is HIS. As this book forcefully argues, that GOD purpose is not to further a tragic apocalyptic end as many believers in the Abrahamic religions would have it. Only human beings lost in the paralysis of their fear of their Creator could think in these terms.

The author found little evidence that the organized Abrahamic religions of this world and their leaders are fully aware of the fragility of our planet and our dependency on a balanced ecosystem. To some degree religious academia is, but not organized religion.

Because they are patterning their thoughts and actions after Gods constructed in ages past, the leaders of the three religions that sprang from Abraham are being held back. Ignorance is holding them back. Pride is holding them back. The comfort of their intellect is holding them back. As a result, we are all suffering. Humanity is suffering. Planet Earth is suffering.

We must find the true GOD of our creation and pattern our thoughts and actions to be in oneness with that true GOD. This is the most important thing any of us can ever do in our lives. In his research to write this book, the author found that very few of those who profess their belief in the God of Judaism, Christianity, or Islam, and most notably those who hold religious and political power in the United States and abroad, have embarked on this search.

We, as an interdependent human civilization must find that true GOD. The writings and lectures noted in this bibliography have convinced the author that how we direct our lives towards that true GOD will determine not only what we as individuals can become during—and after—the lifetime of each but also what in time will become of our earth and our species.

Bibliography

Abdullah Al-Kadhi, Misheal. "Jesus Second Coming and Grace." http://www.sharif.org.uk/jesus4.htm.

Adler, Alfred. *Understanding Human Nature*. Greenwich, Connecticut: Fawcett Publications, 1927.

Aikman, David. "The Great Revival: Understanding Religious Fundamentalism." *New York Times*, August 4, 2003.

Albright, Madeleine. *The Mighty and The Almighty*. New York: HarperCollins, 2006

Angier, Natalie. "The Origin of Religions, From a Distinctly Darwinian View." *New York Times*, December 24, 2002.

Austin, Bill. *The Back of God*. Wheaton, Illinois: Tyndale House, 1980.

Barzun, Jacques. *From Dawn to Decadence, 500 Years of Western Cultural Life*. New York: Harper: Collins Publishers, 2000.

Bauer, Walter. *Orthodoxy and Heresy in Earliest Christianity*. Philadelphia: Fortress Press, 1971.

Bennett, James. "Crossing Jordan, The Exit That Isn't On Bush's Road Map." *New York Times*, May 18, 2003.

———. "Tourism of Sacrilege? Religious Leaders and visitors have opposing views about Jerusalem's Dome of the Rock." *New York Times*.

Berg, Michael. *Becoming Like God Kabbalah and Our Ultimate Destiny*. New York: The Kabbalah Center, 2004.

Berger, Arthur S. LLB. "Life After Death? We Are the First Generation to Know." Lecture sponsored by the Lifelong Learning Society of Florida Atlantic University. Boca Raton, Florida.

Berger, Dr. Allan. "Anti-Semitism: Ancient and Contemporary." Lecture sponsored by the Lifelong Learning Society of Florida Atlantic University. Boca Raton, Florida.

————. "Major Jewish Religious Thinkers of The 20th century." Lecture sponsored by the Lifelong Learning Society of Florida Atlantic University. Boca Raton, Florida.

Berman, Paul. "The Philosopher of Islamic Terror." *New York Times*, March 23, 2003.

Bethke Elshtain, Jean. *Just War Against Terror*. New York: Basic Books, 2003.

Bishop, Eileen. Heightened Dissension within LCMS Remnant of Terrorist Attack, Lutheran Life National News, 10/5/02.

Bly, Robert. *Iron John*. New York: Vintage Books, 1992.

Borg, Marcus. *Jesus & Buddha, The Parallel Sayings*. Berkeley: Seastone, 2002.

Cahill, Thomas. *Desire of The Everlasting Hills*. New York: Anchor Books, 2001.

————. *Sailing The Wine-Dark Sea Why the Greeks Matter*. New York: Doubleday, 2003.

Cary, Professor Phillip. "Kant: Morality as the Basis of Religion Philosophy and Religion in the West." Lecture from the class on *Philosophy and Religion in the West*, Eastern College, recorded by The Teaching Company Limited Partnership.

————. "Kant: Reason Limited to Experience Philosophy and Religion in the West." Lecture from the class on *Philosophy and Religion in the West*, Eastern College, recorded by The Teaching Company Limited Partnership.

————. "Platonist Philosophy and Scriptural Religion Philosophy and Religion in the West." Lecture from the class on *Philosophy and Religion in the West*, Eastern College, recorded by The Teaching Company Limited Partnership.

————. "The Jewish Scriptures: Life with the God of Israel Philosophy and Religion in the West." Lecture from the class on *Philosophy and Religion in the West*, Eastern College, recorded by The Teaching Company Limited Partnership.

————. Lecture class on *Augustine: Philosopher and Saint*, Eastern College, recorded by The Teaching Company Limited Partnership.

————. "Plato's Inquiries: The Gods and the Good Philosophy and Religion in the West." Lecture from the class on *Philosophy and*

Religion in the West, Eastern College, recorded by The Teaching Company Limited Partnership.

————."Plato's Spirituality: The Immortal Soul and the Other World Philosophy and Religion in the West." Lecture from the class on *Philosophy and Religion in the West*, Eastern College, recorded by The Teaching Company Limited Partnership.

————."Plotinus: Neo Platonism and the Ultimate Unity of All Philosophy and Religion in the West." Lecture from the class on *Philosophy and Religion in the West*, Eastern College, recorded by The Teaching Company Limited Partnership.

————."Schleiermacher: Feeling as the Basis of Religion." Lecture from the class on *Philosophy and Religion in the West*, Eastern College, recorded by The Teaching Company Limited Partnership.

Chopra, Deepak. *How To Know God*. New York: Harmony Books, 2000.

Collins, John J. *The Scepter and The Stars: The Messiah of the Dead Sea Scrolls and other Ancient Literature*. Anchor Bible, 1995.

Crab, Larry. *The Safest Place on Earth*. Halifax, Nova Scotia: World Publishing, 1973.

Dali Lama. *How to Practice The Way to a Meaningful Life*. New York: Pocket Books, 2002.

Davey, Monica. "Episcopalians Give Nod for Gay Bishop." *New York Times*, August 4, 2003.

Eck, Professor Diana. "Creating a World: Two Cultures of Ancient India." Lecture given at Harvard University, recorded by The Teaching Company Limited Partnership.

————."Gandhi: All Religions are True." Lecture given at Harvard University, recorded by The Teaching Company Limited Partnership.

————."The Upanishads: Teaching on Wisdom." Lecture given at Harvard University, recorded by The Teaching Company Limited Partnership.

Eckel, Professor Malcolm David. "Buddhist Philosophy." Lecture from the class on *Buddhism*, Boston University, recorded by The Teaching Company Limited Partnership.

————."Emptiness." Lecture from the class on *Buddhism*, Boston

University, recorded by The Teaching Company Limited Partnership.

————."The Story of Buddha." Lecture from the class on *Buddhism*, Boston University, recorded by The Teaching Company Limited Partnership.

————."What is Buddhism?" Lecture from the class on *Buddhism*, Boston University, recorded by The Teaching Company Limited Partnership.

Ehrman, Bart D. *Misquoting Jesus.* San Francisco: HarperSanFrancisco, 2006

Ehrman, Professor Bart D. "Ancient Judaism." Lecture from the class on the *New Testament*, University of North Carolina-Chapel Hill, recorded by The Teaching Company Limited Partnership.

————."John—Jesus the Man from Heaven." Lecture from the class on the *New Testament*, University of North Carolina-Chapel Hill, recorded by The Teaching Company Limited Partnership.

————."Matthew— Jesus the Jewish Messiah." Lecture from the class on the *New Testament*, University of North Carolina-Chapel Hill, recorded by The Teaching Company Limited Partnership.

————."Noncanonical Gospels." Lecture from the class on the *New Testament*, University of North Carolina-Chapel Hill, recorded by The Teaching Company Limited Partnership.

————."Paul, Jesus, and James." Lecture from the class on the *New Testament*, University of North Carolina-Chapel Hill, recorded by The Teaching Company Limited Partnership.

————."Pauline Ethics." Lecture from the class on the *New Testament*, University of North Carolina-Chapel Hill, recorded by The Teaching Company Limited Partnership.

————."The Earliest Traditions About Jesus." Lecture from the class on the *New Testament*, University of North Carolina-Chapel Hill, recorded by The Teaching Company Limited Partnership.

————."The Greco-Roman Context." Lecture from the class on the *New Testament*, University of North Carolina-Chapel Hill, recorded by The Teaching Company Limited Partnership.

————."The Historical Jesus—Sources and Problems." Lecture from the class on the *New Testament*, University of North Carolina-Chapel Hill, recorded by The Teaching Company Limited Partnership.

————."The Early Christians and Their Literature." Lecture from the class on the *New Testament*, University of North Carolina-Chapel Hill, recorded by The

Teaching Company Limited Partnership.

Ehrenreich, Barbara. *Blood Rites*. New York: Henry Holt and Company, 1997.

Fisher, Ian. "Israelis Worry About Terror, by Jews Against Palestinians." *New York Times*, August 19, 2003.

Friedman, Thomas L. "Dinner With the Sayyids." *New York Times*, August 10, 2003.

Friese, Kai. "Hijacking India's History." *New York Times*, December 30, 2002.

Funk, W. Robert. *Honest To Jesus*. SanFrancisco, HarperCollins "A Polebridge Press Book", 1996

Gawain, Shakti. *Creative Visualization*. New York: Bantam Books, 1982.

Gittelson, Dr. Abe. "Contemporary Jewish Movements." Lecture sponsored by the Lifelong Learning Society of Florida Atlantic University. Boca Raton, Florida.

Glynn, Professor Simon. "The Politics and Philosophy of Globalization: Impact on The World Today." Lecture sponsored by the Lifelong Learning Society of Florida Atlantic University. Boca Raton, Florida.

Goodstein, Laurie. "O Ye of Much Faith! A Triple Dose of Trouble, 'Crises in hierarchy, doctrine and identity bedevil three major world religions.'" *New York Times*, June 2, 2002.

Gould, Stephen Jay. *The Structure of Evolutionary Theory*. Boston, Massachusetts: Harvard University Press, 2002.

Gozier, Andre, O.S.B. *15 Days of Prayer with Meister Eckhart*. Liguori, Missouri: Liguori Publications, 2000.

Green, Professor William Scott. "Judaism as a Religion." Lecture from the class *Great World Religions: Beliefs, Practices and Histories* given at the University of Rochester, recorded by The Teaching Company Limited Partnership.

————. "Judaism in Principal: The Shape of Jewish History." Lecture from the class *Great World Religions: Beliefs, Practices and Histories* given at the University of Rochester, recorded by The Teaching Company Limited Partnership.

————. "Levitical Religion." Lecture from the class *Great World Religions: Beliefs, Practices and Histories* given at the University of Rochester, recorded by The Teaching Company Limited Partnership.

————. "Rabbinic Judaism I: The Doctrine of the Dual Torah." Lecture from the class *Great World Religions: Beliefs, Practices and Histories* given at the University of Rochester, recorded by The Teaching Company Limited

Partnership.

————."Rabbinic Judaism: Scripture as a Sacred Object." Lecture from the class *Great World Religions: Beliefs, Practices and Histories* given at the University of Rochester, recorded by The Teaching Company Limited Partnership.

————."The Historical Foundations of Judaism." Lecture from the class *Great World Religions: Beliefs, Practices and Histories* given at the University of Rochester, recorded by The Teaching Company Limited Partnership.

Greene, Brian. *The Elegant Universe.* New York: Vintage Books, 1999.

Halley, Henry H. *Halley's Bible Handbook.* Grand Rapids, Michigan: Zondervan, 1927/1959.

Harris, Sam. *The End of faith.* New York: WW Norton Company, 2005.

Haugk, Kenneth C. *Christian Care Giving A Way of Life.* Minneapolis: Augsburg Publishing House, 1984.

Haugk, Kenneth C., Ruth N. Koch. *Speaking the Truth in Love.* St. Louis, Missouri: Stephen Ministries Publishing, 1992.

Hawking, Stephen W. *A Brief History of Time.* New York: Bantam Books, 1988.

————. *The Universe in a Nutshell.* New York: Bantam Books, 2001.

Hayes, Richard B. *The Faith of Jesus Christ.* Grand Rapids, Michigan: William B. Erdman's Publishing Company, 1983.

Hendricks, Professor Robert. "Buddhism in India and the Beginnings in China." Lecture given at Dartmouth College, recorded by The Teaching Company Limited Partnership.

————."Religion in Ancient China (Before 500 B.C.E.)." Lecture given at Dartmouth College, recorded by The Teaching Company Limited Partnership.

Huntington, Samuel P. *The Clash of Civilizations and the Remaking of World Order.* New York: Simon & Shuster, 1996.

John Paul II, His Holiness. *Crossing The Threshold of Hope.* New York: Alfred A. Knopf, 1994.

Johnson, Professor Luke Timothy. "An Apostle Admired and Despised." Lecture from the class on the *Apostle Paul,* Emory University, recorded by The Teaching Company Limited Partnership.

————."Life and Law: Galatians." Lecture from the class on the *Apostle Paul,* Emory University, recorded by The Teaching Company Limited Partnership.

David Anderson

————."Life in Christ: Second Corinthians." Lecture from the class on the *Apostle Paul*, Emory University, recorded by The Teaching Company Limited Partnership.

————."Paul's Influence." Lecture from the class on the *Apostle Paul*, Emory University, recorded by The Teaching Company Limited Partnership.

————."Problems of Early Christianity." Lecture from the class on the *Apostle Paul*, Emory University, recorded by The Teaching Company Limited Partnership.

Karsh, Efraim *Islamic Imperialism, A History.* New haven and London: Yale University Press, 2006

Kieschick, Gerald B. *The State of the Synod.* Lutheran Church—Missouri Synod, 9/25/02.

Koterski, Father Joseph. Lecture class on *Natural Law and Human Nature*, Fordham University, recorded by The Teaching Company Limited Partnership.

Lathem, Edward Connery. *The Poetry of Robert Frost,* New York: Henry Holt and Company1967 / Leslie Frost Ballantine, 1975

Leaves, Nigel. *The God Problem Alternatives to Fundamentalism.* Santa Rosa, California: Polebridge Press, 2006

Lewin, Kurt. *A Journey Through Illusions.* Santa Barbara, California: Fithian Press, 1994.

Lewis, C. S. *Mere Christianity.* San Francisco: Harper Collins, 1952.

Lewis, Bernard. *The Crisis of Islam.* New York: Random House, 2004.

Lichtenstein, Dr. Murray. "Bible and Babel: Hebrew Bible." Lecture sponsored by the Lifelong Learning Society of Florida Atlantic University. Boca Raton, Florida.

————."How "True" is The Bible?" Lecture sponsored by the Lifelong Learning Society of Florida Atlantic University. Boca Raton, Florida.

————."Judaism and Islam." Lecture sponsored by the Lifelong Learning Society of Florida Atlantic University. Boca Raton, Florida.

Lind, Michael. "The Right Still Has Religion, 'George Bush is president today because the religious right vetoed the nomination of John

McCain.'" *New York Times*, December 9, 2001.

Maltz, Maxwell M.D. *Psycho-Cybernetics & Self-Fulfillment.* New York: Grosset & Dunlap, Prentice Hall, 1960.

Manji, Irshad. *The Trouble With Islam Today.* New York: St. Martin's Griffin, 2005

May, Rollo. *Love and Will.* New York: W.W. Norton Company, 1969.

————. *Man's Search For Himself.* New York: W.W. Norton Company, 1953.

————. *Power and Innocence, A Search for Sources of Violence.* New York: W.W. Norton Company, 1972.

————. *The Courage To Create.* New York: W.W. Norton Company, 1975.

Moorehead, Alan. *No Room in the Ark.* New York: Harper & Brothers Publishers, 1957.

Moyers, Bill. *Facing Evil.* A Co-Production of Public Affairs Television, Inc., KERA/Dallas, 1988

Myrdal, Gynnar. *Challenge To Affluence.* New York: Vintage, 1962.

Nafisi, Azar. *Reading Lolita in Teheran.* New York: Random House, 2003.

Packouz, Rabbi Kalman. "Soul is Essence of Being Human." *Sun-Sentinel*, Ft Lauderdale, November 1, 2002.

Pagels, Elaine. *Beyond Belief, The Secret Gospel of Thomas.* New York: Random House, 2003.

————. *The Gnostic Gospels.* New York: Vintage Books, 1979.

————. *The Origin of Satan.* New York: Vintage Books, 1995.

Phares, Dr. Walid C. "U.S. and Middle East in Post September 11 Era." Lecture sponsored by the Lifelong Learning Society of Florida Atlantic University. Boca Raton, Florida.

————. "America in The Middle East Challenges and Horizons." Lecture sponsored by the Lifelong Learning Society of Florida Atlantic University. Boca Raton, Florida.

. "The Roots of Middle East Rage." Lecture sponsored by the Lifelong Learning Society of Florida Atlantic University. Boca Raton, Florida.

Robinson, James M. *The Nag Hammadi Library in English.* New York:

HarperCollins, 1978.

————*The Gospel of Jesus,* SanFrancisco: Harper Collins, 2006.

Rosenstock-Huessy, Eugen. *I Am An Impure Thinker.* Essex, Vermont: Argo Books, 1970.

————. *Judaism Despite Christianity.* Tuscaloosa, Alabama: University of Alabama Press, 1969.

————. *The Christian Future,* New York: Harper Torchbooks, Charles Scribner & Sons, 1946.

Ruderman, Professor David B. "Abraham Geiger—The Shaping of Reform Judaism." Lecture from the class on *Jewish Intellectual History: 16th to 20th century,* University of Pennsylvania, 2002, recorded by The Teaching Company Limited Partnership.

————. "Abraham Heschel—Mystic and Social Activist." Lecture from the class on *Jewish Intellectual History: 16th to 20th century,* University of Pennsylvania, 2002, recorded by The Teaching Company Limited Partnership.

————. "Mordecai Kaplan and American Judaism." Lecture from the class on *Jewish Intellectual History: 16th to 20th century,* University of Pennsylvania, 2002, recorded by The Teaching Company Limited Partnership.

————."Theological responses to the Nazi Holocaust." Lecture from the class on *Jewish Intellectual History: 16th to 20th century,* University of Pennsylvania, 2002, recorded by The Teaching Company Limited Partnership.

————."Three Zionist Visions." Lecture from the class on *Jewish Intellectual History: 16th to 20th century,* University of Pennsylvania, 2002, recorded by The Teaching Company Limited Partnership.

————."Zionism's Answer to the Jewish Problem." Lecture from the class on *Jewish Intellectual History: 16th to 20th century,* University of Pennsylvania, 2002, recorded by The Teaching Company Limited Partnership.

Ruderman, Professor David B. "Between Cross and Crescent: Jewish Civilization from Mohammed to Spinoza", University of Pennsylvania, 2005, recorded by The Teaching Company Limited Partnership.

Schaefer III, Dr. Henry. "The Real Issue, Stephen Hawking, The Big Bang, and God." Lecture presented at the University of Georgia, Athens, Georgia, Spring 1994.

Scott Peck, M. *People of The Lie, The Hope for Healing Human Evil.* New York: Simon & Schuster, 1983.

Shapiro, Samantha M. "The Unsettlers, 'The radical Young Israelis setting up camp on hilltops in the West bank have no interest in compromise and no plans to slow down.'" *New York Times,* February 16, 2003.

Sheed, F.J. *The Confessions of St. Augustine.* New York: Sheed and Ward, 1942.

Skarsaune, Oskar. *In The Shadow of The Temple, Jewish Influences on Early Christianity.* Downers Grove, Illinois: InterVarsity Press, 2002.

Sobel, Dava. *Galileo's Daughter.* New York: Penguin Books, 1999.

Spencer, Robert. *Islam Unveiled.* San Francisco: Encounter Books, 2002.

_____. *The politically Correct Guide to Islam.* Washington, DC: Regency Publishing, 2005.

Spong, John Shelby. *Rescuing the Bible from Fundamentalism.* New York: HarperCollins, 1991.

_____. *Liberating The Gospels.* San Francisco: HarperCollins, 1996.

_____. *The Sins of Scripture.* San Francisco: HarperCollins, 2005.

Stagg, Frank. *New Testament Theology.* Broadman Press, 1962.

Steindl-Rast, David O.S.B. *Meister Eckhart from Whom God Hid Nothing.* Boston & London: Shambhala Publications, 1996.

Stern, Jessica. "How America Created a Terrorist Haven." *New York Times,* August 20, 2003.

Sullivan, Nancy. *The Treasure of American Poetry.* New York: Dorset Press, 1978.

Sun-Sentinel, "Nothing Left, 'Witnesses recall horror in Bali as death toll nears 200.'" October 14, 2002.

Swanson, Professor John. "Intellectual and Mystical Forces within Medieval Islam." Lecture given at The American University of Cairo, recorded by The Teaching Company Limited Partnership.

David Anderson

————."Islam; Past, Present and Future." Lecture given at The American University of Cairo, recorded by The Teaching Company Limited Partnership.

————. "Islamic Response to Western Predominance." Lecture given at The American University of Cairo, recorded by The Teaching Company Limited Partnership.

————. "The History of Islam and the Emergence of the Schia." Lecture given at The American University of Cairo, recorded by The Teaching Company Limited Partnership.

————. "The Rise of an Islamic Institution." Lecture given at The American University of Cairo, recorded by The Teaching Company Limited Partnership.

Tarnas, Richard. *The Passion of the Western Mind*, New York: Ballantine Books, 1991

Telchin, Stan. *Betrayed.* Grand Rapids, Michigan: Chosen Books, 1981.

Tillich, Paul. *The Eternal Now.* New York: Charles Scribner's Sons, 1963.

————. *The Shaking of the Foundations.* New York: Charles Scribner's Sons, 1948.

Time Warner Company, "*Passion* testing Jewish-Christian links," CNN. com, http:// www.cnn.com.

Tuchmann, Barbara W., *Bible and Sword.* New York: Ballantine Books, 1984.

Walker, Ethan III. *The Mystic Christ.* Norman, OK: Devi Press, 2003.

Warshal, Rabbi Bruce. "Judaism, nice Jewish boys and gay rights." *Jewish Journal*, July 31, 2003.

Wheatcroft, Andrew. *Infidels.* New York: Random House, 2005.

Weisman, Steven R. and Greg Myre. "Israel plans 600 homes on West bank site." *New York Times*, October 3, 2003.

Weiss, Rabbi Avi. "Who wrote the Book of Deuteronomy?" *Jewish Journal*, July 31, 2003.

Wilson, Edward O., *The Future of Life*. New York: Random House, 2002.

Zacharias, Ravi. *Jesus Among Other Gods.* Nashville, Tennessee: W
Publishing Group, 2000. aphy

Sexuality and the Religions of Abraham

inerrant *adj.*, inerrancy *n.*

"not wandering, not erring, making no mistakes, infallible"

Webster's New World Dictionary

The use of the masculine form *mankind* to designate the human species and the words *HIM*, *Him* and *His* to designate GOD are used throughout this book only to avoid having to invent words that are gender neutral.

GOD'S nature in the Hebrew Bible was revealed using images and symbols that could be understood within the social conventions of an historical time period. This was a period when men were considered to be the intellectually dominant members of society. Women were subject to them, and as leaders were seldom heard from. Abraham was a man. Moses was a man. David was a man.

The dominance of the male begins at the very first page of Jewish/ Christian as well as Muslim history. The Book of Genesis reads in 1:26:

And God said; let us make man in our image, after our likeness.

And then in: 2:21-22:

And the Lord God caused a deep sleep to fall upon Adam, and he slept; and he took one of his ribs, And the rib, which the Lord God had taken from man, made he a women.

Many of those who believe in the inerrancy of every word of the Bible and the Koran will declare that since GOD made *Man* in His own *image*; therefore, GOD must look like man. And, as woman was *taken out of man*, she therefore must be secondary to man.

The words in Genesis referring to GOD making man in his own image are GOD'S revelation to men and women of the human species that they were created like HIM, not in bodily form, but in mind. The words mean that each of us is a reflection of the mind of GOD. We are a part of HIM. HE is a part of us.

The Genesis story does not stop there. It goes on to explain that not all of us are like HIM. WE have a capacity that He does not have. We have the capacity to choose evil. Therefore, our human nature is not all like HIM. This is the revelation coming from Genesis. It is a story explaining the duality of human nature. This is its meaning. It has nothing to do with sexual dominance or difference.

The words of the Torah for centuries were not written, but were passed from generation to generation by word of mouth. Storytellers revealed what they considered to be GOD'S message, using the language of Myth. Many of the biblical images found in the Torah—including the Garden of Eden itself—extend back another 2000 years into early Sumerian times, before the Jewish people had existed as a unified tribe. Many other images grew out of the mythology of prior generations of other tribes and nations in the Mesopotamian area.

The early Jewish writers used these images to explain the revelation of GOD as they interpreted it within the context of their own understanding of themselves and their relationship to Him. Theirs was a culture of dominant men, as other cultures had been. Males therefore were dominant in their Myths.

Males were dominant when Jesus preached, but he made no distinction between Man and Woman. He looked with equanimity on both. Women played an important role in his life, and in fact women defined much of his ministry.

For Islam, 600, years after Jesus, Muhammad adopted the Hebraic view of male and female.

It was the Apostle Paul, not Jesus, who defined the role of women in the early Christian Church. He gave the Christian community hard and fast choices as to how to behave. These choices were deeply rooted in his pharisaic religious bias. They were also in sympathy with the prevailing social structure of the Roman society from which conversions were taking place. Paul's rhetorical hardball was intended for a far less enlightened audience than we see in today's world. We must therefore view the statements of Paul in the context of the period in which he lived and the challenges he faced. We must view them in the context of his own pharisaic background, his temperament, and his own questionable sexual orientation.

Men and women in the 21st century and beyond must search for the ultimate truth about GOD and their relationship to GOD, without the literal constraints of past mythology. They are physiologically different, but their souls are not. They were both made in the image of GOD. Like Adam and Eve after the fall, both men and women have a capacity for good as well as for evil. They have to make choices every day of their lives between good and evil. Both were given the freedom to contribute to society according to their abilities as mothers and fathers and mentors—as well as Priests, Pastors, Mullahs, Rabbis, CEOs, Artists, Electricians, Plumbers, and Presidents.

We are all, each of us, GOD'S chosen ONES in a *human society* with

David Anderson

no sexual dividing lines. Each of us was born into this world to add to it, to use for GOD'S purposes what He has given us, each according to his or her individual ability. Biological sexual form—or even orientation—is not relevant.

Jesus told us in the Gospel of Thomas (24) and the Gospel of Matthew (25:15-30) that what matters in the mind of GOD is what we make of our lives. If Judaism, Christianity and Islam do not elevate their theologies and the scriptures that support them to acknowledge this, in time they will cease to be.

About the Author

The author is a geopolitical scientist and theologian who, over a lifetime, observed the role of religion as a major underlying force directing human social behavior. In this book he draws conclusions as to the extent of all three of the religions of Abraham—Judaism, Christianity and Islam—sharing culpability for present world conflict.

Made in the USA
Las Vegas, NV
30 July 2021